Start
a Business
in
Florida

Eighth Edition

Mark Warda

Attorney at Law

SPHINX® PUBLISHING
AN IMPRINT OF SOURCEBOOKS, INC.®
NAPERVILLE, ILLINOIS
www.SphinxLegal.com

Eighth Edition: 2006

Published by: **Sphinx® Publishing, An Imprint of Sourcebooks, Inc.®**

Naperville Office
P.O. Box 4410
Naperville, Illinois 60567-4410
630-961-3900
Fax: 630-961-2168
www.sourcebooks.com
www.SphinxLegal.com

This publication is designed to provide accurate and authoritative information in regard to the subject matter covered. It is sold with the understanding that the publisher is not engaged in rendering legal, accounting, or other professional service. If legal advice or other expert assistance is required, the services of a competent professional person should be sought.

From a Declaration of Principles Jointly Adopted by a Committee of the American Bar Association and a Committee of Publishers and Associations

This product is not a substitute for legal advice.

Disclaimer required by Texas statutes.

Library of Congress Cataloging-in-Publication Data
Warda, Mark.
  Start a business in Florida / by Mark Warda.-- 8th ed.
     p. cm.
  Rev. ed. of: How to Start a business in Florida. 7th ed. 2003.
  Includes index.
  ISBN-13: 978-1-57248-538-9 (pbk. : alk. paper)
  ISBN-10: 1-57248-538-8 (pbk. : alk. paper)
 1. New business enterprises--Law and legislation--Florida--Popular works.
2. New business enterprises--Taxation--Law and legislation--Florida--Popular works. I. Warda, Mark. How to start a business in Florida. II. Title.

KFF205.Z9W37 2006
346.759'065--dc22
                                                                 2006002279

Printed and bound in the United States of America.
SB — 10 9 8 7 6 5 4 3 2

Contents

Using Self-Help Law Books

Before using a self-help law book, you should realize the advantages and disadvantages of doing your own legal work and understand the challenges and diligence that this requires.

The Growing Trend

Rest assured that you will not be the first or only person handling your own legal matter. For example, in some states, more than 75% of the people in divorces and other cases represent themselves. Because of the high cost of legal services, this is a major trend, and many courts are struggling to make it easier for people to represent themselves. However, some courts are not happy with people who do not use attorneys and refuse to help them in any way. For some, the attitude is, "Go to the law library and figure it out for yourself."

We write and publish self-help law books to give people an alternative to the often complicated and confusing legal books found in most law libraries. We have made the explanations of the law as simple and easy to understand as possible. Of course, unlike an attorney advising an individual client, we cannot cover every conceivable possibility.

Cost/Value Analysis

Whenever you shop for a product or service, you are faced with various levels of quality and price. In deciding what product or service to buy, you make a cost/value analysis on the basis of your willingness to pay and the quality you desire.

When buying a car, you decide whether you want transportation, comfort, status, or sex appeal. Accordingly, you decide among choices such as a Neon, a Lincoln, a Rolls Royce, or a Porsche. Before making a decision, you usually weigh the merits of each option against the cost.

When you get a headache, you can take a pain reliever (such as aspirin) or visit a medical specialist for a neurological examination. Given this choice, most people, of course, take a pain reliever, since it costs only pennies; whereas a medical examination costs hundreds of dollars and takes a lot of time. This is usually a logical choice because it is rare to need anything more than a pain reliever for a headache. But in some cases, a headache may indicate a brain tumor, and failing to see a specialist right away can result in complications. Should everyone with a headache go to a specialist? Of course not, but people treating their own illnesses must realize that they are betting on the basis of their cost/value analysis of the situation. They are taking the most logical option.

The same cost/value analysis must be made when deciding to do one's own legal work. Many legal situations are very straightforward, requiring a simple form and no complicated analysis. Anyone with a little intelligence and a book of instructions can handle the matter without outside help.

But there is always the chance that complications are involved that only an attorney would notice. To simplify the law into a book like this, several legal cases often must be condensed into a single sentence or paragraph. Otherwise, the book would be several hundred pages long and too complicated for most people. However, this simplification necessarily leaves out many details and nuances that would apply to special or unusual situations. Also, there are many ways to interpret most legal questions. Your case may come before a judge who disagrees with the analysis of our authors.

Therefore, in deciding to use a self-help law book and to do your own legal work, you must realize that you are making a cost/value analysis. You have decided that the money you will save in doing it yourself outweighs the chance that your case will not turn out to your satisfaction. Most people handling their own simple legal matters never have a problem, but occasionally people find that it ended up costing them more to have an attorney straighten out the situation than it would have if they had hired an attorney in the beginning. Keep this in mind while handling your case, and be sure to consult an attorney if you feel you might need further guidance.

Local Rules   The next thing to remember is that a book which covers the law for the entire nation, or even for an entire state, cannot possibly include every procedural difference of every jurisdiction. Whenever possible, we provide the exact form needed; however, in some areas, each county, or even each judge, may require unique forms and procedures. In our state books, our forms usually cover the majority of counties in the state or provide examples of the type of form that will be required. In our national books, our forms are sometimes even more general in nature but are designed to give a good idea of the type of form that will be needed in most locations. Nonetheless, keep in mind that your state, county, or judge may have a requirement, or use a form, that is not included in this book.

You should not necessarily expect to be able to get all of the information and resources you need solely from within the pages of this book. This book will serve as your guide, giving you specific information whenever possible and helping you to find out what else you will need to know. This is just like if you decided to build your own backyard deck. You might purchase a book on how to build decks. However, such a book would not include the building codes and permit requirements of every city, town, county, and township in the nation; nor would it include the lumber, nails, saws, hammers, and other materials and tools you would need to actually build the deck. You would use the book as your guide, and then do some work and research involving such matters as whether you need a permit of some kind, what type and grade of wood is available in your area, whether to use hand tools or power tools, and how to use those tools.

Before using the forms in a book like this, you should check with your court clerk to see if there are any local rules of which you should be aware or local forms you will need to use. Often, such forms will require the same information as the forms in the book but are merely laid out differently or use slightly different language. They will sometimes require additional information.

Besides being subject to local rules and practices, the law is subject to change at any time. The courts and the legislatures of all fifty states are constantly revising the laws. It is possible that while you are reading this book, some aspect of the law is being changed.

In most cases, the change will be of minimal significance. A form will be redesigned, additional information will be required, or a waiting period will be extended. As a result, you might need to revise a form, file an extra form, or wait out a longer time period. These types of changes will not usually affect the outcome of your case. On the other hand, sometimes a major part of the law is changed, the entire law in a particular area is rewritten, or a case that was the basis of a central legal point is overruled. In such instances, your entire ability to pursue your case may be impaired.

Introduction

Florida is booming! Nearly 1,000 people move to the state each day, and the demand for new products and services keeps growing. Some have said Florida is now what California was to the 1960s—a thriving, trend-setting center of activity where little shops can bloom into expansive enterprises.

The best way to take part in this boom is to run your own business. Each year, over a quarter of a million corporations and limited liability companies are registered in Florida. Be your own boss and be as successful as you dare to be—but always obey the law.

If you do not follow the laws of the state, your progress can be slowed or stopped by government fines, civil judgments, or even criminal penalties.

This book is intended to give you the framework for legally opening a business in Florida. It also includes information on where to find special rules for each type of business. If you have problems that are not covered by this book, you should seek out an attorney who can be available for your ongoing needs.

In order to cover all of the aspects of any business you are thinking of starting, you should read through this entire book, rather than skipping to the parts that look most interesting. Many laws that may not sound like they apply to you do have provisions that will affect your business.

In recent years, the government bureaucracies have been amending and lengthening their forms regularly. The forms included in this book were the most recent available at the time of publication. It is possible that some may be revised at the time you read this book, but in most cases, previous versions of the forms will still be accepted.

Deciding to Start a Business

If you are reading this book, then you have probably made a serious decision to take the plunge and start your own business. Hundreds of thousands of people make the same decision each year, and many of them become very successful. A lot of them also fail. Knowledge can only help your chances of success. You need to know why some businesses succeed while others fail. Some of what follows may seem obvious, but to someone wrapped up in a new business idea, some of this information is occasionally overlooked.

KNOW YOUR STRENGTHS

The last thing a budding entrepreneur wants to hear is that he or she is not cut out for running a business. You might avoid those "do you have what it takes" quizzes because you are not sure you want hear the answer. However, you can be successful if you know where to get the skills you lack.

You should consider all of the skills and knowledge that running a successful business requires, and decide whether you have what it takes. If you do not, it does not necessarily mean you are doomed to be an employee all your life. Perhaps you just need a partner who has the skills you lack. Perhaps you can hire someone with the skills you need, or you can structure your business to avoid areas where you are weak. If those tactics do not work, maybe you can learn the skills.

For example, if managing employees is not your strong suit, you can:

- handle product development yourself, and have a partner or manager deal with employees;

- take seminars in employee management; or,

- structure your business so that you do not need employees (use independent contractors or set yourself up as an independent contractor).

When planning your business, consider the following factors.

- *If it takes months or years before your business turns a profit, do you have the resources to hold out?* Businesses have gone under or have been sold just before they were about to take off. Staying power is an important ingredient to success.

- *Are you willing to put in a lot of overtime to make your business a success?* Owners of businesses do not set their own hours—the business sets hours for the owner. Many business owners work long hours seven days a week. You have to enjoy running your business and be willing to make some personal time sacrifices.

- *Are you willing to do the dirtiest or most unpleasant work of the business?* Emergencies come up and employees are not always dependable. You might need to mop up a flooded room, spend a weekend stuffing 10,000 envelopes, or work Christmas if someone calls in sick.

- *Do you know enough about the product or service?* Are you aware of the trends in the industry and what changes new technology might bring? Think of the people who started typesetting or printing businesses just before type was replaced by laser printers.

✪ *Do you know enough about accounting and inventory to manage the business?* Do you have a good "head for business"? Some people naturally know how to save money and do things profitably. Others are in the habit of buying the best or the most expensive of everything. The latter can be fatal to a struggling new business.

✪ *Are you good at managing employees?* If your business has employees (or will have in the future), managing them is an unavoidable part of running the business.

✪ *Do you know how to sell your product or service?* You can have the best product on the market, but people will not know about it unless you tell them about it. If you are a wholesaler, shelf space in major stores is hard to get, especially for a new company without a record, a large line of products, or a large advertising budget.

✪ *Do you know enough about getting publicity?* The media receives thousands of press releases and announcements each day, and most are thrown away. Do not count on free publicity to put your name in front of the public.

KNOW YOUR BUSINESS

Not only do you need to know the concept of a business, but you need the experience of working in a business. Maybe you always dreamed of running a bed and breakfast or having your own pizza place. Have you ever worked in such a business? If not, you may have no idea of the day-to-day headaches and problems of the business. For example, do you really know how much to allow for theft, spoilage, and unhappy customers?

You might feel silly taking an entry-level job at a pizza place when you would rather start your own, but it might be the most valuable preparation you do. A few weeks of seeing how a business operates could mean the difference between success and failure.

Working in a business as an employee is one of the best ways to be a success at running such a business. People with new ideas can revolutionize established industries with obvious improvements that no one before dared to try.

SOURCES FOR FURTHER GUIDANCE

There are many things to consider as you prepare to start your own business. Most likely, you will have numerous questions that need to be answered before opening your doors for the first time. Luckily, there are many resources available for help. The sources discussed in this section offer free or low-cost guidance for new businesses.

SCORE   Florida is a haven for retired people, and many of them are glad to give free guidance to new businesses. To facilitate this, the *Small Business Administration* (SBA) has developed a group, known as the *Service Corps of Retired Executives* (SCORE), that provides invaluable assistance to new business ventures. There are several local SCORE offices throughout Florida.

Florida SCORE Chapters
www.score.org

Bay County SCORE
Lynn Haven
850-271-1108
Fax: 850-271-1109
www.nfci.org/score.htm

Central Florida SCORE
Lakeland
863-619-5783

Charlotte/DeSoto County SCORE
Punta Gorda
941-743-6179
www.charlotte-florida.com/
business/scorepg01.htm

Citrus County SCORE
Lecanto
352-621-0775
www.scorecitrus.org

Fort Lauderdale SCORE
Fort Lauderdale
954-356-7263
Fax: 954-356-7145
www.score17.org

Gainesville SCORE
Gainesville
352-375-8278
Fax: 352-375-5340
www.scoregainesville.org

Hillsborough SCORE
Tampa
813-988-1435
Fax: 813-914-4027
www.tampascore.org

Jacksonville SCORE
Jacksonville
904-443-1900
Fax: 904-443-1980
www.scorejax.org

Lake Sumter SCORE
Eustis
352-589-2250
www.score414.org

Manasota SCORE
Sarasota
941-955-1029
Fax: 941-955-5581
www.score-suncoast.org

Miami-Dade SCORE
Miami
305-536-5521 x150
Fax: 305-536-5058
www.scoremiami.org

Naples/Collier SCORE
Naples
239-430-0081
Fax: 239-430-0082
www.scorenaples.org

Ocala SCORE
Ocala
352-629-5959

Orlando SCORE
Orlando
407-420-4844
Fax: 407-420-4849
www.scoreorlando.org

Palm Beach SCORE
West Palm Beach
561-833-1672
Fax: 561-833-1470
www.wpbscore.org

Pasco/Hernando County SCORE
New Port Richey
727-842-4638
Fax: 727-841-7266
www.score439.org

South Broward/North Dade SCORE
Hollywood
954-966-8415
Fax: 954-966-2313

South Palm Beach SCORE
Boca Raton
561-981-5180
Fax: 561-981-5391
www.score-chapter412.org

Southwest Florida SCORE
Fort Myers
941-489-2935
Fax: 941-489-1170
www.score219.org

Space Coast SCORE
Melbourne
321-254-2288
www.spacecoastscore.org

Suncoast/Pinellas SCORE
Clearwater
727-532-6800
www.score115.org

Treasure Coast SCORE
Fort Pierce
772-489-0548
www.score308.com

Suwannee Valley SCORE
Lake City
386-755-9026

Volusia/Flagler SCORE
Holly Hill
386-255-6889
Fax: 386-255-0229
www.score87.org

Small Business Development Centers

Educational programs for small businesses are offered through the *Small Business Development Centers* (SBDCs) at many Florida colleges and universities. You should see if they have any that could help you in any areas in which you are weak. To find an SBDC near you, review the following list.

Florida Small Business Development Centers (SBDCs)
www.floridasbdc.com

State Director's Office
401 East Chase Street
Suite 100
Pensacola, FL 32502
850-473-7800
Fax: 850-473-7813
www.floridasbdc.com

Florida Atlantic University
777 Glades Road
Building T-10
Boca Raton, FL 33431
561-297-1140
Fax: 561-297-1141
www.fausbdc.com

Fort Lauderdale (Broward
   Library), 954-357-8068
Key West, 305-292-2396
Miami, 786-388-9040

Florida A & M University
1363 East Lafayette Street
Tallahassee, FL 32301
850-599-3407
Fax: 850-561-2049
www.sbdcatfamu.org

Madison, 850-973-1637
Perry, 850-584-5366

Florida Gulf Coast University
12751 Westlinks Drive
Building 3, #8
Fort Myers, FL 33913
239-225-4220
Fax: 239-225-4221
http://cli.fgcu.edu/sbdc

Cape Coral, 239-573-2737

Gulf Coast Community College
2500 Minnesota Avenue
Lynn Haven, FL 32444
850-271-1108
Fax: 850-271-1109
www.northfloridabiz.com

University of South Florida
1101 Channelside Drive
Suite 210
Tampa, FL 33602
813-905-5800
Fax: 813-905-5801
http://sbdc.usf.edu

Bartow, 863-534-2503
Largo, 727-549-6393
Venice, 941-408-1413

University of Central Florida
315 East Robinson Street
Suite 100
Orlando, FL 32801
407-420-4850
Fax: 407-420-4862
www.sbdcorlando.com

Daytona Beach, 386-506-4723
    www.sbdcdaytona.com
Kissimmee, 407-847-2452
Melbourne, 321-433-5570
    www.bcctraining.com
Sanford, 407-321-3495
    http://sbdc.scc-fl.edu

University of North Florida
12000 Alumni Drive
Jacksonville, FL 32224
904-620-2476
Fax: 904-620-2567
www.sbdc.unf.edu

Gainesville, 352-334-7230
Ocala, 352-622-8763

University of West Florida
401 East Chase Street
Suite 100
Pensacola, FL 32502
850-473-7830
www.sbdc.uwf.edu

Fort Walton Beach, 850-833-9400

County Economic Development Centers

While not all counties have SCORE offices or Small Business Development Centers, every county has an organization that is involved with economic development. Some will be more helpful than others, but you should at least see what your local office has to offer. The following list will help you find an office near you.

ALACHUA

    Gainesville Council for
      Economic Outreach
    352-378-7300
    www.gceo.com

    Alachua County Office of
      Planning and Development
    352-374-5249

    Gainesville Area Chamber of
      Commerce
    352-334-7100

    City of Hawthorne
    352-481-2432

    City of Newberry
    352-472-6611

BAKER

    Baker County Chamber
      of Commerce
    904-259-6433
    www.bakerchamberfl.com

BAY

    Bay County Economic
      Development Alliance
    850-785-5206
    www.baycountyeda.org

    Panama City Beaches
      Chamber of Commerce
    850-234-7634

BRADFORD

    North Florida Regional
      Chamber of Commerce
    904-964-5278
    www.northfloridachamber.com

BREVARD

    Economic Development
      Commission of Florida's
      Space Coast
    800-535-0203
    www.spacecoastedc.org

    City of Cocoa Office of
      Economic Development
    321-459-2200
    www.cocoafl.org

    City of Melbourne
    321-639-7577

    City of Palm Bay
    321-952-3426
    www.palmbayflorida.org

    Space Coast Economic
      Development Commission
    800-749-3224

    City of Titusville
    321-383-5775
    www.titusville.com

BROWARD

    Broward Alliance
    954-524-3113
    www.browardalliance.org

    Broward County Office of
      Economic Development
    954-357-6155

    Coral Springs Economic
      Development Foundation
    954-346-6996

Town of Davie—
Office of Economic
Development
954-797-2087

City of Fort Lauderdale
954-828-4515

Hollywood Business Council
954-927-0277

City of Lauderhill
Neighborhood City Business
Council
954-730-3036

Oakland Park & Wilton
Manors Chamber of
Commerce
954-568-7755

City of Plantation
954-797-2622
www.plantation.org

City of Pompano Beach
954-786-4049

City of Sunrise
954-746-3430

City of Tamarac
954-724-1292

Weston Area Chamber of
Commerce
954-389-0600

CALHOUN
Calhoun County Chamber of
Commerce
850-674-4519
www.calhounco.org

CHARLOTTE
Charlotte County
Economic Development Office
800-729-5836
www.pureeconomics.org

CITRUS
Citrus County Economic
Development Council
352-795-2000
www.citrusedc.com

CLAY
Clay County Economic
Development Council
904-264-7373
www.clayedo.com

COLLIER
Economic Development
Council of Collier County
239-263-8989
www.enaplesflorida.com

Collier County
239-403-2398

COLUMBIA
Lake City—Columbia County
Chamber of Commerce
386-752-3690
www.lakecitychamber.com

DESOTO
DeSoto County Economic
Development Office
863-993-4800
www.co.desoto.fl.us

DIXIE
Dixie County Chamber
of Commerce
352-498-5454
www.dixiecounty.org

DUVAL
Jacksonville Regional
Chamber of Commerce
904-366-6680
www.coj.net

Jacksonville Economic
Development Commission
904-630-1858

ESCAMBIA
Pensacola Bay Area Chamber
Committee of 100
850-438-4081
www.pensacolachamber.com

City of Pensacola
850-435-1603

Pensacola Area Chamber
of Commerce
850-438-4081

FLAGLER
Enterprise Flagler
800-899-7962
www.enterpriseflagler.org

FRANKLIN
Apalachicola Bay Chamber
of Commerce
850-653-9419
www.apalachicolabay.org

GADSDEN
Gadsden County Chamber
of Commerce
850-627-9231
www.gadsdengov.net

GILCHRIST
Gilchrist County Development
Authority
352-463-3467
www.gilchristcounty.com

GLADES
Glades County Economic
Development Council
863-946-0300
www.gladescountyedc.com

GULF
Gulf County Economic
Development Council
850-229-1901
www.gulfcountyedc.org

HAMILTON
Hamilton County Office of
Economic Development
386-792-6828
www.hamiltoncountyflorida.com

HARDEE
Hardee County Economic
Development Office
863-773-3030
www.hardeebusiness.com

HENDRY

Hendry County Economic
Development Council
863-675-6007
www.hendrycountyedc.com

HERNANDO

Hernando County Office of
Business Development
352-540-6400
www.hernandobusiness.com

HIGHLANDS

Highlands County Economic
Development Commission
863-385-1025
www.highlandsedc.com

HILLSBOROUGH

Greater Tampa Chamber of
Commerce
Committee of 100
813-228-7777
www.tampachamber.com

Greater Brandon Chamber
of Commerce
813-689-1221

Hillsborough County Economic
Development Department
813-272-7232
www.hillsboroughcounty.org

Greater Plant City Chamber
of Commerce
813-754-3707

City of Tampa, Economic
Development
813-274-7315

HOLMES

Holmes County Development
Commission
850-547-4682
www.holmescountyonline.com

INDIAN RIVER

Indian River Chamber
of Commerce
772-567-3491
www.indianriverchamber.com

JACKSON

Jackson County Development
Council
850-526-4005
www.phonl.com/jcdc

JEFFERSON

Jefferson County Economic
Development Council
850-342-0187
www.co.jefferson.fl.us

LAFAYETTE

Lafayette County
Development Authority
386-294-1805

LAKE

Metro Orlando Economic
Development Commission
352-728-0899
www.orlandoedc.com

Lake County Economic
Development and Tourism
352-429-3673

City of Leesburg—
    Economic Development
    Department
352-728-9708
www.leesburgflorida.gov

City of Tavares
352-742-6209

LEE

Lee County Office of
    Economic Development
239-338-3161
www.leecountybusiness.com

City of Cape Coral
239-574-0444
www.bizcapecoral.com

LEON

Tallahassee Area Chamber of
    Commerce & Tallahassee
    Economic Development
    Council
850-224-8116
www.taledc.com

City of Tallahassee
850-891-8886

LEVY

Nature Coast Business
    Development Council
352-486-5470
www.naturecoast.org

LIBERTY

Bristol-Liberty County
    Chamber of Commerce
850-643-2359

MADISON

Greater Madison County
    Chamber of Commerce
850-973-2788
www.madisonfl.org

MANATEE

Economic Development
    Council
Manatee Chamber of
    Commerce
941-748-3411
www.manateeedc.com

MARION

Ocala/Marion County
    Economic Development
    Corporation
352-291-4410
www.ocalaedc.org

MARTIN

Business Development Board
    of Martin County
772-221-1380
www.bdbmc.org

MIAMI-DADE

The Beacon Council
305-579-1300
www.beaconcouncil.com

City of Hialeah
Department of Grants
    and Human Services
305-883-5839

City of Homestead
    Community Redevelopment
    Agency
305-224-4481

Greater Miami Chamber
of Commerce
305-350-7700
www.miamichamber.com

Miami-Dade County
Industrial Development
Authority
305-579-0070

City of North Miami—
Office of Economic
Development
305-893-6511

Perrine-Cutler Ridge Council
305-378-9470

MONROE
South Florida Regional
Planning Council
954-985-4416
www.monroecounty-fl.gov

Islamorada Chamber
of Commerce
305-664-4503

NASSAU
Nassau County Economic
Development Board
904-225-8878
www.nassaucountyfla.com

OKALOOSA
Economic Development
Council of Okaloosa County
800-995-7374
www.florida-edc.org

OKEECHOBEE
Okeechobee County
863-763-9312

ORANGE
Metro Orlando Economic
Development Commission
407-422-7159
www.orlandoedc.com

Orange County
407-836-5417

City of Orlando
407-656-1304

West Orange Chamber
of Commerce
407-656-1304

OSCEOLA
Osceola County Economic
Development Department
407-343-4050
www.idoteam.com

Metro Orlando Economic
Development Commission
407-422-7159
www.orlandoedc.com

PALM BEACH
Business Development Board
of Palm Beach County
561-835-1008
www.bdb.org

Greater Delray Beach
Chamber of Commerce
561-279-1380

City of Palm Beach Gardens
561-799-4136

PASCO

Pasco Economic Development
Council
813-996-4075
www.pascoedc.com

PINELLAS

Pinellas County Economic
Development
888-759-5627
www.siliconbay.org

City of Clearwater
727-562-4040

City of Pinellas Park
727-541-0702

City of St. Petersburg
727-893-7100

City of Tarpon Springs
727-942-5638

POLK

Central Florida Development
Council of Polk County
www.cfdc.org
863-534-4370

Haines City Economic
Development Council
863-422-2525

Lakeland Economic
Development Council
863-687-3788

Lake Wales Area Chamber of
Commerce
863-676-3445

PUTNAM

Putnam County Chamber
of Commerce/Economic
Development Authority
386-328-5401
www.putnamcountychamber.org

SANTA ROSA

Team Santa Rosa Economic
Development Council
850-623-0174
www.teamsantarosa.com

Santa Rosa County Board of
County Commissioners
850-983-1876

SARASOTA

Economic Development
Corporation of Sarasota
County
941-309-1200
www.edcsarasotacounty.org

City of North Port
941-423-3181

Sarasota County
941-861-5344

SEMINOLE

Metro Orlando Economic
Development Commission
407-665-2903
www.orlandoedc.com

Seminole County
407-665-7132

ST. JOHNS

St. Augustine/St. Johns
County Chamber of
Commerce
904-829-5681
www.staugustinechamber.com

ST. LUCIE

Economic Development
Council of St. Lucie County
772-879-4144
www.edcstlucie.org

City of Port St. Lucie
772-344-4185

St. Lucie County Chamber of
Commerce
772-595-9999

St. Lucie County Economic
Development Division
772-462-1564

SUMTER

Sumter County Economic
Development Council
352-793-3003
www.sumtercountytoday.com

SUWANNEE

Suwannee County Economic
Alliance
386-362-3071
www.suwanneechamber.com

TAYLOR

Perry-Taylor County Chamber
of Commerce and County
Development Authority
850-584-5627
www.taylorcountychamber.com

UNION

North Florida Regional
Chamber of Commerce
904-964-5278
www.northfloridachamber.com

VOLUSIA

Volusia County Department of
Economic Development
386-248-8048
www.floridabusiness.org

City of Daytona Beach
386-671-8120

Daytona Beach/
Halifax Area Chamber
386-255-0981

City of New Smyrna Beach
386-424-2287

City of Ormond Beach
386-676-3266

WAKULLA

Wakulla County Chamber
of Commerce
850-926-1848
www.wakullacounty.com

WALTON

Walton County Economic
Development Council
850-892-0555
www.waltonbusiness.com

WASHINGTON

Washington County Chamber
of Commerce
850-638-4157
www.washcomall.com

Other Offices   You may still need further help or have a question that goes beyond your local area. In those cases, the federal Small Business Administration has two offices in Florida.

North Florida District Office
7825 Baymeadows Way
Suite 100B
Jacksonville, FL 32256
904-443-1900
Fax: 904-443-1980
904-443-1909 TDD
www.sba.gov/fl/north

North Florida District Office
100 South Biscayne Boulevard
7th Floor
Miami, FL 33131
305-536-5521
Fax: 305-536-5058
www.sba.gov/fl/south

The following offices help businesses that plan to export U.S. goods overseas.

U.S. Export Assistance Center, Miami
5835 Blue Lagoon Drive
Suite 203
Miami, FL 33126
305-526-7425

U.S. Export Assistance Center, Ft. Lauderdale
200 East Las Olas Boulevard
Suite 1600
Ft. Lauderdale, FL 33301
954-356-6640

chapter 2

Choosing the Form of Your Business

Before starting your business, you should choose the form of your business. That is, you should choose whether you will do business in your own name, with a partner, or as a legal entity such as a corporation or LLC. In Florida, forming and maintaining an artificial entity is very inexpensive, so most lawyers advise using one for any type of business to protect yourself against liability.

BASIC FORMS OF DOING BUSINESS

The five most common forms for a business in Florida are proprietorship, partnership, limited partnership, corporation, and limited liability company. The characteristics, advantages, and disadvantages of each are discussed in this section.

Proprietorship

A *proprietorship* is one person doing business in his or her own name or under a fictitious name.

Advantages. Simplicity is a proprietorship's greatest advantage. There is also no organizational expense and no extra tax forms or reports.

Disadvantages. The proprietor is personally liable for all debts and obligations. There is also no continuation of the business after death. All profits are directly taxable, which is certainly a disadvantage for the proprietor, and business affairs are easily mixed with personal affairs.

General Partnership

A *general partnership* involves two or more people carrying on a business together to share the profits and losses.

Advantages. Partners can combine expertise and assets. A general partnership allows liability to be spread among more persons. Also, the business can be continued after the death of a partner if bought out by a surviving partner.

Disadvantages. Each partner is liable for acts of other partners within the scope of the business. This means that if your partner harms a customer or signs a million-dollar credit line in the partnership's name, you can be personally liable. Even if you leave all profits in the business, those profits are taxable. Control is shared by all parties, and the death of a partner may result in liquidation. In a general partnership, it is often hard to get rid of a bad partner.

Limited Partnership

A *limited partnership* has characteristics similar to both a corporation and a partnership. There are general partners who have the control and personal liability, and there are limited partners who only put up money and whose liability is limited to what they paid for their share of the partnership (like corporate stock). A new type of limited partnership, a *limited liability limited partnership*, allows all partners to avoid liability.

Advantages. Capital can be contributed by limited partners who have no control of the business or liability for its debts.

Disadvantages. A great disadvantage is high start-up costs. Also, an extensive partnership agreement is required because general partners are personally liable for partnership debts and for the acts of each other. (One solution to this problem is to use a corporation as the general partner.)

Corporation

A *corporation* is an artificial legal "person" that carries on business through its officers for its shareholders. Laws covering corporations are contained in the Florida Statutes (Fla. Stat.), Chapter (Ch.) 607. This legal person carries on business in its own name, and shareholders are not necessarily liable for its acts. In Florida, one person may form a corporation and be its sole shareholder and officer.

An *S corporation* is a corporation that has filed Internal Revenue Service (IRS) Form 2553, thus choosing to have all profits taxed to the shareholders, rather than to the corporation. An S corporation files a tax return, but pays no federal or state tax. The profit shown on the S corporation tax return is reported on the owners' tax returns.

A *C corporation* is any corporation that has not elected to be taxed as an S corporation. A C corporation pays income tax on its profits. The effect of this is that when dividends are paid to shareholders, they are taxed twice—once for the corporation and once when they are paid to the shareholders. In Florida, a C corporation must also pay corporate income tax.

A *professional service corporation* is a corporation formed by professionals, such as doctors or accountants. Florida has special rules for professional service corporations that differ slightly from those of other corporations. These rules are included in Florida Statutes, Chapter 621. There are also special tax rules for professional service corporations.

A *nonprofit corporation* is usually used for organizations such as religious groups and condominium associations. However, with careful planning, some types of businesses can be set up as nonprofit corporations and save a lot in taxes. While a nonprofit corporation cannot pay dividends, it can pay its officers and employees fair salaries. Some of the major American nonprofit organizations pay their officers well over $100,000 a year. Florida's special rules for nonprofit corporations are included in Florida Statutes, Chapter 617.

Advantages. If a corporation is properly organized, shareholders have no liability for corporate debts and lawsuits, and officers usually have no personal liability for their corporate acts. The existence of a corporation may be perpetual. There are tax advantages allowed only to corporations. There is prestige in owning a corporation. Two of the most important advantages to doing business as a corporation are the ability to raise capital by issuing stock and the ease of transferring ownership upon death.

A small corporation can be set up as an S corporation to avoid corporate taxes, but still retain corporate advantages. Some types of businesses can be set up as nonprofit corporations that provide significant tax savings.

Disadvantages. The start-up costs for forming a corporation are certainly a disadvantage. Plus, there are certain formalities to comply with, such as annual meetings, separate bank accounts, and more complicated tax forms. Unless a corporation registers as an S corporation, it must pay federal income tax separate from the tax paid by the owners, and must pay Florida income tax. Over the years, there have occasionally been proposals to tax S corporations with an exemption for small operations, but none have passed the legislature.

Limited Liability Company

Florida was the second state in the United States to allow business owners to form *limited liability companies* (LLCs). An LLC is like a limited partnership without general partners. It has characteristics of both a corporation and a partnership—none of the partners have liability and all can have some control. LLCs are exempt from Florida corporate income tax. Florida's LLC law also allows professionals to form *professional limited liability companies*, which are used for such businesses as doctors and lawyers. LLCs are governed by Florida Statutes, Chapter 608.

NOTE: *Florida no longer has limited liability partnerships.*

Advantages. The limited liability company offers the tax benefits of a partnership with the protection from liability of a corporation. While both a corporation and an LLC offer a business owner protection from business debts, the LLC also offers protection of the company's assets from the debts of an owner. It offers more tax benefits than an S corporation, because it may pass through more depreciation and deductions, have different classes of ownership, have an unlimited number of members, and have aliens as members. It is similar to a Latin-American *Limitada* or a German *GmbH,* and is expected to attract foreign investment to Florida.

Disadvantages. An LLC that is set up as a disregarded entity might pay more Social Security taxes on business income than a S corporation. This can be eliminated by opting to be taxed as an S corporation.

START-UP PROCEDURES

Except for a sole proprietorship, you must prepare some paperwork to start your business, and for some types, you must file the paperwork and pay a registration fee.

Proprietorship In a proprietorship, all accounts, property, and licenses are taken in the name of the owner. See Chapter 3 for a discussion of fictitious names.

Partnership To form a partnership, a written agreement should be prepared to spell out the rights and obligations of the parties. It may be registered with the secretary of state, but this is not required. Most accounts, property, and licenses can be in either the partnership name or the partners' names.

Limited Partnership A written *limited partnership agreement* must be drawn up and registered with the secretary of state in Tallahassee, and a lengthy disclosure document given to all prospective limited partners. Because of the complexity of securities laws and the criminal penalties for violation, it is advantageous to have an attorney organize a limited partnership.

Corporation To form a corporation, *articles of incorporation* must be filed with the secretary of state in Tallahassee, along with $70 in filing fees. An organizational meeting is then held. At the meeting, officers are elected, stock issued, and other formalities are complied with in order to avoid the corporate entity being set aside later and treated as though it never was formed. Licenses and accounts are titled in the name of the corporation. One person or more may form a for-profit corporation, but at least three persons are needed to form a nonprofit corporation.

Limited Liability Corporation One or more persons may form a limited liability company by filing *articles of organization* with the secretary of state in Tallahassee. Licenses and accounts are titled in the name of the company.

FOREIGN NATIONALS

Persons who are not citizens or legal permanent residents of the United States are free to start any type of business organization in Florida. The type that would be most advantageous would be the LLC, because federal tax law allows it to have foreign owners (unlike an S corporation) and it avoids corporate taxation (unlike a C corporation).

Two legal issues that foreign persons should be concerned with when starting a business in Florida are their immigration status and the proper reporting of the business's foreign owners.

The ownership of a U.S. business does not automatically confer rights to enter or remain in the United States. Different types of visas are available to investors and business owners, and each of these has strict requirements.

A visa to enter the United States may be permanent or temporary. Permanent visas for business owners usually require investments to be from $500,000 to $1,000,000 and to result in the creation of new jobs. However, there are ways to obtain visas for smaller investments, if structured right. For more information on this area, consult an immigration specialist or a book on immigration.

Temporary visas may be used by business owners to enter the United States. However, these are hard to get, because in most cases, the foreign person must prove that there are no U.S. residents qualified to take the job.

Reporting   Businesses in the U.S. that own real property and are controlled by foreigners are required to file certain federal reports under the *International Investment Survey Act*, the *Agricultural Foreign Investment Disclosure Act*, and the *Foreign Investment in Real Property Tax Act* (FIRPTA). If these laws apply to your business, you should consult an attorney who specializes in foreign ownership of U.S. businesses.

BUSINESS COMPARISON CHART

	Sole Proprietorship	General Partnership	Limited Partnership	Limited Liability Co.	Corporation C or S	Nonprofit Corporation
Liability Protection	No	No	For limited partners	For all members	For all shareholders	For all members
Taxes	Pass through	Pass through	Pass through	Pass through or corporate	S corps. pass through, C corps. pay tax	None on 501(c)(3) charities, Employees pay on wages
Minimum # of members	1	2	2	1	1	3
Start-up fee	None	$50 optional	$1000	$125	$70	$70
Annual fee	None	$25 optional	$500	$50	$150	$61.25
Different classes of ownership	No	Yes	Yes	Yes	S corps. No C corps. Yes	No ownership, Diff. classes of membership
Survives after Death	No	No	Yes	Yes	Yes	Yes
Best for	One person, low-risk business, or no assets	Low-risk business	Low-risk business with silent partners	All types of business	All types of business	Educational

research the

(1) county

(2) Secretary of State
Tallahassee

Sunbiz.org

Naming Your Business

Before deciding upon a name for your business, you should be sure that it is not already being used by someone else. Many business owners have spent thousands of dollars on publicity and printing, only to throw it all away because another company owned the name. A company that owns a name can take you to court and force you to stop using that name. It can also sue you for damages if it thinks your use of the name cost it a financial loss.

Even if you will be running a small local shop with no plans for expansion, you should at least check out whether the name has been trademarked. If someone else is using the same name anywhere in the country and has registered it as a federal trademark, they can sue you if you use it. If you plan to expand or to deal nationally, then you should do a thorough search of the name.

The first places to look are the local phone books and official records of your county. Next, you should check with the secretary of state's office in Tallahassee to see if someone has registered a fictitious or corporate name that is the same as, or confusingly similar to, the one you have chosen. This can be done either by calling them or by visiting their website at:

www.sunbiz.org

To do a national search, you should check trade directories and phone books of major cities. These can be found at many libraries and are usually reference books that cannot be checked out. The *Trade Names Directory* is a two-volume set of names, compiled from many sources, published by Gale Research Co.

With Internet access, you can search all of the Yellow Page listings in the U.S. at a number of sites at no charge. One website, **www.superpages.com**, offers free searches of Yellow Pages for all states at once. You can also use **www.google.com** to see if your company name is used anywhere on the Internet.

To be sure that your use of the name does not violate someone else's trademark rights, you should have a trademark search done of the mark in the *United States Patent and Trademark Office* (PTO). In the past, this required a visit to their offices or the hiring of a search firm for over a hundred dollars. However, in 1999, the PTO put its trademark records online, and you can now search them at **www.uspto.gov.**

Even if you do not have access to the Internet, you might be able to search at a public library or have one of their employees order an online search for you for a small fee. If this is not available to you, you can have the search done through a firm. One such firm, Government Liason Services, Inc., offers searches of 100 trade directories and 4800 phone books.

Government Liaison Services, Inc.
200 North Glebe Road
Suite 321
Arlington, VA 22203
800-642-6564
www.trademarkinfo.com

No matter how thorough your search is, there is no guarantee that there is not a local user somewhere with rights to the mark. If, for example, you register a name for a new chain of restaurants and later find out that someone in Tucumcari, New Mexico has been using the name longer than you, that person will still have the right to use the name, but just in his or her local area. If you do not want this restaurant to cause confusion with your chain, you can try to buy him or her out. Similarly, if you are operating a small business under a unique name and a law firm in New York writes and offers to buy the right to your name, you can assume that some large corporation wants to start a major expansion under that name.

The best way to make sure a name you are using is not already owned by someone else is to make one up. Names such as Xerox, Kodak, and Exxon were made up and did not have any meaning prior to their use. Remember that there are millions of businesses, and even something you make up may already be in use. Do a search just to be sure.

FICTITIOUS NAMES

In Florida, as in most states, unless you do business in your own legal name, you must register the name you are using, called a *fictitious name*. When you use a fictitious name, you are *doing business as* (d/b/a) whatever name you are using. The name must be registered with the secretary of state's office in Tallahassee. Previously, registrations of fictitious names were handled by each county. Businesses that had been registered with their county were supposed to reregister with the secretary of state between January 1, 1991 and December 31, 1992. Because some did not do so, but may still be in business, you should be sure to check the county records as well as the state.

A fictitious name registration is good for five years and expires on December 31st of the fifth year. It can be renewed for additional five-year periods.

Requirements and Exemptions

It is a misdemeanor to fail to register a fictitious name, and you may not sue anyone unless you are registered. If someone sues you and you are not registered, you may have to pay their attorney's fees and court costs.

If your name is *John Doe* and you are operating a masonry business, you may operate your business as *John Doe, Mason* without registering it. But any other use of a name should be registered, such as:

Doe Masonry	Doe Masonry Company
Doe Company	Florida Sunshine Masonry

Legally, you would use the full name "John Doe d/b/a Doe Masonry."

You cannot use the words "corporation," "incorporated," "corp.," or "inc." unless you are a corporation. However, corporations do not have to register the name they are using unless it is different from their registered corporate name. (See "Corporate Names" on p.29 for more information on this subject.)

Attorneys and professionals licensed by the Department of Professional Regulation do not have to register the names under which they practice their profession.

Obtaining a Fictitious Name

To register a fictitious name, you must first place an ad announcing your intent to use the name. Place the ad in a newspaper of general circulation for the county in which you will be maintaining your principal place of business. The ad only has to be run once. The ad would typically be placed in the classified section under "Legal Notices" and could be worded as follows:

FICTITIOUS NAME NOTICE

Notice is hereby given that the undersigned, desiring to engage in business under the name of DOE COMPANY, intend to register the name with the Clerk of the Circuit Court of Liberty County, Florida.
JOHN DOE   75% Owner
JIM DOE   25% Owner
John Doe, 123 Main Street, Libertyville, FL 32101

You should compare ad rates before placing the ad. Many counties have weekly newspapers that specialize in legal ads and charge a third of what the large newspapers charge. Check the newsstands, especially around the courthouse.

After the ad has appeared, you must file an **APPLICATION FOR REGISTRATION OF FICTITIOUS NAME** with the secretary of state. (see form 2, p.233.) Unlike corporate names and trademarks, which are carefully screened by the secretary of state to avoid duplication, fictitious name registrations are accepted without regard to who else is using the name. If you apply for registration of a trademark or corporate name, the secretary of state will check all other registrations and refuse registration if the name or a similar name is already registered. However, the registration of a fictitious name does not bestow any rights to the name upon the registrant—it merely notifies the world of who is behind the business. The secretary of state will allow anyone to register any name, even if 100 others have already registered that name.

As discussed previously, you should do some research to see if the name you intend to use is already being used by anyone else. Even persons who have not registered a name can acquire some legal rights to the name through mere use.

Some businesses have special requirements for registration of their fictitious names. For example, prior to obtaining its license from the state, a private investigative agency must obtain permission from the Department of Business and Professional Regulation for the use of its proposed name. Other businesses may have similar requirements. See Chapter 7 for a list of state-regulated professions with references to the laws that apply to them.

Appendix B has a sample filled-in **APPLICATION FOR REGISTRATION OF FICTITIOUS NAME**. A blank form and instructions are included in Appendix C. (see form 2, p.233.)

CORPORATE NAMES

A corporation does not have to register a fictitious name because it already has a legal name. The name of a corporation must contain one of the following words:

Incorporated	Inc.
Corporation	Corp.
Company	Co.

It is not advisable to use only the word "Company" or "Co.," because unincorporated businesses also use these words; therefore, a person dealing with you might not realize you are incorporated. If this happens, you might end up with personal liability for corporate debts. You may use a combination of two of the words, such as ABC Co., Inc.

If the name of the corporation does not contain one of the above words it will be rejected by the secretary of state. It will also be rejected if the name is already taken, is similar to the name of another corporation, or if it uses a forbidden word such as "Bank" or "Trust." To check on a name, use the secretary of state's website:

www.sunbiz.org/corpweb/inquiry/cormenu.html

If a name you pick is taken by another company, you may be able to change it slightly and have it accepted. For example, if there is already a Tri-City Upholstery, Inc., and it is in a different county, you may be allowed to use Tri-City Upholstery of Liberty County, Inc. However, even if this is approved by the secretary of state, you might get sued by the other company if your business is close to theirs or there is a likelihood of confusion.

Do not have anything printed with your business name on it until you have final approval. If you register online, you will get an email approval that the articles are filed. If you file by mail, you should wait until you receive the copy back with the filing date stamped on it.

If a corporation wants to do business under a name other than its corporate name, it can register a fictitious name, such as "Doe Corporation d/b/a Doe Industries." However, if the name leads people to believe that the business is not a corporation, the right to limited liability may be lost. If you use such a name, it should always be accompanied by the corporate name.

PROFESSIONAL ASSOCIATIONS

Professionals such as attorneys, doctors, dentists, life insurance agents, and architects can form corporations or limited liability companies in which to practice. These are better than general partnerships because they protect the professional from the malpractice of his or her coworkers. These professional corporations and professional limited liability companies are covered by Florida Statutes, Chapter 621.

Under Florida law, a professional corporation cannot use the usual corporate designations (Inc., Corp., or Co.), but must use the designations "Professional Association," "P.A.," or "Chartered." Other states use abbreviations such as P.C. (professional corporation) or P.S.C. (professional service corporation), but neither of these is legal in Florida.

A professional LLC can use "chartered," "professional limited company," "P.L.," or "L.C."

THE WORD *LIMITED*

The word *limited* or the abbreviation *ltd.* should not be used unless the entity is a limited partnership or limited liability company. If a corporation wishes to use the word *limited* in its name, it must still use one of the corporate words or abbreviations, such as *incorporated* or *corp.*

TRADEMARKS

As your business builds goodwill, its name will become more valuable and you will want to protect it from others who may wish to copy it. To protect a name used to describe your goods or services, you can register it as a *trademark* (for goods) or a *service mark* (for services) with either the secretary of state of Florida or with the United States Patent and Trademark Office (or both).

You cannot obtain a trademark for the name of your business, but you can trademark the name you use on your goods and services. In most cases, you use your company name on your goods as your trademark. In effect, it protects your company name. Another way to protect your company name is to incorporate. A particular corporate name can only be registered by one company in Florida.

State registration would be useful if you only expect to use your trademark within the state of Florida. Federal registration would protect your mark anywhere in the country. The registration of a mark gives you exclusive use of the mark for the types of goods for which it is registered. The only exception is for people who have already been using the mark. You cannot stop people who have been using the mark prior to your registration.

State Registration

The procedure for state registration is simple and the cost is $87.50. First, you should check the availability of the name with the secretary of state's office. This can be done by checking their website at **www.sunbiz.org.** From the drop-down menu, select "Fictitious Names."

Before a mark can be registered, it must be used in Florida. For goods, this means it must be used on the goods themselves, or on containers, tags, labels, or displays of the goods. For services, it must be used in the sale or advertising of the services. The use must be in an actual transaction with a customer. A sample mailed to a friend is not an acceptable use.

The $87.50 fee will register the mark in only one class of goods. If the mark is used on more than one class of goods, a separate registration must be filed. The registration is good for ten years. Six months prior to its expiration, it must be renewed. The renewal fee is $87.50 for each class of goods.

In Appendix B there is a sample, filled-in **APPLICATION FOR THE REGISTRATION OF A TRADEMARK OR SERVICE MARK**. A blank form and instructions are in Appendix C of this book. (see form 3, p.235.) For questions about filing the application, call 850-488-9000.

Federal Registration

For federal registration, the procedure is a little more complicated. There are two types of applications, depending upon whether you have already made *actual use* of the mark or whether you merely have an *intention to use* the mark in the future. For a trademark that has been in use, you must file an application form along with specimens showing actual use and a drawing of the mark that complies with all of the rules of the United States Patent and Trademark Office. For an intent to use application, you must file two separate forms—one when you make the initial application and the other after you have made actual use of the mark—as well as the specimens and a drawing. Before a mark can be entitled to federal registration, the use of the mark must be in *interstate commerce—*

commerce with another state. The fee for registration is $335, but if you file an intent to use application there is a second fee of $100 for the filing after actual use.

DOMAIN NAMES

With the Internet changing so rapidly, all of the rules for Internet names have not yet been worked out. Originally, the first person to reserve a name owned it, and enterprising souls bought up the names of most of the Fortune 500 corporations. Then a few of the corporations went to court and the rule was developed that if a company had a trademark for a name, that company could stop someone else from using it if the other person did not have a trademark. More recently, Congress made it illegal for cybersquatters to register the names of famous persons and companies. Once you have a valid trademark, you will be safe using it for your domain name.

In recent years, several new *top-level domains* (TLDs) have been created. TLDs are the last letters of the URL (uniform resource locator), such as ".com," ".org," and ".net." Now you can also register names with the following TLDs.

.biz	.pro
.cc	.aero
.info	.coop
.name	.museum

One of the best places to register a domain name is **www.registerfly .com**. If your name is taken, they automatically suggest related names that might work for you, and their registration fees are lower than most other sites.

To find out if a domain name is available, go to **www.whois.net**.

fruitylicious

Preparing a Business Plan

Not everyone needs a business plan to start a business, but if you have one it might help you avoid mistakes and make better decisions. For example, if you think it would be a great idea to start a candle shop in a little seaside resort, you might find out after preparing a business plan that considering the number of people who might stop by, you could never sell enough candles to pay the rent.

A business plan lets you look at the costs, expenses, and potential sales, and see whether or not your plan can be profitable. It also allows you to find alternatives that might be more profitable. In the candle shop example, you might find that if you chose a more populous location or if you sold something else in addition to the candles, you would be more likely to make a profit.

ADVANTAGES AND DISADVANTAGES OF A BUSINESS PLAN

Other than helping you figure out if your business will be profitable, a business plan would also be useful if you hope to borrow money or have investors buy into your business. Lenders and equity investors always require a business plan before they will provide money to a business.

If your idea is truly unusual, a business plan may discourage you from starting your business. A business idea might look like a failure on paper, but if in your gut you know it would work, it might be worth trying without a business plan.

Example:

When Chester Carlson invented the first photocopy machine, he went to IBM. They spent $50,000 to analyze the idea and concluded that nobody needed a photocopy machine because people already had carbon paper—which was cheaper. However, he believed in his machine and started Xerox Corporation, which became one of the biggest and hottest companies of its time.

However, even with a great concept, you need to at least do some basic calculations to see if the business can make a profit.

- ✪ If you want to start a retail shop, figure out how many people are close enough to become customers and how many other stores will be competing for those customers. Visit some of those other shops and see how busy they are. Without giving away your plans to compete, ask some general questions like "how's business?" and maybe they will share their frustrations or successes.

- ✪ Whether you sell a good or a service, do the math to find out how much profit is in it. For example, if you plan to start a house painting company, find out what you will have to pay to hire painters, what it will cost you for all of the insurance, what bonding and licensing you will need, and what the advertising will cost you. Figure out how many jobs you can do per month and what other painters are charging. In some industries, in different areas of the state there may be a large margin of profit, while in other areas there may be almost no profit.

✪   Find out if there is a demand for your product or service. Suppose you have designed a beautiful new kind of candle and your friends all say you should open a shop because "everyone will want them." Before making a hundred of them and renting a store, bring a few to craft shows or flea markets and see what happens.

✪   Figure out what the income and expenses would be for a typical month of your new business. List monthly expenses, such as rent, salaries, utilities, insurance, taxes, supplies, advertising, services, and other overhead. Then, figure out how much profit you will average from each sale. Next, figure out how many sales you will need to cover your overhead and divide by the number of business days in the month. Can you reasonably expect that many sales? How will you get those sales?

Most types of businesses have trade associations, which often have figures on how profitable its members are. Some even have start-up kits for people wanting to start businesses. One good source of information on such organizations is the *Encyclopedia of Associations* published by Gale Research Inc., available in many library reference sections. Suppliers of products to the trade often give assistance to small companies getting started, to win their loyalty. Contact the largest suppliers of the products your business will be using and see if they can be of help.

OUTLINE FOR YOUR BUSINESS PLAN

While you may believe that you do not need a business plan, conventional wisdom says you do and it only makes good business sense to have one. A typical business plan has sections that cover topics such as the following:

✪   executive summary;

✪   product or service;

✪   market;

- ✪ competition;

- ✪ marketing plan;

- ✪ production plan;

- ✪ organizational plan;

- ✪ financial projections;

- ✪ management team; and,

- ✪ risks.

The following is an explanation of each.

Executive Summary This is an overview of what the business will be and why it is expected to be successful. If the business plan will be used to lure investors, this section is the most important, since many might not read any further if they are not impressed with the summary.

Product or Service This is a detailed description of what you will be selling. You should describe what is different about it and why people would need it or want it.

Market The market should analyze who the potential buyers of your product or service are. Describe both the physical location of the customers and their demographics. For example, a bodybuilding gym would probably mostly appeal to males in the 18 to 40 age bracket in a ten to twenty mile radius, depending on the location.

If you will sell things from a retail shop, you might also want to sell from mail order catalogs or over the Internet if your local customer base would not be large enough to support the business. Describe what you will be doing for those ventures.

If you are manufacturing things, you should find out who the wholesalers and distributors are, and their terms. This information should also be included in this section.

Competition Before opening your business, you should know who and where your competitors are. If you are opening an antique shop, you might want to be near other antique shops so more customers come by your place, since antiques are unique and do not really compete with other antiques. However, if you open a florist shop, you probably do not want to be near other florist shops since most florists sell similar products and a new shop would just dilute the customer base.

If you have a truly unique way of selling something, you might want to go near other similar businesses to grab their existing customer base and expand your market share. However, if they could easily copy your idea, you might not take away the business for long and end up diluting the market for each business. (see Chapter 6.)

Marketing Plan Many a business has closed just a few months after opening because not enough customers showed up. How do you expect customers to find out about your business? Even if you get a nice write-up in the local paper, not everyone reads the paper, many people do not read every page, and lots of people forget what they read.

Your marketing plan describes how you will advertise your business. List how much the advertising will cost, and describe how you expect people to respond to the advertising.

Production Plan The production plan needs to address and answer questions such as the following.

- ✪ If you are manufacturing a product, do you know how you will be able to produce a large quantity of them?

- ✪ Do you know all the costs and the possible production problems that could come up?

- ✪ If Wal-Mart orders 100,000 of them, could you get them made in a reasonable time?

The production plan needs to anticipate the normal schedule you intend to use, as well as how to handle any changes, positive or negative, to that schedule.

If you are selling a service and will need employees to perform those services, your production plan should explain how you will recruit and train those employees.

Organizational Plan

If your business will be more than a mom and pop operation, what will the organizational plan be? How many employees will you need and who will supervise whom? How much of the work will be done by employees and how much will be hired out to other businesses and independent contractors? Will you have a sales force? Will you need manufacturing employees? Will your accounting, web site maintenance, and office cleaning and maintenance be contracted out or done by employees?

Financial Projections

Tying all the previously discussed topics together is what your financial plan will discuss. You should know how much rent, utilities, insurance, taxes, marketing, and product costs or wages for labor will cost you for the first year. Besides listing known, expected expenses, you should calculate your financial well-being under a number of different possible scenarios. Some of the questions to think about and answer will be, *how long would you be in business if you have very few customers the first few months?*, and *if Wal-Mart does order 100,000 of your products, could you afford to manufacture them, knowing you won't be paid for months?*

Management Team

If you will be seeking outside funding, you will need to list the experience and skills of the management of the business. Investors want to know that the people have experience and know what they are doing.

Risks

A good business plan weighs all the risks of the new enterprise. Is new technology in the works that will make the business obsolete? Would a rise in the price of a particular needed supply eliminate all your profits? What are the chances of a new competitor entering the market if you show some success, and what are you going to do about it? Part of your analysis should be to look at all of the possible things that could happen in the field you chose and to gauge the likelihood of success.

Gathering Information

Some of the sections of your business plan require a lot of research. People sometimes take years to prepare them. Today, the Internet puts a nearly infinite amount of information at your fingertips, but you might also want to do some personal research.

Sometimes the best way to get the feel for a business is to get a job in a similar business. At a minimum, you should visit similar businesses and perhaps sit outside of one, and see how many customers they have and how much business they do. There are startup guides for many types of businesses, which can be found at Amazon.com, your local bookstores, and library. Your local chamber of commerce, business development office, or SCORE office might also have materials to help your research.

SAMPLE BUSINESS PLAN

The following plan is one for a simple one-person business that will use its owner's assets to start. Of course, a larger business, or one which needs financing, will need a much longer and more detailed plan.

A website with sixty sample business plans and information on business plan software is **www.bplans.com**.

Executive Summary

This is the plan for a new business, Reardon Computer Repair, LLC by Henry Reardon, to be started locally and then expanded throughout the state and perhaps further if results indicate this is feasible. The mission of Reardon Computer Repair (RCR) is to offer fast, affordable repairs to office and home computers. The objective is to become profitable within the first three months and to grow at a quick but manageable pace.

In order to offer customers the quickest service, RCR will rely on youthful computer whizzes who are students and have the time and expertise to provide the service. They will also have the flexibility to arrive quickly and the motivation to show off their expertise.

To reach customers, we will use limited advertising, but primarily the Internet and word of mouth from happy customers.

With nearly every business and family having several computers and lack of fast service currently available, it is expected this business could be successful quickly and could grow rapidly.

Product or Service

The company will offer computer repair services both at its shop and at customers' offices and homes. It will sell computer parts as necessary to complete the repairs and it will also carry upgrades, accessories, and peripherals, which will most likely be of value to customers needing repairs.

Market

The market would be nearly every business and family at every address in the city, state, and country, since today nearly everyone has a computer. Figures show nearly 250 million computers in use in America, and that number is expected to grow to over 300 million in five years.

The market for the initial shop would be a fifteen-mile radius, which is a reasonable driving distance for our employees. The population in that area is 300,000, people which would mean 240,000 potential customers, based on the current level of 800 computers per 1,000 people.

The market would not include new computers, which typically come with a one-year guarantee. It would also not include people who bought extended guarantees.

The growth trend for the industry is 8-10% for the next decade.

Competition

The competition would be the authorized repair shops working with the computer manufacturers. While these have the advantage of being authorized, research and experience has shown that they are slow and do not meet customers' need for an immediate repair.

There is one computer repair shop within a ten-mile radius of the proposed shop and two more within a twenty-five-mile radius. Average wait time for a dropped off repair is one week. The two closest repair services offer no on-site repair. Shipping a computer to a dealer for repair takes one to two weeks. Most customers need their computer fixed within a day or two.

One potential source for competition would be from employees or former employees who are asked to work for customers "on the side" at a reduced rate. To discourage this, the company will have a contract with employees with a non-compete agreement that specifies that they will pay the company three times what they earn. Also, agreements with customers will include a clause that they have the option to hire away one of our employees for a one-time $2,000 fee.

Marketing Plan

The business will be marketed through networking, Internet marketing, advertising, and creative marketing.

Networking will be through the owner's contacts and local computer clubs and software stores. Some local retailers do not offer service and they have already indicated that they would promote a local business that could offer fast repairs.

A website would be linked to local businesses and community groups, and to major computer repair referral sites.

Advertising would include the Yellow Pages and local computer club newsletters. Studies have shown that newspaper and television advertising would be too expensive and not cost effective for this type of business.

Creative advertising would include vinyl lettering on the back window of owner's vehicle.

Production Plan

The company will be selling the services of computer technicians and computer parts. The owner will supply most of the services in the beginning and then add student technicians as needed.

The parts will all be purchased ready-made from the manufacturers, except for cables, which can be made on an as-needed basis much cheaper than ready-made ones.

Employees

The employees will be students who are extremely knowledgeable about computers. Some would call them computer "geeks"—in a nice way. They have extensive knowledge of the workings of computers, have lots of free time, need money, and would love to show off how knowledgeable they are.

As students, they already have health insurance and do not need full-time work. They would be available as needed. The company would pay them $12 an hour plus mileage, which is more than any other jobs available to students, but is not cost prohibitive, considering the charge to customers of $50 per hour.

Financial Projections
The minimum charge for a service call will be $75 on-site and $50 in-shop, which will include one hour of service. The parts markup will be the industry standard of 20%. The average customer bill will be estimated to be $100 including labor and markup.

The labor cost is estimated to be $30 per call including time, taxes, insurance, and mileage. The owner will be estimated to handle 75% of the work the first six months and 50% the second six months.

Rent, utilities, insurance, taxes, and other fixed costs is estimated to be $3,000 per month.

Advertising and promotion expenses are expected to be $3,000 per month.

Estimated number of customers will be:

First three months:	10 per week
Second three months:	20 per week
Third three months:	35 per week
Fourth three months:	50 per week

Estimated monthly revenue:

First three months:	$4,000
Second three months:	$8,000
Third three months:	$14,000
Fourth three months:	$20,000

Monthly income and expense projection:

First three months:

Income	$4,000
Labor	$300
Fixed costs	$3,000
Advertising	$3,000
Net	$2,300 loss per month

Second 3 months:

Income	$8,000
Labor	$600
Fixed costs	$3,000
Advertising	$3,000
Net	$1,400 profit per month

Third 3 months:

Income	$14,000
Labor	$2,100
Fixed costs	$3,000
Advertising	$3,000
Net	$5,900 profit per month

Fourth 3 months:

Income	$20,000
Labor	$3,000
Fixed costs	$3,000
Advertising	$3,000
Net	$11,000 profit per month

Organization Plan

The business will start with the owner, Henry Reardon, and three students who are experts at computer repair and available as part time workers on an as-needed basis.

The owner will manage the business and do as many repairs as are possible with the time remaining in the week.

One of the students, Peter Galt, will work after school in the shop, and the others, Dom Roark and Howard Taggert, are willing to work on an on-call basis, either at the shop or at customers' homes.

As business grows, the company will recruit more student employees through the school job placement offices and at computer clubs.

Management Team

The owner, Henry Reardon, will be the sole manager of the company. He will use the accounting services of his accountant, Dave Burton. The owner anticipates being able to supervise up to ten employees. When there are more than ten, the company will need a manager to take over scheduling and some of other management functions.

Risks

Because the business does not require a lot of capital, there will be a low financial risk in the beginning. The biggest reason for failure would be an inability to get the word out that the company exists and can fill a need when it arises. For this reason, the most important task in the beginning will be marketing and promotion.

As the company grows, the risk will be that computers will need fewer repairs, become harder to repair, and become so cheap they are disposable. To guard against this possibility, the company will add computer consulting services as it grows so that it will always have something to offer computer owners.

Financing Your Business

The way to finance your business is determined by how fast you want your business to grow and how much risk of failure you are able to handle. Letting the business grow with its own income is the slowest but safest way to grow. Taking out a personal loan against your house to expand quickly is the fastest but riskiest way to grow.

GROWING WITH PROFITS

Many successful businesses have started out with little money and used the profits to grow bigger and bigger. If you have another source of income to live on (such as a job or a spouse's job), you can plow all the income of your fledgling business into growth.

Some businesses start as hobbies or part-time ventures on the weekend while the entrepreneur holds down a full-time job. Many types of goods or service businesses can start this way. Even some multi-million dollar corporations, such as Apple Computer, started out this way.

This allows you to test your idea with little risk. If you find you are not good at running that type of business, or the time or location was not right for your idea, all you are out is the time you spent and your start-up capital.

However, a business can only grow so big from its own income. In many cases, as a business grows, it gets to a point where the orders are so big that money must be borrowed to produce the product to fill them. With this kind of order, there is the risk that if the customer cannot pay or goes bankrupt, the business will also go under. At such a point, a business owner should investigate the creditworthiness of the customer and weigh the risks. Some businesses have grown rapidly, some have gone under, and others have decided not to take the risk and stayed small. You can worry about that down the road.

USING YOUR SAVINGS

If you have savings you can tap to get your business started, that is the best source. You will not have to pay high interest rates and you will not have to worry about paying someone back. This section discusses some options for using your own savings to start your business, and potential pitfalls for each.

Home Equity

If you have owned your home for several years, it is possible that the equity has grown substantially and you can get a second mortgage to finance your business. If you have been in the home for many years and have a good record of paying your bills, some lenders will make second mortgages that exceed the equity. Just remember, if your business fails, you may lose your house.

Retirement Accounts

Be careful about borrowing from your retirement savings. There are tax penalties for borrowing from or against certain types of retirement accounts. Also, your future financial security may be lost if your business does not succeed.

Having Too Much Money

It probably does not seem possible to have too much money with which to start a business, but many businesses have failed for that reason. With plenty of start-up capital available, a business owner does not need to watch expenses and can become wasteful. Employees get used to lavish spending. Once the money runs out and the business must run on its own earnings, it fails.

Starting with the bare minimum forces a business to watch its expenses and be frugal. It necessitates finding the least expensive solutions to problems that crop up and creative ways to be productive.

BORROWING MONEY

It is extremely tempting to look to others to get the money to start a business. The risk of failure is less worrisome and the pressure is lower, but that is a problem with borrowing. If it is others' money, you do not have quite the same incentive to succeed as you do if everything you own is on the line.

Actually, you should be even more concerned when using the money of others. Your reputation is at risk, and if you do not succeed, you probably will still have to pay back the loan.

Family Depending on how much money your family can spare, it may be the most comfortable or most uncomfortable source of funds for you. If you have been assured a large inheritance and your parents have more funds than they need to live on, you may be able to borrow against your inheritance without worry. It will be your money anyway, and you need it much more now than you will ten or twenty years from now. If you lose it all, it is your own loss.

However, if you are asking your widowed mother to cash in a CD she lives on to finance your get-rich-quick scheme, you should have second thoughts about it. Stop and consider all the real reasons your business might not take off and what your mother would do without the income.

Friends Borrowing from friends is like borrowing from family members. If you know they have the funds available and could survive a loss, you may want to risk it, but if they would be loaning you their only resources, do not chance it.

Financial problems can be the worst thing for a relationship, whether it is a casual friendship or a long-term romantic involvement. Before you borrow from a friend, try to imagine what would happen if you could not pay it back and how you would feel if it caused the end of your relationship.

The ideal situation is if your friend were a co-venturer in your business and the burden would not be totally on you to see how the funds were spent. Still, realize that such a venture will put extra strain on the relationship.

Banks

In a way, a bank can be a more comfortable party from which to borrow, because you do not have a personal relationship with them as you do with a friend or family member. If you fail, they will write your loan off rather than disown you. However, a bank can also be the least comfortable party to borrow from because they will demand realistic projections (your business plan) and be on top of you to perform. If you do not meet their expectations, they may call your loan just when you need it most.

The best thing about a bank loan is that they will require you to do your homework. You must have plans that make sense to a banker. If they approve your loan, you know that your plans are at least reasonable.

Bank loans are not cheap or easy. You will be paying a good interest rate, and you will have to put up collateral. If your business does not have equipment or receivables, the bank may require you to put up your house and other personal property to guarantee the loan.

Banks are a little easier to deal with when you get a Small Business Administration (SBA) loan. That is because the SBA guarantees that it will pay the bank if you default on the loan. SBA loans are obtained through local bank branches.

Credit Cards

Borrowing against a credit card is one of the fastest growing ways of financing a business, but it can be one of the most expensive ways. The rates can go higher than 20%, although many cards offer lower rates. Some people are able to get numerous cards. Some successful businesses have used credit cards to get off the ground or to weather through a cash crunch, but if the business does not begin to generate the cash to make the payments, you could soon end up in bankruptcy. A good strategy is only to use credit cards for a long-term asset, like a computer, or for something that will quickly generate cash, like buying inventory to fill an order. Do not use credit cards to pay expenses that are not generating revenue.

GETTING A RICH PARTNER

One of the best business combinations is a young entrepreneur with ideas and ambition, and a retired investor with business experience and money. Together, they can supply everything the business needs.

How to find such a partner? Be creative. You should have investigated the business you are starting and know others who have been in such businesses. Have any of them had partners retire over the last few years? Are any of the partners planning to phase out of the business?

SELLING SHARES OF YOUR BUSINESS

Silent investors are the best source of capital for your business. You retain full control of the business, and if it happens to fail, you have no obligation to them. Unfortunately, few silent investors are interested in a new business. It is only after you have proven your concept to be successful and built up a rather large enterprise that you will be able to attract such investors.

The most common way to obtain money from investors is to issue stock to them. For this, the best type of business entity is the corporation. It gives you almost unlimited flexibility in the number and kinds of shares of stock you can issue.

Enterprise Florida is a group that has helped Florida businesses find capital. You can visit their website at **www.eflorida.com**, or find their offices at the following locations.

Enterprise Florida, Inc.—Headquarters
390 North Orange Avenue
Suite 1300
Orlando, FL 32801
407-316-4600
Fax: 407-316-4599

Enterprise Florida, Inc.—Government Relations
325 John Knox Road
Atrium Building
Suite 201
Tallahassee, FL 32303
850-488-6300
Fax: 850-922-9595

Enterprise Florida, Inc.—
International Trade & Business Development
2801 Ponce de Leon Boulevard
Suite 700
Coral Gables, FL 33134
305-569-2650
Fax: 305-569-2686

UNDERSTANDING SECURITIES LAWS

There is one major problem with selling stock in your business, and that is all of the federal and state regulations with which you must comply. Both the state and federal governments have long and complicated laws dealing with the sales of securities. There are also hundreds of court cases attempting to explain what these laws mean. A thorough explanation of this area of law is obviously beyond the scope of this book.

Basically, *securities* have been held to exist in any case in which a person provides money to someone with the expectation that he or she will get a profit through the efforts of that person. This can apply to any situation where someone buys stock in, or makes a loan to, your business. What the laws require is disclosure of the risks involved, and in some cases, registration of the securities with the government. There are some exemptions, such as for small amounts of money and for limited numbers of investors.

Penalties for violation of securities laws are severe, including triple damages and prison terms. You should consult a specialist in securities laws before issuing any security. You can often get an introductory consultation at a reasonable rate to learn your options.

USING THE INTERNET TO FIND CAPITAL

The Internet can also be a great resource for finding and marketing to investors. However, before attempting to market your company's shares on the Internet, be sure to get an opinion from a securities lawyer or do some serious research into securities law. The immediate accessibility of the Internet makes it very easy for you to get ahead of yourself and unintentionally violate state and federal securities laws. The Internet contains a wealth of information that can be useful in finding sources of capital. The following sites may be helpful.

America's Business Funding Directory
www.businessfinance.com

Small Business Administration
www.sba.gov

Inc. Magazine
www.inc.com

NVST
www.nvst.com

The Capital Network
www.thecapitalnetwork.com

Locating Your Business

The right location for your business will be determined by what type of business it is and how fast you expect it to grow. For some types of businesses, the location will not be important to your success or failure—in others, it will be crucial.

WORKING OUT OF YOUR HOME

Many small businesses get started out of the home. Chapter 7 discusses the legalities of home businesses. This section discusses the practicalities.

Starting a business out of your home can save you the rent, electricity, insurance, and other costs of setting up at another location. For some people this is ideal, and they can combine their home and work duties easily and efficiently. For other people it is a disaster. A spouse, children, neighbors, television, and household chores can be so distracting that no other work gets done.

Since residential rates are usually lower than business lines, many people use their residential telephone line or add a second residential line to conduct business. However, if you wish to be listed in the Yellow Pages, you will need to have a business line in your home. If you are running two or more types of businesses, you can probably add their names as additional listings on the original number and avoid paying for another business line.

You also should consider whether the type of business you are starting is compatible with a home office. For example, if your business mostly consists of calling clients, then the home may be an ideal place to run it. If your clients need to visit you, or you will need daily pickups and deliveries by truck, then the home may not be a good location. This is discussed in more detail in the next chapter.

CHOOSING A RETAIL SITE

For most types of retail stores the location is of prime importance. Things to consider include how close it is to your potential customers, how visible it is to the public, and how easily accessible it is to both autos and pedestrians. The attractiveness and safety of the site should also be considered.

Location would be less important for a business that was the only one of its kind in the area. For example, if there was only one moped parts dealer or Armenian restaurant in a metropolitan area, people would have to come to wherever you are if they want your products or services. However, even with such businesses, keep in mind that there is competition. People who want moped parts can order them by mail and restaurant customers can choose another type of cuisine.

You should look up all the businesses similar to the one you plan to run in the phone book and mark them on a map. For some businesses, like a cleaners, you would want to be far from the others. However, for other businesses, like antique stores, you would want to be near the others. (Antique stores usually do not carry the same things, they do not compete, and people like to go to an antique district and visit all the shops.)

CHOOSING OFFICE, MANUFACTURING, OR WAREHOUSE SPACE

If your business will be the type where customers will not come to you, then locating it near customers is not as much of a concern and you can probably save money by locating away from the high-traffic central business districts. However, you should consider the convenience for employees, and not locate in an area that would be unattractive to them or too far from where they would likely live.

For manufacturing or warehouse operations, you should consider your proximity to a post office, trucking company, or rail line. When several sites are available, you might consider which one has the earliest or most convenient pickup schedule for the carriers you plan to use.

LEASING A SITE

A lease of space can be one of the biggest expenses of a small business, so you should do a lot of homework before signing one. There are a lot of terms in a commercial lease that can make or break your business. The most critical terms are discussed in the following pages.

Zoning

Before signing a lease, you should be sure that everything that your business will need to do is allowed by the zoning of the property. Check the city and county zoning regulations.

Restrictions

In some shopping centers, existing tenants have guarantees that other tenants do not compete with them. For example, if you plan to open a restaurant and bakery, you may be forbidden to sell carryout baked goods if the supermarket next door has a bakery and a non-compete clause.

Signs

Business signs are regulated by zoning laws, sign laws, and property restrictions. If you rent a hidden location with no possibility for adequate signage, your chances for success are less than with a more visible site or much larger sign.

ADA Compliance

The *Americans with Disabilities Act* (ADA) requires that reasonable accommodations be made to make businesses accessible to the disabled.

When a business is remodeled, many more changes are required than if no remodeling is done. Be sure that the space you rent complies with the law, or that the landlord will be responsible for compliance. Be aware of the full costs you will bear.

Expansion   As your business grows, you may need to expand your space. The time to find out about your options is before you sign the lease. Perhaps you can take over adjoining units when those leases expire.

Renewal   Location is a key to success for some businesses. If you spend five years building up a clientele, you do not want someone to take over your locale at the end of your lease. Therefore, you should have a renewal clause on your lease. Usually, this allows an increase in rent based on inflation.

Guarantee   Most landlords of commercial space will not rent to a small corporation without a personal guarantee of the lease. This is a very risky thing for a new business owner to do. The lifetime rent on a long-term commercial lease can be hundreds of thousands of dollars, and if your business fails the last thing you want to do is be personally responsible for five years of rent.

Where space is scarce or a location is hot, a landlord can get the guarantees he or she demands, and there is nothing you can do about it (except perhaps set up an asset protection plan ahead of time). However, where several units are vacant or the commercial rental market is soft, often you can negotiate out of the personal guarantee. If the lease is five years, maybe you can get away with a guarantee of just the first year.

Duty to Open   Some shopping centers have rules requiring all shops to be open certain hours. If you cannot afford to staff it the whole time required, or if you have religious or other reasons that make this a problem, you should negotiate it out of the lease or find another location.

Sublease   At some point, you may decide to sell your business, and in many cases the location is the most valuable aspect of it. For this reason, you should be sure that you have the right to either assign your lease or to sublease the property. If this is impossible, one way around a prohibition is to incorporate your business before signing the lease, and then when you sell the business, sell the stock. However, some lease clauses prohibit transfer of *any interest* in the business, so read the lease carefully.

BUYING A SITE

If you are experienced with owning rental property, you will probably be more inclined to buy a site for your business. If you have no experience with real estate, you should probably rent and not take on the extra cost and responsibility of property ownership.

One reason to buy your site is that you can build up equity. Rather than pay rent to a landlord, you can pay off a mortgage and eventually own the property.

Separating the Ownership

One risk in buying a business site is that if the business gets into financial trouble, the creditors may go after the building as well. For this reason, most people who buy a site for their business keep the ownership out of the business. For example, the business will be a corporation and the real estate will be owned personally by the owner or by a trust unrelated to the business.

Expansion

Before buying a site, you should consider the growth potential of your business. If it grows quickly, will you be able to expand at that site or will you have to move? Might the property next door be available for sale in the future if you need it? Can you get an option on it?

If the site is a good investment whether or not you have your business, then by all means buy it. However, if its main use is for your business, think twice.

Zoning

Some of the concerns when buying a site are the same as when renting. You will want to make sure that the zoning permits the type of business you wish to start, or that you can get a variance without a large expense or delay. Be aware that just because a business is now using the site does not mean that you can expand or remodel the business at that site. Check with the zoning department of your local government and find out exactly what is allowed.

Signs   Signs are another concern. Some cities have regulated signs and do not allow new or larger ones. Some businesses have used these laws to get publicity. A car dealer who was told to take down a large number of American flags on his lot filed a federal lawsuit and rallied the community behind him.

ADA Compliance   ADA compliance is another concern when buying a commercial building. Find out from the building department if the building is in compliance or what needs to be done to put it in compliance. If you remodel, the requirements may be more strict.

> **NOTE:** *When dealing with public officials, keep in mind that they do not always know what the law is, or do not accurately explain it. They often try to intimidate people into doing things that are not required by law. Read the requirements yourself and question the officials if they seem to be interpreting it incorrectly. Seek legal advice if officials refuse to reexamine the law or move away from an erroneous position.*
>
> *Also, consider that keeping them happy may be worth the price. If you are already doing something they have overlooked, do not make a big deal over a little thing they want changed, or they may subject you to a full inspection or audit.*

CHECKING GOVERNMENTAL REGULATIONS

When looking for a site for your business, you should investigate the different governmental regulations in your area. For example, a location just outside the city or county limits might have a lower licensing fee, a lower sales tax rate, and less strict sign requirements.

Licensing Your Business

The federal and state legislatures and local governments have an interest in protecting consumers from bad business practices. In order to ensure that consumers are protected from unscrupulous business people and to require a minimum level of service to the public, the federal, state, and local governments have developed hundreds of licensing requirements that cover occupations and services ranging from attorneys to barbers to day care providers.

OCCUPATIONAL LICENSES AND ZONING

Some Florida counties and cities require you to obtain an occupational license. If you are in a city, you may need both a city and a county license. Businesses that do work in several cities, such as builders, must obtain a license from each city in which they do work. This does not have to be done until you actually begin a job in a particular city.

County occupational licenses can be obtained from the tax collector in the county courthouse. City licenses are usually available at city hall. Be sure to find out if zoning allows your type of business before buying or leasing property. The licensing departments will check the zoning before issuing your license.

If you will be preparing or serving food, you will need to check with the local health department to be sure that the premises comply with their regulations. In some areas, if food has been served on the premises in the past, there is no problem getting a license. If food has never been served on the premises, then the property must comply with all the newest regulations. This can be very costly.

Home Businesses

Problems occasionally arise when people attempt to start businesses in their homes. Small, newer businesses cannot afford to pay rent for commercial space, and cities often try to forbid business in residential areas. Getting a county occupational license or advertising a fictitious name often gives notice to the city that a business is being conducted in a residential area.

Some people avoid the problem by starting their businesses without occupational licenses, figuring that the penalties for not having a license (if they are caught) are less expensive than the cost of office space. Others get the county license and ignore the city rules. If a person regularly parks commercial trucks and equipment on his or her property, has delivery trucks coming and going, or has employee cars parked along the street, there will probably be complaints from neighbors and the city will probably take legal action. However, if a person's business consists merely of making phone calls out of the home and keeping supplies there, the problem may never become an issue.

If a problem does arise regarding a home business that does not disturb the neighbors, a good argument can be made that the zoning law that prohibits the business is unconstitutional. When zoning laws were first instituted, they were not meant to stop people from doing things in a residence that had historically been part of the life in a residence. Consider an artist. Should a zoning law prohibit a person from sitting at home and painting pictures? Does selling them for a living there make a difference? Can the government force the rental of commercial space just because the artist decides to sell the paintings?

Similar arguments can be made for many home businesses. For hundreds of years people performed income-producing activities in their homes. On the other hand, court battles with a city are expensive and probably not worth the effort for a small business. The best course of action is to keep a low profile. Using a post office box for the business is sometimes helpful in diverting attention away from the residence.

STATE-REGULATED PROFESSIONS

Many professionals require special state licenses. You will probably be called upon to produce such a license when applying for an occupational license.

If you are in a regulated profession, you should be aware of all the laws that apply to your activities. The following is a list of statutes and regulations covering various professions in Florida. You can make copies of the statutes and regulations at your local library or you can download them from state websites.

The statutes can be found at **www.flsenate.gov/statutes/index.cfm**.

Regulations in the Florida Administrative Code can be found at **http://fac.dos.state.fl.us**.

For up-to-date contact information and information on the regulations affecting your profession, visit the Florida Business and Professional Regulation website at **www.myflorida.com/dbpr/index.shtml**.

The list on pages 66–67 provides the sections of the Florida statutes for many of the state's regulated professions. Florida Administrative Code Sections can also provide for those professions with code regulations.

Profession	Fla. Stats.	F.A.C.
Accountancy	455, 473	61H1
Acupuncture	457	61F1
Alcoholic Beverages	210, 561–569	61A
Architecture	481	61G1
Asbestos Consultants	469	61E1
Athlete Agents	468	61-24
Athlete Trainers	468	61-25
Attorneys	454	
Auctioneers	468	61G2
Barbering	476	61G3
Chiropractic	460	61F2
Clinical Social Workers	491	61F4
Construction Contracting	489	61G4
Cosmetology	477	61G5
Dentistry	466	61F5
Electrical Contracting	489	61G6
Employee Leasing	468	61G7
Engineering	471	61G15
Fire Equipment	633	
Fishing, Freshwater	372	
Fishing, Saltwater	370	
Funeral Directing	470	61G8, 61E-5
Geologists	492	61G16
Health Testing Services	483	
Hearing Aid Sales	468	61G9
Hotels	509	61C
Hypnotists	456	
Interior Designers	481	61G1
Land Sales	475, 498	61B
Land Surveying	472, 177	61G17
Landscape Architects	481	61G10
Massage Practice	480	61G11
Medical Doctors	458	61F6
Midwifery	467	61E8
Mobile Home Parks	723	61B
Mortgage Brokers	494	
Naturopathy	462	
Nursing	464	61F7
Nursing Homes	400, 468	61G12
Opticians	484	61G13
Optometry	463	61F8
Osteopathy	459	61F9
Pharmacy	465	61F10
Pilot Commissioners	310	61G14
Plumbing	469	

Podiatry	461	61F12
Private Investigators	493	
Physical Therapy	486	61F11
Psychological Services	490	61E9, 61F13
Radiologic Technologists	468	
Real Estate Appraisal	475	61J1
Real Estate Brokerage	475	61J2
Restaurants	509	61C
Secondhand Dealers	538	
Septic Tank Contracting	489	
Speech Pathology & Audiology	468	61F14
Surveyors and Mappers	455, 472	61G17
Talent Agencies	468	61-19
Time-shares	721	61B
Veterinary Medicine	474	61G18

FEDERAL LICENSES

Few businesses require federal registration. If you are in any of the types of businesses in the following list, you should check with the federal agency connected with it.

✪ Radio or television stations or manufacturers of equipment emitting radio waves:

Federal Communications Commission
445 12th Street, SW
Washington, DC 20554
www.fcc.gov

✪ Manufacturers of alcohol, tobacco, or firearms:

Bureau of Alcohol, Tobacco, Firearms, and Explosives
Office of Public and Governmental Affairs
650 Massachusetts Avenue, NW
Room 8290
Washington, DC 20226
www.atf.treas.gov

✪   Securities brokers and providers of investment advice:

SEC
100 F Street, NW
Washington, DC 20549
www.sec.gov

✪   Manufacturers of drugs and processors of meat:

Food and Drug Administration
5600 Fishers Lane
Rockville, MD 20857
www.fda.gov

✪   Interstate carriers:

Surface Transportation Board
1925 K Street, NW
Washington, DC 20423
www.stb.dot.gov

✪   Exporters:

Bureau of Industry and Security
Department of Commerce
14th Street & Constitution Avenue, NW
Washington, DC 20230
www.bis.doc.gov

Contract Laws

As a business owner, you will need to know the basics of forming a simple contract for your transactions with both customers and vendors. There is a lot of misunderstanding about what the law is, and people may give you erroneous information. Relying on it can cost you money. This chapter gives you a quick overview of the principles that apply to your transactions and the pitfalls to avoid. If you face more complicated contract questions, you should consult a law library or an attorney familiar with small business law.

TRADITIONAL CONTRACT LAW

One of the first things taught in law school is that a contract is not legal unless three elements are present—offer, acceptance, and consideration. The rest of the semester dissects exactly what may be a valid offer, acceptance, and consideration. For your purposes, the important things to remember are as follows.

- ❂ If you make an offer to someone, it may result in a binding contract, even if you change your mind or find out it was a bad deal for you.

○ Unless an offer is accepted and both parties agree to the same terms, there is no contract.

○ A contract does not always have to be in writing. Some laws require certain contracts to be in writing, but as a general rule, an oral contract is legal. The problem is in proving that the contract existed.

○ Without *consideration* (the exchange of something of value or mutual promises), there is not a valid contract.

Basic Contract Rules

Some of the most important contract rules for a business owner are as follows.

○ *An advertisement is not an offer.* Suppose you put an ad in the newspaper offering "New IBM computers only $995," but there is a typo in the ad and it says $9.95. Can people come in and say "I accept, here's my $9.95," creating a legal contract? Fortunately, no. Courts have ruled that an ad is not an offer that a person can accept. It is an invitation to come in and make offers, which the business can accept or reject.

○ *The same rule applies to the price tag on an item.* If someone switches price tags on your merchandise, or if you accidentally put the wrong price on it, you are not required by law to sell it at that price. However, many merchants honor a mistaken price, because refusing to do so would constitute bad will and probably lose a customer. If you intentionally put a lower price on an item, intending to require a buyer to pay a higher price, you may be in violation of *bait and switch* laws.

○ *When a person makes an offer, several things may happen.* It may be accepted, creating a legal contract; it may be rejected; it may expire before it has been accepted; or, it may be withdrawn before acceptance. A contract may expire either by a date made in the offer ("This offer remains open until noon on January 29, 2007") or after a reasonable amount of time. What is reasonable is a legal question that a court must decide. If someone makes you an offer to sell goods, clearly you cannot come back five years later and accept. Can you accept a week later or a month later and create a legal contract? That depends on the type of goods and the circumstances.

✪ *A person accepting an offer cannot add any terms to it.* If you offer to sell a car for $1,000, and the other party says he or she accepts as long as you put new tires on it, there is no contract. An acceptance with changed terms is considered a rejection and a counteroffer.

✪ *When someone rejects your offer and makes a counteroffer, a contract can be created by your acceptance of the counteroffer.*

These rules can affect your business on a daily basis. Suppose you offer to sell something to one customer over the phone, and five minutes later another customer walks in and offers you more for it. To protect yourself, you should call the first customer and withdraw your offer before accepting the offer of the second customer. If the first customer accepts before you have withdrawn your offer, you may be sued if you have sold the item to the second customer.

Exceptions There are a few exceptions to the basic rules of contracts. Some of the important exceptions you need to know are as follows.

✪ *Consent to a contract must be voluntary.* If it is made under a threat, the contract is not valid. If a business refuses to give a person's car back unless they pay $500 for changing the oil, the customer could probably sue and get the $500 back.

✪ *Contracts to do illegal acts or acts against public policy are not enforceable.* If an electrician signs a contract to put some wiring in a house that is not legal, the customer could probably not force him or her to do it, because the court would refuse to require an illegal act.

✪ *If either party to an offer dies, then the offer expires and cannot be accepted by the heirs.* If a painter is hired to paint a portrait, and dies before completing it, his wife, for example, cannot finish it and require payment. However, a corporation does not die, even if its owners die. If a corporation is hired to build a house and the owner of the corporation dies, the heirs may take over the corporation, finish the job, and require payment.

✪ *Contracts made under misrepresentation are not enforceable.* For example, if someone tells you a car has 35,000 miles on it and you later discover it has 135,000 miles, you may be able to rescind the contract for fraud and misrepresentation.

✪ *If there was a mutual mistake a contract may be rescinded.* For example, if both you and the seller thought the car had 35,000 miles on it and both relied on that assumption, the contract could be rescinded. However, if the seller knew the car has 135,000 miles on it, but you assumed it had 35,000 and did not ask, you probably could not rescind the contract.

STATUTORY CONTRACT LAW

The previous section discussed the basics of contract law and some of the additional rules for when a contract can be made unenforeceable. These are not usually stated in the statutes, but are the legal principles decided by judges over the past hundreds of years. In recent times, the legislatures have made numerous exceptions to these principles. In most cases, these laws have been passed when the legislature felt that traditional law was not fair.

Statutes of Fraud

Statutes of fraud state when a contract must be in writing to be valid. Some people believe a contract is not valid unless it is in writing, but that is not so. Only those types of contracts mentioned in the statutes of fraud must be in writing. Of course, an oral contract is much harder to prove in court than one that is in writing.

In Florida, some of the contracts that must be in writing, and the applicable statute sections, are as follows:

✪ sales of any interest in real estate (Fla. Stat. Secs. 689.01 and 725.01);

✪ leases of real estate over one year (Fla. Stat. Sec. 725.01);

- ✪ guarantees of debts of another person (Fla. Stat. Sec. 725.01);

- ✪ subscriptions to newspapers and periodicals (Fla. Stat. Sec. 725.01);

- ✪ sales of goods of $500 or more (Fla. Stat. Sec. 672.201);

- ✪ sales of personal property of $5,000 or more (Fla. Stat. Sec. 671.206);

- ✪ agreements that take over one year to complete (Fla. Stat. Sec. 725.01);

- ✪ sales of securities (Fla. Stat. Sec. 678.319); and,

- ✪ guarantees by doctors, dentists, and chiropractors for certain results. (Fla. Stat. Sec. 725.01.)

Due to the alleged unfair practices by some types of businesses, laws have been passed controlling the types of contracts they may use. Most notable among these are health clubs and door-to-door solicitations. The laws covering these businesses usually give the consumer a certain time to cancel the contract. These advertising and promotion laws are described in Chapter 13.

PREPARING YOUR CONTRACTS
Before you open your business, you should obtain or prepare the contracts or policies you will use in your business. In some businesses, such as a restaurant, you will not need much. Perhaps you will want a sign near the entrance stating "shirt and shoes required" or "diners must be seated by 10:30 p.m."

However, if you are a building contractor or a similar business, you will need detailed contracts to use with your customers. If you do not clearly spell out your rights and obligations, you may end up in court and lose thousands of dollars in profits.

Of course, the best way to have an effective contract is to have an attorney experienced on the subject prepare one to meet the needs of your business. However, since this may be too expensive for your new operation, you may want to go elsewhere. Three sources for the contracts you will need are other businesses like yours, trade associations, and legal form books. You should obtain as many different contracts as possible, compare them, and decide which terms are most comfortable for you.

Insurance

There are few laws requiring you to have insurance, but if you do not have insurance you may face liability that may ruin your business. You should be aware of the types of insurance available and weigh the risks of a loss against the cost of a policy.

Be aware that there can be a wide range of prices and coverage in insurance policies. You should get at least three quotes from different insurance agents and ask each one to explain the benefits of his or her policy.

WORKERS' COMPENSATION

If you have four or more employees, or if you are in the construction industry and have one or more employees, you are required by law to carry workers' compensation insurance.

The term *employee* is specifically defined in Florida Statutes, Chapter 440. You should read this law carefully if you think you need to comply with this law. For example, part-time employees, students, aliens, or illegal workers count as employees. However, under certain conditions, volunteers, real estate agents, musical performers, taxi cab or limo drivers, officers of a corporation, casual workers, and persons who transport property by vehicle are not considered employees. *Independent contractors,* as defined in Florida Statutes, Chapter 440, are also not considered employees.

To protect yourself from litigation, you may wish to carry workers' compensation insurance even if you are not required to have it. This insurance can be obtained from most insurance companies and, at least for low-risk occupations, it is not expensive. If you have such coverage, you are protected against potentially ruinous claims by employees or their heirs in case of accident or death.

For high-risk occupations, such as roofing, it can be very expensive— sometimes thirty to fifty cents for each dollar of payroll. For this reason, construction companies try all types of ways to become exempt from the requirement to carry workers' compensation, such as hiring independent contractors or only having a few employees who are also officers of the business. However, the requirements for the exemptions are strict. Anyone intending to obtain an exemption should first check with an attorney specializing in workers' compensation to be sure to do it right.

Failure to provide workers' compensation insurance when required is considered serious. It could result in a fine of up to $500, up to a year in prison, and an injunction against employing anyone. Failure to obtain the insurance within ninety-six hours of written notification can result in a fine of $100 per day. If a person is injured on a job, even if another employee caused it or the injured person contributed to his or her own injury, you may be required to pay for all resulting losses.

There are other requirements of the workers' compensation law, such as reporting any on-the-job deaths of workers within twenty-four hours. Also, it is a misdemeanor to deduct the amount of the premiums from the employees' wages.

Those who are exempt from the law are supposed to file an affidavit each year with the state showing that they are exempt. Also, a notice must be posted in the workplace stating that employees are not entitled to workers' compensation benefits.

This law has been subject to frequent change lately, so you should check with the Division of Workers' Compensation for the latest requirements. Ask for the booklet *Employers' Rights and Responsibilities*, or their latest publication. Call 800-342-1741 or write to the following address.

Division of Workers' Compensation
200 East Gaines Street
Tallahassee, FL 32399
850-413-1600
www.fldfs.com/wc

LIABILITY INSURANCE

In most cases, you are not required to carry liability insurance. A notable exception is for physicians, who must carry malpractice insurance in order to be licensed. (Fla. Stat. Sec. 458.320.)

Liability insurance can be divided into two main areas—coverage for injuries on your premises and by your employees, and coverage for injuries caused by your products or services.

Coverage for the first type of injury is usually very reasonably priced. Injuries in your business or by your employees (such as in an auto accident) are covered by standard premises or auto policies. However, coverage for injuries by products may be harder to find and more expensive. The current trend in liability cases is for juries to award extremely high judgments for accidents involving products that sometimes had little impact on the accidents.

Asset Protection   If insurance is unavailable or unaffordable, you can go without and use a corporation and other asset protection devices to protect yourself from liability. The best way to find out if insurance is available for your type of business is to check with other businesses. If there is a trade group for your industry, their newsletter or magazine may contain ads for insurers.

Umbrella Policy   As a business owner, you will be a more visible target for lawsuits, even if there is little merit to them. Lawyers know that a nuisance suit is often settled for thousands of dollars. Because of your greater exposure, you should consider getting a personal umbrella policy. This is a policy that covers you for claims of up to a million—or even two or five million—dollars, and is very reasonably priced.

HAZARD INSURANCE

One of the worst things that can happen to your business is a fire, flood, or other disaster. With lost customer lists, inventory, and equipment, many businesses have been forced to close after such a disaster.

The premium for such insurance is usually reasonable and could protect you from losing your business. You can even get business interruption insurance, which will cover your losses while your business is getting back on its feet.

HOME BUSINESS INSURANCE

There is a special insurance problem for home businesses. Most homeowner and tenant insurance policies do not cover business activities. In fact, under some policies, you may be denied coverage if you use your home for a business.

If you merely use your home to make business phone calls and send letters, you will probably not have a problem and not need extra coverage. However, if you own equipment or have dedicated a portion of your home exclusively to the business, you could have a problem. Check with your insurance agent for the options that are available to you.

If your business is a sole proprietorship and you have, say, a computer that you use both personally and for your business, it would probably be covered under your homeowners policy. If you incorporated your business and bought the computer in the name of the corporation, coverage might be denied. If a computer is your main business asset, you could get a special insurance policy in the company name covering just the computer. One company that offers such a policy is Safeware, and you can call them at 800-800-1492.

AUTOMOBILE INSURANCE

If you or any of your employees will be using an automobile for business purposes, be sure that such use is covered. Sometimes, a policy may contain an exclusion for business use. Check to be sure your liability policy covers you if one of your employees causes an accident while running a business errand.

HEALTH INSURANCE

While new businesses can rarely afford health insurance for their employees, the sooner they can obtain it, the better chance they will have to find and keep good employees. As a business owner, you will certainly need health insurance for yourself (unless you have a working spouse who can cover the family), and you can sometimes get a better rate if you purchase a small business package.

Florida has a nonprofit organization, Community Health Purchasing Alliance, that helps businesses with under fifty employees locate affordable health insurance plans. They can be reached at 800-469-2472.

SALES TAX BONDS

For some businesses, the Florida Department of Revenue will require a bond to guarantee payment of sales taxes. This can be obtained from your insurance agent.

EMPLOYEE THEFT

If you fear employees may be able to steal from your business, you may want to have them *bonded*. This means that you pay an insurance company a premium to guarantee employees' honesty, and if they cheat you, the insurance company pays you damages. This can cover all existing and new employees.

Your Business and the Internet

The Internet has opened up a world of opportunities for businesses. It was not long ago that getting national visibility cost a fortune. Today, a business can set up a Web page for a few hundred dollars, and with some clever publicity and a little luck, millions of people around the world will see it.

This new world has new legal issues and new liabilities. Not all of them have been addressed by laws or by the courts. Before you begin doing business on the Internet, you should know the existing rules and the areas where legal issues exist.

DOMAIN NAMES

A *domain name* is the address of your website. For example, **www.apple.com** is the domain name of Apple Computer Company. The last part of the domain name, the ".com" (or "dot com") is the *top-level domain*, or TLD. Dot com is the most popular, but others are currently available in the United States, including .net and .org. (Originally, .net was only available to network service providers and

.org only to nonprofit organizations, but regulations have eliminated those requirements.)

It may seem like most words have been taken as a dot-com name, but if you combine two or three short words or abbreviations, a nearly unlimited number of possibilities are available. For example, if you have a business dealing with automobiles, most likely someone has already registered **automobile.com** and **auto.com**. You can come up with all kinds of variations, using adjectives or your name, depending on your type of business:

autos4u.com	joesauto.com	autobob.com
myauto.com	yourauto.com	onlyautos.com
greatauto.com	autosfirst.com	usautos.com
greatautos.com	firstautoworld.com	4autos.com

One site that provides both low-cost registrations and suggestions for name variations is **www.registerfly.com**.

When the Internet first began, some individuals realized that major corporations would soon want to register their names. Since the registration was easy and cheap, people registered names they thought would ultimately be used by someone else.

At first, some companies paid high fees to buy their names from the registrants. One company, Intermatic, filed a lawsuit instead of paying. The owner of the domain name they wanted had registered numerous domain names, such as **britishairways.com** and **ussteel.com**. The court ruled that since Intermatic owned a trademark on the name, the registration of their name by someone else violated that trademark, and that Intermatic was entitled to it.

Since then, people have registered names that are not trademarks, such as **CalRipkin.com**, and have attempted to charge the individuals with those names to buy their domain. In 1998, Congress passed the *Anti-Cybersquatting Consumer Protection Act*, making it illegal to register a domain with no legitimate need to use it.

This law helped a lot of companies protect their names, but then some companies started abusing it and tried to stop legitimate users of names similar to theirs. This is especially likely against small companies. An organization that has been set up to help small companies protect their domains is the *Domain Name Rights Coalition.* Its website is **www.netpolicy.com**. Some other good information on domain names can be found at **www.bitlaw.com/internet/domain.html**.

Registering a domain name for your own business is a simple process. There are many companies that offer registration services. For a list of those companies, visit the site of the *Internet Corporation for Assigned Names and Numbers* (ICANN) at **www.icann.org**. You can link directly to any member's site and compare the costs and registration procedures required for the different top-level domains.

WEB PAGES

There are many new companies eager to help you set up a website. Some offer turnkey sites for a low, flat rate, while custom sites can cost tens of thousands of dollars. If you have plenty of capital, you may want to have your site handled by one of these professionals. However, setting up a website is a fairly simple process, and once you learn the basics, you can handle most of it in-house.

If you are new to the Web, you may want to look at **www.learn thenet.com** and **www.webopedia.com**, which will familiarize you with the Internet jargon and give you a basic introduction to the Web.

Site Setup   There are seven steps to setting up a website: site purpose, design, content, structure, programming, testing, and publicity. Whether you do it yourself, hire a professional site designer, or employ a college student, the steps toward creating an effective site are the same.

Before beginning your own site, you should look at other sites, including those of major corporations and of small businesses. Look at the sites of all the companies that compete with you. Look at hundreds of sites and click through them to see how they work (or do not work).

Site purpose. To know what to include on your site, you must decide what its purpose will be. Do you want to take orders for your products or services, attract new employees, give away samples, or show off your company headquarters? You might want to do several of these things.

Site design. After looking at other sites, you can see that there are numerous ways to design a site. It can be crowded, or open and airy; it can have several windows (frames) open at once or just one; and, it can allow long scrolling or just click-throughs.

You will have to decide whether the site will have text only; text plus photographs and graphics; or, text plus photos, graphics, and other design elements, such as animation or Java script. Additionally, you will begin to make decisions about colors, fonts, and the basic graphic appearance of the site.

Site content. You must create the content for your site. For this, you can use your existing promotional materials, new material just for the website, or a combination of the two. Whatever you choose, remember that the written material should be concise, free of errors, and easy for your target audience to read. Any graphics (including photographs) and written materials not created by you require permission. You should obtain such permission from the lawful copyright holder in order to use any copyrighted material. Once you know your site's purpose, look, and content, you can begin to piece the site together.

Site structure. You must decide how the content (text plus photographs, graphics, animation, etc.) will be structured—what content will be on which page, and how a user will link from one part of the site to another. For example, your first page may have the business name and then choices to click on, such as "about us," "opportunities," or "product catalog." Have those choices connect to another page containing the detailed information, so that a user will see the catalog when he or she clicks on "product catalog." Your site could also have an option to click on a link to another website related to yours.

Site programming and setup. When you know nothing about setting up a website, it can seem like a daunting task that will require an expert. However, *programming* here means merely putting a site together. There are inexpensive computer programs available that make it very simple.

Commercial programs such as Microsoft FrontPage, Dreamweaver, Pagemaker, Photoshop, MS Publisher, and PageMill allow you to set up Web pages as easily as laying out a print publication. These programs will convert the text and graphics you create into HTML, the programming language of the Web. Before you choose Web design software and design your site, you should determine which Web hosting service you will use. Make sure that the design software you use is compatible with the host server's system. The Web host is the provider who will give you space on their server and who may provide other services to you, such as secure order processing and analysis of your site to see who is visiting and linking to it.

If you have an America Online (AOL) account, you can download design software and a tutorial for free. You do not have to use AOL's design software in order to use this service. You are eligible to use this site whether you design your own pages, have someone else do the design work for you, or use AOL's templates. This service allows you to use your own domain name and choose the package that is appropriate for your business.

If you have used a page layout program, you can usually get a simple Web page up and running within a day or two. If you do not have much experience with a computer, you might consider hiring a college student to set up a Web page for you.

Site testing. Some of the website setup programs allow you to thoroughly check your new site to see if all the pictures are included and all the links are proper. There are also websites you can go to that will check out your site. Some even allow you to improve your site, such as by reducing the size of your graphics so they download faster. Use a major search engine listed on page 86 to look for companies that can test your site before you launch it on the Web.

Site publicity. Once you set up your website, you will want to get people to look at it. *Publicity* means getting your site noticed as much as possible by drawing people to it.

The first thing to do to get noticed is to be sure your site is registered with as many *search engines* as possible. These are pages that people use to find things on the Internet, such as Yahoo and Google. They do not automatically know about you just because you created a website. You must tell them about your site, and they must examine and catalog it.

For a fee, there are services that will register your site with numerous search engines. If you are starting out on a shoestring, you can easily do it yourself. While there are hundreds of search engines, most people use a dozen or so of the bigger ones. If your site is in a niche area, such as genealogy services, then you would want to be listed on any specific genealogy search engines. Most businesses should be mainly concerned with getting on the biggest ones.

By far the biggest and most successful search engine today is Google (**www.google.com**). Some of the other big ones are:

www.altavista.com	www.hotbot.com
www.excite.com	www.lycos.com
www.fastsearch.com	www.metacrawler.com
www.go.com	www.northernlight.com
www.goto.com	www.webcrawler.com

Most of these sites have a place to click to "add your site" to their system. Some sites charge hundreds of dollars to be listed. If your site contains valuable information that people are looking for, you should be able to do well without paying these fees.

Getting Your Site Known

A *meta tag* is an invisible subject word added to your site that can be found by a search engine. For example, if you are a pest control company, you may want to list all of the scientific names of the pests you control and all of the treatments you have available, but you may not need them to be part of the visual design of your site. List these words as meta tags when you set up your page so people searching for those words will find your site.

Some companies thought that a clever way to get viewers would be to use commonly searched names, or names of major competitors, as meta tags to attract people looking for those big companies. For example, a small delivery service that has nothing to do with UPS or FedEx might use those company names as meta tags so people looking for them would find the smaller company. While it may sound like a good idea, it has been declared illegal trademark infringement. Today many companies have computer programs scanning the Internet for improper use of their trademarks.

Once you have made sure that your site is passively listed in all the search engines, you may want to actively promote your site. However, self-promotion is seen as a bad thing on the Internet, especially if its purpose is to make money.

Newsgroups are places on the Internet where people interested in a specific topic can exchange information. For example, expectant mothers have a group where they can trade advice and experiences. If you have a product that would be great for expectant mothers, that would be a good place for it to be discussed. However, if you log into the group and merely announce your product, suggesting people order it from your website, you will probably be *flamed* (sent a lot of hate mail).

If you join the group, however, and become a regular, and in answer to someone's problem, mention that you "saw this product that might help," your information will be better received. It may seem unethical to plug your product without disclosing your interest, but this is a procedure used by many large companies. They hire *buzz agents* to plug their product all over the Internet and create positive *buzz* for the product. So, perhaps it has become an acceptable marketing method and consumers know to take plugs with a grain of salt. Let your conscience be your guide.

Keep in mind that Internet publicity works both ways. If you have a great product and people love it, you will get a lot of business. If you sell a shoddy product, give poor service, and do not keep your customers happy, bad publicity on the Internet can kill your business. Besides being an equalizer between large and small companies, the Internet can be a filtering mechanism between good and bad products.

Spamming   Sending unsolicited email advertising (called spam) started out as a mere breach of internet etiquette (netiquette) but has now become a state and federal crime. The ability to reach millions of people with advertising at virtually no cost was too good for too many businesses to pass up and this resulted in the clogging of most users' email boxes and near shut down of some computer systems. Some people ended up with thousand of offers every day.

To prevent this, many states passed anti-spamming laws and Congress passed the CAN-SPAM Act. This law:

- bans misleading or false headers on email;

- bans misleading subject lines;

- requires allowing recipients to opt out of future mailings;

- requires the email be identified as advertising; and,

- requires the email include a valid physical address.

Each violation can result in up to an $11,000 fine and the fines can be raised if advertisers violate other rules such as not harvesting names and not using permutations of existing names. More information can be found on the Federal Trade Commission's website (**www.ftc.gov**).

Advertising   Advertising on the Internet has grown in recent years. At first, small, thin rectangular ads appeared at the top of websites; these are called *banner ads*. Lately they have grown bigger, can appear anywhere on the site, and usually blink or show a moving visual.

The fees can be based on how many people view an ad, how many click on it, or both. Some larger companies, such as Amazon.com, have affiliate programs in which they will pay a percentage of a purchase if a customer comes from your site to theirs and makes a purchase. For sites that have thousands of visitors the ads have been profitable—some sites reportedly make over $100,000 a year.

Example:
One financially successful site is Manolo's Shoe Blog (**http://shoeblogs.com**). It is written by a man who loves shoes, has a great sense of humor, and writes in endearing broken English. Because he is an expert in his field, his suggestions are taken by many readers who click through to the products and purchase them.

LEGAL ISSUES

Before you set up a Web page, you should consider the many legal issues associated with it.

Jurisdiction   *Jurisdiction* is the power of a court in a particular location to decide a particular case. Usually, you have to have been physically present in a jurisdiction or have done business there before you can be sued there. Since the Internet extends your business's ability to reach people in faraway places, there may be instances when you could be subject to legal jurisdiction far from your own state (or country). There are a number of cases that have been decided in this country regarding the Internet and jurisdiction, but very few cases have been decided on this issue outside of the United States.

In most instances, U.S. courts use the pre-Internet test—whether you have been present in another jurisdiction or have had enough contact with someone in the other jurisdiction. The fact that the Internet itself is not a "place" will not shield you from being sued in another state when you have shipped you company's product there, have entered into a contract with a resident of that state, or have defamed a foreign resident with content on your website.

According to the court, there is a spectrum of contact required between you, your website, and consumers or audiences. (*Zippo Manufacturing Co. v. Zippo Dot Com, Inc.,* 952 F. Supp. 1119 (W.D. Pa 1997).) The more interactive your site is with consumers, the more you target an audience for your goods in a particular location, and the farther you reach to send your goods out into the world, the more it becomes possible for someone to sue you outside of your own jurisdiction—so weigh these risks against the benefits when constructing and promoting your website.

The law is not even remotely final on these issues. The American Bar Association, among other groups, is studying this topic in detail. At present, no final, global solution or agreement about jurisdictional issues with websites exists.

One way to protect yourself from the possibility of being sued in a faraway jurisdiction would be to state on your website that those using the site or doing business with you agree that "jurisdiction for any actions regarding this site" or your company will be in your home county.

For extra protection, you can have a preliminary page that must be clicked before entering your website. However, this may be overkill for a small business with little risk of lawsuits. If you are in any business for which you could have serious liability, you should review some competitors' sites and see how they handle the liability issue. They often have a place to click for "legal notice" or "disclaimer" on their first page.

You may want to consult with an attorney to discuss the specific disclaimer you will use on your website, where it should appear, and whether you will have users of your site actively agree to this disclaimer or just passively read it. However, these disclaimers are not enforceable everywhere in the world. Until there is global agreement on jurisdictional issues, this may remain an area of uncertainty for some time to come.

Libel   *Libel* is any publication that injures the reputation of another. This can occur in print, writing, pictures, or signs. All that is required for publication is that you transmit the material to at least one other person. When putting together your website, you must keep in mind that it is visible to millions of people all over the planet and that if you libel a person or company, you may have to pay damages. Many countries do not have the freedom of speech that we do, and a statement that is not libel in the United States may be libelous elsewhere. If you are concerned about this, alter the content of your site or check with an attorney about libel laws in the country you think might take action against you.

Copyright Infringement   It is so easy to copy and borrow information on the Internet that it is easy to infringe copyrights without even knowing it. A *copyright* exists for a work as soon as the creator creates it. There is no need to register the copyright or to put a copyright notice on it. Therefore, practically everything on the Internet belongs to someone.

Some people freely give their works away. For example, many people have created Web artwork (*gifs* and *animated gifs*) that they freely allow people to copy. There are numerous sites that provide hundreds or thousands of free gifs that you can add to your Web pages. Some require you to acknowledge the source and some do not. You should always be sure that the works are free for the taking before using them.

Linking and Framing

One way to violate copyright laws is to improperly link other sites to yours, either directly or with framing. *Linking* is when you provide a link that takes the user to the linked site. *Framing* occurs when you set up your site so that when you link to another site, your site is still viewable as a frame around the linked-to site.

While many sites are glad to be linked to others, some, especially providers of valuable information, object. Courts have ruled that linking and framing can be a copyright violation. One rule that has developed is that it is usually okay to link to the first page of a site, but not to link to some valuable information deeper within the site. The rationale for this is that the owner of the site wants visitors to go through the various levels of their site (viewing all the ads) before getting the information. By linking directly to the information, you are giving away their product without the ads.

The problem with linking to the first page of a site is that it may be a tedious or difficult task to find the needed page from there. Many sites are poorly designed and make it nearly impossible to find anything.

If you wish to link to another page, the best solution is to ask permission. Email the webmaster or other person in charge of the site, if an email address is given, and explain what you want to do. If they grant permission, be sure to print out a copy of their email for your records.

Privacy

Since the Internet is such an easy way to share information, there are many concerns that it will cause a loss of individual privacy. The two main concerns arise when you post information that others consider private, and when you gather information from customers and use it in a way that violates their privacy.

While public actions of politicians and celebrities are fair game, details about their private lives are sometimes protected by law, and details about persons who are not public figures are often protected. The laws in each state are different, and what might be allowable in one state could be illegal in another. If your site will provide any personal information about individuals, you should discuss the possibility of liability with an attorney.

Several well-known companies have been in the news lately for violations of their customers' privacy. They either shared what the customer was buying or downloading, or looked for additional information on the customer's computer. To let customers know that you do not violate certain standards of privacy, you can subscribe to one of the privacy codes that have been created for the Internet. These allow you to put a symbol on your site guaranteeing to your customers that you follow the code.

The following are the websites of two organizations that offer this service and their fees at the time of this publication.

www.privacybot.com	$100
www.bbbonline.com	$200 to $7,000

Protecting Yourself The easiest way to protect yourself personally from the various possible types of liability is to set up a corporation or limited liability company to own the website. This is not foolproof protection since, in some cases, you could be sued personally as well, but it is one level of protection.

COPPA If your website is aimed at children under the age of thirteen, or if it attracts children of that age, then you are subject to the federal *Children Online Privacy Protection Act of 1998* (COPPA). This law requires such websites to:

- ✪ give notice on the site of what information is being collected;

- ✪ obtain verifiable parental consent to collect the information;

- ✪ allow the parent to review the information collected;

- ✪ allow the parent to delete the child's information or to refuse to allow the use of the information;

- ✪ limit the information collected to only that necessary to participate on the site; and,

- ✪ protect the security and confidentiality of the information.

HIRING A WEBSITE DESIGNER

If you hire someone to design your website, you should make sure of what rights you are buying. Under copyright law, when you hire someone to create a work, you do not get all rights to that work unless you clearly spell that out in a written agreement.

For example, if your designer creates an artistic design to go on your website, you may have to pay extra if you want to use the same design on your business cards or letterhead. Depending on how the agreement is worded you may even have to pay a yearly fee for the rights.

If you spend a lot of money promoting your business and a logo or design becomes important to your image, you would not want to have to pay royalties for the life of your business to someone who spent an hour or two putting together a design. Whenever you purchase a creative work from someone, be sure to get a written statement of what rights you are buying. If you are not receiving all rights for all uses for all time you should think twice about the purchase.

If the designer also is involved with hosting your site, you should be sure you have the right to take the design with you if you move to another host. You should get a backup of your site on a CD in case it is ever lost or you need to move it to another site.

FINANCIAL TRANSACTIONS

The existing services for sending money over the Internet, such as PayPal, usually offer more risk and higher fees than traditional credit card processing. Under their service agreements, you usually must agree that they can freeze your account at any time and can take money out of your bank account at any time. Some do not offer an appeal process. Before signing up for any of these services, you should read their service agreement carefully and check the Internet for other peoples' experiences with them. For example, for PayPal you can check **www.nopaypal.com**.

For now, the easiest way to exchange money on the Internet is through traditional credit cards. Because of concerns that email can be abducted in transit and read by others, most companies use a secure site in which customers are guaranteed that their card data is encrypted before being sent.

When setting up your website, you should ask the provider if you can be set up with a secure site for transmitting credit card data. If they cannot provide it, you will need to contract with another software provider. Use one of the major search engines listed on page 86 to look for companies that provide credit card services to businesses on the Internet.

As a practical matter, there is very little to worry about when sending credit card data by email. If you do not have a secure site, another option is to allow purchasers to fax or phone in their credit card data. However, keep in mind that this extra step will lose some business unless your products are unique and your buyers are very motivated.

The least effective option is to provide an order form on the site that can be printed out and mailed in with a check. Again, your customers must be really motivated or they will lose interest after finding out this extra work is involved.

FTC RULES

Because the Internet is an instrument of interstate commerce, it is a legitimate subject for federal regulation. The *Federal Trade Commission* (FTC) first said that all of its consumer protection rules applied to the Internet, but lately it has been adding specific rules and issuing publications. The following publications are available from the FTC website at **www.ftc.gov/bcp/menu-internet.htm** or by mail from:

Consumer Response Center
Federal Trade Commission
600 Pennsylvania, NW
Room H-130
Washington, DC 20580

✪ *Advertising and Marketing on the Internet: The Rules of the Road*

✪ *Appliance Labeling Rule Homepage*

✪ *BBB-Online: Code of Online Business Practices*

✪ *Big Print. Little Print. What's the Deal? How to Disclose the Details*

✪ *Businessperson's Guide to the Mail and Telephone Order Merchandise Rule*

✪ *CAN-SPAM Act: Requirements for Commercial Emailers*

✪ *Complying with the Telemarketing Sales Rule*

✪ *Disclosing Energy Efficiency Information: A Guide for Online Sellers of Appliances*

✪ *Dot Com Disclosures: Information About Online Advertising*

✪ *Electronic Commerce: Selling Internationally. A Guide for Business*

✪ *How to Comply With The Children's Online Privacy Protection Rule*

✪ *Frequently Asked Questions About the Children's Online Privacy Protection Rule*

✪ *Internet Auctions: A Guide for Buyer and Sellers*

✪ *"Remove Me" Responses and Responsibilities: Email Marketers Must Honor "Unsubscribe" Claims*

✪ *Securing Your Server—Shut the Door on Spam*

✪ *Security Check: Reducing Risks to Your Computer Systems*

✪ *Selling on the Internet: Prompt Delivery Rules*

- *TooLate.Com: The Lowdown on Late Internet Shipments*

- *Website Woes: Avoiding Web Service Scams*

- *What's Dot and What's Not: Domain Name Registration Scams*

- *You, Your Privacy Policy & COPPA*

FRAUD

Because the Internet is somewhat anonymous, it is a tempting place for those with fraudulent schemes to look for victims. As a business consumer, you should exercise caution when dealing with unknown or anonymous parties on the Internet.

The U.S. Department of Justice, the FBI, and the National White Collar Crime Center jointly launched the Internet Crime Complaint Center (ICCC). If you suspect that you are the victim of fraud online, whether as a consumer or a business, you can report incidents to the ICCC on their website, **www.ic3.gov**. The ICCC is currently staffed by FBI agents and representatives of the National White Collar Crime Center, and will work with state and local law enforcement officials to prevent, investigate, and prosecute high-tech and economic crime online.

chapter 11

Health and Safety Laws

As a reaction to the terrible work conditions prevalent in the factories and mills of the nineteenth century industrial age, Congress and the states developed many laws intended to protect the health and safety of the nation's workers. These laws are difficult to understand and often seem to be very unfair to employers. Therefore, this is an area that you need to pay particular attention to as a new business. Failure to do so can result in terrible consequences for you.

FEDERAL LAWS

The federal government's laws regarding health and safety of workers are far-reaching and very important to consider in running your business, especially if you are a manufacturer or in the oil and gas, food production, or agriculture industries.

OSHA The point of the *Occupational Safety and Health Administration* (OSHA) is to place the duty on the employer to keep the workplace free from recognized hazards that are likely to cause death or serious bodily injury to workers. The regulations are not as cumbersome for small businesses as for larger enterprises. If you have ten or fewer employees, or if you are in a certain type of business, you do not have to keep a record of illnesses, injuries, and exposure to hazardous substances of employees. If you have eleven or more employees, OSHA's rules will apply. One important rule to know is that within forty-eight hours of an on-the-job death of an employee or injury of five or more employees on the job, the area director of OSHA must be contacted.

For more information, write or call an OSHA office.

Fort Lauderdale Area Office
8040 Peters Road
Building H-100
Fort Lauderdale, FL 33324
954-424-0242
Fax: 954-424-3073

Jacksonville Area Office
Ribault Building
Suite 227
1851 Executive Center Drive
Jacksonville, FL 32207
904-232-2895
Fax: 904-232-1294

Tampa Area Office
5807 Breckenridge Parkway
Suite A
Tampa, FL 33610
813-626-1177
Fax: 813-626-7015

You can also visit their website, **www.osha.gov**, to obtain copies of their publications, *OSHA Handbook for Small Business* (OSHA 2209) and *OSHA Publications and Audiovisual Programs Catalog* (OSHA 2019). They also have a poster that is required to be a posted in the workplace. Find it at **www.osha.gov/publications/poster.html**.

The *Hazard Communication Standard* requires that employees be made aware of the hazards in the workplace. (Code of Federal Regulations (C.F.R.), Title 29, Section (Sec.) 1910.1200.) It is especially applicable to those working with chemicals, but this can even include offices that use copy machines. Businesses using hazardous chemicals must have a comprehensive program for informing employees of the hazards and for protecting them from contamination.

For more information, you can contact OSHA at the previously-mentioned addresses, phone numbers, or websites. They can supply a copy of the regulation and a booklet called *OSHA 3084,* which explains the law.

EPA The *Worker Protection Standard for Agricultural Pesticides* requires safety training, decontamination sites, and of course, posters. The *Environmental Protection Agency* (EPA) will provide information on compliance with this law. They can be reached at 800-490-9198, or on their website at **www.epa.gov**.

They can also be reached by mail at:

Environmental Protection Agency
Atlanta Federal Center
61 Forsyth Street, SW
Atlanta, GA 30303
404-562-9900
800-241-1754
Fax: 404-562-8174
850-245-2118 Florida office

FDA The *Pure Food and Drug Act of 1906* prohibits the misbranding or adulteration of food and drugs. It also created the *Food and Drug Administration* (FDA), which has promulgated many regulations and which must give permission before a new drug can be introduced into the market. If you will be dealing with any food or drugs, you should keep abreast of their policies. Their website is **www.fda.gov**. The FDA's small business site is **www.fda.gov/ora/fed_state/small_business** and their regional small business representative is at:

Small Business Representative (HFR-SE17)
FDA, Southeast Region
60 Eighth Street, NE
Atlanta, GA 30309
404-253-2238
Fax: 404-253-1207

Hazardous Materials Transportation

There are regulations that control the shipping and packing of hazardous materials. For more information, contact:

Office of Hazardous Materials Safety
Research and Special Programs Administration
U.S. Department of Transportation
400 7th Street, SW
Washington, DC 20590

For an organizational structure and phone contacts, visit **http://hazmat.dot.gov/contact/org/org&ct.htm**.

CPSC

The *Consumer Product Safety Commission* (CPSC) has a set of rules that cover the safety of products. The commission feels that because its rules cover products, rather than people or companies, they apply to everyone producing such products. However, federal laws do not apply to small businesses that do not affect interstate commerce. Whether a small business would fall under a CPSC rule would depend on the size and nature of your business.

The CPSC rules are contained in the Code of Federal Regulations, Title 16 in the following parts.

Product	Part
Antennas, CB, and TV	1402
Architectural Glazing Material	1201
Articles Hazardous to Children Under 3	1501
Baby Cribs—Full Size	1508
Baby Cribs—Non-Full Size	1509
Bicycle Helmets	1203
Bicycles	1512
Carpets and Rugs	1630, 1631
Cellulose Insulation	1209, 1404
Cigarette Lighters	1210
Citizens Band Base Station Antennas	1204

Coal and Wood Burning Appliances	1406
Consumer Products Containing Chlorofluorocarbons	1401
Electrically Operated Toys	1505
Emberizing Materials Containing Asbestos (banned)	1305
Extremely Flammable Contact Adhesives (banned)	1302
Fireworks	1507
Garage Door Openers	1211
Hazardous Lawn Darts (banned)	1306
Hazardous Substances	1500
Human Subjects	1028
Lawn Mowers, Walk-Behind	1205
Lead-Containing Paint (banned)	1303
Matchbooks	1202
Mattresses	1632
Pacifiers	1511
Patching Compounds Containing Asbestos (banned)	1304
Poisons	1700
Rattles	1510
Self-Pressurized Consumer Products	1401
Sleepwear—Children's	1615, 1616
Swimming Pool Slides	1207
Toys, Electrical	1505
Unstable Refuse Bins (banned)	1301

Search the CPSC's site at **http://cpsc.gov** for more information on these rules.

Additional Regulations

Every day there are proposals for new laws and regulations. It would be impossible to include every conceivable one in this book. To be up-to-date on the laws that affect your type of business, you should belong to a trade association for your industry and subscribe to newsletters that cover your industry. Attending industry conventions is a good way to learn more about federal regulations and to discover new ways to increase your profits.

FLORIDA LAWS

In additional to federal laws, the State of Florida has statutes and regulations designed to protect the health and safety of workers and consumers.

Hazardous Occupations
Under Florida Statutes, Chapter 769, hazardous occupations include railroading; operating street railways; generating and selling electricity; telegraph and telephone business; express business; blasting and dynamiting; operating automobiles for public use; and, boating, when the boat is powered by steam, gas, or electricity. The owners of such enterprises are liable for injuries or death of their employees, because there is a presumption that they did not use reasonable care. They must be able to rebut this presumption in order to be found not liable. In cases where the employee is at fault, the damages are *apportioned*, or divided, according to fault. Employers may not contract with employees to avoid the liability of this law.

Smoking
In 2002, Florida voters passed a constitutional amendment banning smoking in indoor workplaces. The amendment was implemented by Florida Statutes, Chapter 386, Sections 386.201 through 386.2125.

Smoking is not allowed in any indoor work area, including bars and restaurants, except those exempted in Section 386.2045, which are:

- Private residences not being used for child care, adult care, or health care;

- Retail tobacco shops as defined in Fla. Stat. §386.203(8);

- Designated smoking rooms in lodging establishments as defined in Fla. Stat. §386.203(4);

- Stand-alone bars as defined in Fla. Stat. §386.203(11);

- Smoking cessation facilities if signs comply with Fla. Stat. §386.206; and,

- U.S. Customs smoking room in an airport subject to restrictions in Fla. Stat. §386.205.

Additional rules are contained in Chapter 61A of Florida's Administrative Code, which can be downloaded at **www.myflorida. com/dbpr/os/hot_topics/amendment6**. This site also has form DBPR ABT-6039, which is used by a stand-alone bar to elect to allow smoking.

Violation of the law can result in fines of $100 for the first violation and $500 for subsequent violations. Some establishments have been in the news for actively violating the law and simply paying the fines when cited. Obviously, for the health of your workers and the maintenance of your reputation, you should comply with Florida's smoking law.

Employment and Labor Laws

As they have with health and safety laws, Congress and the states have heavily regulated the actions that employers can take with regard to hiring and firing, improper employment practices, and discrimination. Because the penalties can be severe, educate yourself on the proper actions to take and consult a labor and employment lawyer, if necessary, prior to making important employee decisions.

HIRING AND FIRING LAWS

For small businesses, there are not many rules regarding who you may hire or fire. The ancient law that an employee can be fired at any time (or may quit at any time) still prevails for small businesses. In certain situations and as you grow, however, you will come under a number of laws that affect your hiring and firing practices.

One of the most important things to consider when hiring someone is that if you fire him or her, that fired employee may be entitled to unemployment compensation. If so, your unemployment compensation tax rate will go up and it can cost you a lot of money. Therefore, you should only hire people you are sure you will keep, and you should avoid situations where your former employees can make claims against your company.

One way this can be done is by hiring only part-time employees. The drawback to this is that you may not be able to attract the best employees. When hiring dishwashers or busboys this may not be an issue, but when hiring someone to develop a software product, you do not want him or her to leave halfway through the development.

A better solution is to screen applicants to begin with and only hire those who you feel certain will work out. Of course, this is easier said than done. Some people interview well but then turn out to be incompetent at the job.

The best record to look for is someone who has stayed a long time at each of his or her previous jobs. Next best is someone who has not stayed as long (for good reasons), but has always been employed. The worst type of hire would be someone who is or has been collecting unemployment compensation.

The reason those who have collected compensation are a bad risk is that if they collect in the future, even if it is not your fault, your employment of them could make you chargeable for their claim. For example, you hire someone who has been on unemployment compensation and he or she works out well for a year, but then quits to take another job, and is fired after a few weeks. In this situation, you would be chargeable for most of his or her claim, because the last five quarters of work are analyzed. Look for a steady job history.

Often, the intelligence of an employee is more important than his or her experience. An employee with years of typing experience may be fast, but unable to figure out how to use your new computer, whereas an intelligent employee can learn the equipment quickly and eventually gain speed. Of course, common sense is important in all situations.

The bottom line is that you cannot know if an employee will be able to fill your needs from a résumé and interview. Once you have found someone who you think will work out, offer that person a job with a ninety-day probationary period. If you are not completely satisfied with the employee after the ninety days, offer to extend the probationary period for ninety additional days rather than end the relationship immediately. Of course, all of this should be in writing.

Background Checks

Beware that a former boss may be a good friend or even a relative. It has always been considered acceptable to exaggerate on résumés, but in recent years, some applicants have been found to be completely fabricating sections of their education and experience. Checking references is important.

Polygraph Tests

Under the federal *Employee Polygraph Protection Act,* you cannot require an employee or prospective employee to take a polygraph test unless you are in the armored car, guard, or pharmaceutical business.

Drug Tests

Under the Americans with Disabilities Act (ADA), drug testing can only be required of applicants who have been offered jobs conditioned upon passing the drug test. Under Florida law, employers are allowed to test employees before and after they are hired. (Fla. Stat. Sec. 440.102.) They can obtain discounts on drug tests if they qualify under the drug-free workplace program. (Fla. Stat. Sec. 627.0915.) Employers can also deny medical and indemnity benefits for failure to pass a test.

FIRING

In most cases, unless you have a contract with an employee for a set time period, you can fire him or her at any time. This is only fair, since the employee can quit at any time. This type of employment is called *at will.* You should make it clear when offering a job to someone that, upon acceptance, he or she will be an at-will employee. The exceptions to this are if you fired someone based on illegal discrimination, for filing some sort of health or safety complaint, or for refusing your sexual advances.

NEW HIRE REPORTING

In order to track down parents who do not pay child support, a federal law was passed in 1996 that requires the reporting of new hires. The *Personal Responsibility and Work Opportunity Reconciliation Act of 1996* (PRWORA) provides that such information must be reported by employers to their state government.

Within twenty days of hiring a new employee, an employer must provide the state with information about the employee, including the name, Social Security number, and address. This information can be submitted in several ways, including mail, fax, magnetic tape, or over the Internet. There is a special form that can be used for this reporting; however, an employer can simply use the **EMPLOYEE'S WITHHOLDING ALLOWANCE CERTIFICATE (IRS FORM W-4)** for this purpose. (see form 7, p.261.) Since this form must be filled out for all employees anyway, it would be pointless to use a separate form for the new hire reporting. A copy of the **IRS FORM W-4** is included in Appendix C. This may be faxed to 850-656-0528 or toll-free at 888-854-4762, or mailed to:

Florida New Hire Reporting Program
P.O. Box 6500
Tallahassee, FL 32314

For more information about the program, you can call them at 850-656-3343 or toll-free at 888-854-4791, write to them at the above address, or visit their website at **www.fl-newhire.com**.

EMPLOYMENT AGREEMENTS

To avoid misunderstanding with employees, you should use an employment agreement or an employee handbook. These can spell out in detail the policies of your company and the rights of your employees. These agreements can protect your trade secrets and spell out clearly that employment can be terminated at any time by either party.

Make sure that your agreement is fair and clear, because you have the upper hand in this situation and you would not want a court to find that you abused that bargaining power with an unreasonable employee agreement.

If having an employee sign an agreement is awkward, you can usually obtain the same rights by putting the company policies in an employee manual. Each existing and new employee should be given a copy along with a letter stating that the rules apply to all employees, and that by accepting or continuing employment at your company, they agree to abide by the rules. Having an employee sign a receipt for the letter and manual is proof that he or she received it.

One danger of an employment agreement or handbook is that it may be interpreted to create a long-term employment contract. To avoid this, be sure that you clearly state in the agreement or handbook that the employment is at will and can be terminated at any time by either party.

Some other things to consider in an employment agreement or handbook are:

- ✪   what the salary and other compensation will be;

- ✪   what the hours of employment will be;

- ✪   what the probationary period will be;

- ✪   that the employee cannot sign any contracts binding the employer; and,

- ✪   that the employee agrees to arbitration rather than filing a lawsuit if serious disagreements arise.

INDEPENDENT CONTRACTORS

One way to avoid problems with employees and taxes at the same time is to have all of your work done through independent contractors. This can relieve you of most of the burdens of employment laws, as well as the obligation to pay Social Security and Medicare taxes for the workers.

An independent contractor is, in effect, a separate business that you pay to do a job. You pay them just as you pay any company from which you buy products or services. At the end of the year, if the amount paid exceeds $600, you must issue a 1099 form, which is similar to the W-2 that you would issue to employees.

This may seem too good to be true, and in some situations it is. The IRS does not like independent contractor arrangements, because it is too easy for the independent contractors to cheat on their taxes. To limit the use of independent contractors, the IRS has strict regulations on who may and may not be classified as an independent contractor. Also, companies who do not appear to pay enough in wages for their field of business are audited.

Using independent contractors for jobs not traditionally done by independent contractors puts you at high risk for an IRS audit. For example, you could not get away with hiring a secretary as an independent contractor. One of the most important factors considered in determining if a worker can be an independent contractor is the amount of control the company has over his or her work. If you need someone to paint your building and you agree to pay a certain price to have it done according to the painter's own methods and schedule, you can pay the painter as an independent contractor. However, if you tell the painter when and how to do the work, and provide the tools and materials, the painter will be classified as an employee.

If you just need some typing done and you take it to a typing service and pick it up when it is ready, you will be safe in treating those workers as independent contractors. However, if you need someone to come into your office to type on your machine at your schedule, you will probably be required to treat that person as an employee for tax purposes.

The IRS has a form you can use in determining if a person is an employee or an independent contractor, called **DETERMINATION OF WORKER STATUS (IRS FORM SS-8)**. It is included in Appendix C of this book along with instructions. (see form 6, p.255.)

Independent Contractors vs. Employees

In deciding whether to make use of independent contractors or employees, you should weigh the following advantages and disadvantages.

Advantages.

✪ Lower taxes. You do not have to pay Social Security, Medicare, unemployment, or other employee taxes.

✪ Less paperwork. You do not have to handle federal withholding deposits or the monthly employer returns to the state or federal government.

✪ Less insurance. You do not have to pay workers' compensation insurance or insurance against their possible liabilities.

✪ More flexibility. You can use independent contractors only when you need them.

Disadvantages.

✪ The IRS and state tax offices are strict about which workers can be qualified as independent contractors. They will audit companies whose use of independent contractors does not appear to be legitimate.

✪ If your use of independent contractors is found to be improper, you may have to pay back taxes and penalties, and may have problems with your pension plan.

✪ While employees usually cannot sue you for their injuries (if you have covered them with workers' compensation), independent contractors can sue you if their injuries were your fault.

✪ If you are paying someone to produce a creative work (writing, photography, artwork), you receive fewer rights to the work of an independent contractor.

✪ You have less control over the work of an independent contractor and less flexibility in terminating him or her if you are not satisfied that the job is being done the way you require.

✪ You have less loyalty from an independent contractor who works sporadically for you and possibly others than you have from your own full-time employees.

For some businesses, the advantages outweigh the disadvantages. For others, they do not. Consider your business plans and the consequences from each type of arrangement. Keep in mind that it will be easier to start with independent contractors and switch to employees than to hire employees and have to fire them to hire independent contractors.

TEMPORARY WORKERS

Another way to avoid the hassles of hiring employees is to get workers from a temporary agency. In this arrangement, you may pay a higher amount per hour for the work, but the agency will take care of all of the tax and insurance requirements. Since these can be expensive and time-consuming, the extra cost may be well worth it.

Whether or not temporary workers will work for you depends upon the type of business you are in and tasks you need performed. For such jobs as sales management, you would probably want someone who will stay with you long-term and develop relationships with the buyers, but for order fulfillment, temporary workers might work out well.

Another advantage of temporary workers is that you can easily stop using those who do not work out well for you. Conversely, if you find one who is ideal, you may be able to hire him or her on a full-time basis.

In recent years, a new wrinkle has developed in the temporary worker area. Many large companies are beginning to use them because they are so much cheaper than paying the benefits demanded by full-time employees. For example, Microsoft Corp. had as many as 6,000 temporary workers, some of whom worked for them for years. Some of the temporary workers won a lawsuit that declared they are really employees and are entitled to the same benefits of other employees (such as pension plans).

The law is not yet settled in this area, regarding what arrangements will result in a temporary worker being declared an employee. That will take several more court cases, some of which have already been filed. A few things you can do to protect yourself include the following.

- ✪   Be sure that any of your benefit plans make it clear that they do not apply to workers obtained through temporary agencies.

- ✪   Do not keep the same temporary workers for longer than a year.

- ✪   Do not list temporary workers in any employee directories or hold them out to the public as your employees.

- ✪   Do not allow them to use your business cards or stationery.

DISCRIMINATION LAWS

There are numerous federal laws forbidding discrimination based upon race, sex, pregnancy, color, religion, national origin, age, or disability. The laws apply to both hiring and firing, and to employment practices such as salaries, promotions, and benefits. Most of these laws only apply to an employer who has fifteen or more employees for twenty weeks of a calendar year, or has federal contracts or subcontracts. Therefore, you most likely will not be required to comply with the law immediately upon opening your business. However, there are similar state laws that may apply to your business that have a lower employee threshold.

One exception to the fifteen or more employees rule is the *Equal Pay Act*. This act applies to employers with two or more employees, and requires that women be paid the same as men in the same type of job.

Employers with fifteen or more employees are required to display a poster regarding discrimination. This poster is available from the Equal Employment Opportunity Commission on their website at **www.dol.gov/esa/regs/compliance/posters/eeo.htm**. Employers with 100 or more employees are required to file an annual report with the EEOC.

Discriminatory Interview Questions

When hiring employees, some questions are illegal or inadvisable to ask. The following data *should not* be collected on your employment application or in your interviews, unless the information is somehow directly tied to the duties of the job.

✪ Do not ask about an applicant's citizenship or place of birth. However, after hiring an employee, you must ask about his or her right to work in this country.

✪ Do not ask a female applicant her maiden name. You can ask if she has been known by any other name in order to do a background check.

✪ Do not ask if applicants have children, plan to have them, or have child care. You can ask if an applicant will be able to work the required hours.

✪ Do not ask if the applicant has religious objections for working Saturday or Sunday. You can mention if the job requires such hours and ask whether the applicant can meet this job requirement.

✪ Do not ask an applicant's age. You can ask if an applicant is age 18 or over, or if it is a liquor-related job, you can ask if the applicant is age 21 or over.

✪ Do not ask an applicant's weight.

✪ Do not ask if an applicant has AIDS or is HIV positive.

✪ Do not ask if the applicant has filed a workers' compensation claim.

✪ Do not ask about the applicant's previous health problems.

✪ Do not ask if the applicant is married or whether the spouse would object to the job, hours, or duties.

✪ Do not ask if the applicant owns a home, furniture, or car, as it is considered racially discriminatory.

✪ Do not ask if the applicant was ever arrested. You can ask if the applicant was ever convicted of a crime.

ADA

Under the *Americans with Disabilities Act of 1990* (ADA), employers who do not make *reasonable accommodations* for disabled employees will face fines of up to $100,000, as well as other civil penalties and civil damage awards.

While the goal of creating more opportunities for the disabled is a good one, the result has put all of the costs of achieving this goal on businesses that are faced with disabled applicants. In fact, studies done since the law was passed have shown that employers have hired fewer disabled applicants than before the law was passed, possibly due to the costs of reasonable accommodations and the fear of being taken to court.

The ADA is very vague. When it passed, some feared it could be taken to ridiculous lengths—such as forcing companies to hire blind applicants for jobs that require reading, and then forcing them to hire people to read for the blind employees. In the years since its enactment, some of the critics' fears have been met. In some famous rulings, the EEOC said:

✪ rude, disruptive, and chronically late employees could be protected by the ADA if they had some type of mental disability;

✪ recovering drug addicts and alcoholics are protected by the ADA;

✪ obesity can be a disability covered by the ADA;

✪ workers who are disturbed by the sight of other workers because of emotional imbalance must be given private work areas; and,

✪ airlines cannot discriminate against persons blind in one eye when hiring pilots.

When the ADA was passed, it was estimated that 3 million Americans were blind, deaf, or in wheelchairs, but it has been estimated that the ADA now applies to 49 million Americans with every type of physical or mental impairment. Of the ADA cases that go to court, 92% are won by businesses. While this may sound good, considering the cost of going to court, the expense of this litigation is devastating for the businesses. Many of these lawsuits occur because the law is worded so vaguely.

Some lawyers in the Miami area have been sending disabled people around the state to see if businesses comply with the ADA. When they find a violation, they immediately file a lawsuit. Because defending such a suit is expensive, the businesses routinely settle with the law firm for several thousand dollars. One newspaper discovered that once the settlement is paid, the law firms rarely care if the business complies with the law—they just move to the next town and file more suits.

If your business is the victim of such a scheme, you should consider getting together with other businesses and fighting the cases. This type of activity was not what the ADA was meant for, and perhaps it could be ruled to be extortion or even a violation of racketeering laws.

The ADA currently applies to employers with fifteen or more employees. Employers who need more than fifteen employees might want to consider contracting with independent contractors to avoid problems with this law, particularly if the number of employees is only slightly larger than fifteen.

For more information on how this law affects your business, see the U.S. Department of Justice website at **www.usdoj.gov/crt/ada/business.htm**.

Tax Benefits   There are three types of tax credits to help small businesses with the burden of these laws.

- ✪ Businesses can deduct up to $15,000 a year for making their premises accessible to the disabled and can depreciate the rest. (Internal Revenue Code (I.R.C.) Section 190.)

- ✪ Small businesses (under $1,000,000 in revenue and under thirty employees) can get a tax credit each year for 50% of the cost of making their premises accessible to the disabled, but this only applies to the amount between $250 and $10,500.

- ✪ Small businesses can get a credit of up to 40% of the first $6,000 of wages paid to certain new employees who qualify through the Pre-Screening Notice and Certification Request (IRS form 8850).

Records

To protect against potential claims of discrimination, all employers should keep detailed records showing reasons for hiring or not hiring applicants, and for firing employees.

Florida Law

Florida has its own laws regarding discrimination in employment practices. The *Florida Civil Rights Act of 1992* prohibits discrimination or classification based upon race, color, religion, sex, national origin, age, handicap, or marital status. An employer who violates this law can be sued and be required to pay back pay, damages, and punitive damages. (Fla. Stat. Sec. 760.10.)

Equal pay. Florida Statutes Section 448.07 is Florida's counterpart to the federal law providing for equal pay to both sexes for the same job. This state statute is meant to fill the gap of workers not covered by federal law. Therefore, it does not apply to workers who are covered by the *Fair Labor Standards Act*, which is the federal wage and hour law discussed on page 120.

Sickle-cell anemia. Florida Statutes Sections 448.075 and 448.076 prohibit discrimination based upon the sickle-cell trait and prohibit a requirement of screening for sickle-cell trait as a basis for employment.

HIV. Florida Statutes Section 760.50 forbids firing, segregating, or refusing to hire people on the basis of a person being HIV positive or having taken an HIV test. The employer has the burden of proving that being HIV-free is a necessary condition of the job. A person unknowingly violating this law is subject to a minimum $1,000 fine plus attorney's fees, and a person who knowingly violates it is subject to a minimum $5,000 fine plus attorney's fees.

SEXUAL HARASSMENT

As an employer you can be liable for the acts of your employees. One of the latest types of acts that employers have been help liable for is sexual harassment of customers, employees, and others. While you cannot control every act of every employee, if you indicate to employees that such behavior is unacceptable and set up a system to resolve complaints, you will do much to protect yourself against lawsuits.

The EEOC has held the following in sexual harassment cases.

- ✪ The victim as well as the harasser may be a woman or a man.

- ✪ The victim does not have to be of the opposite sex.

- ✪ The harasser can be the victim's supervisor, an agent of the employer, a supervisor in another area, a coworker, or a nonemployee.

- ✪ The victim does not have to be the person harassed, but could be anyone affected by the offensive conduct.

- ✪ Unlawful sexual harassment may occur without economic injury to or discharge of the victim.

- ✪ The harasser's conduct must be unwelcome.

Some of the actions that have been considered harassment are:

- ✪ displaying sexually explicit posters in the workplace;

- ✪ requiring female employees to wear revealing uniforms;

- ✪ rating the sexual attractiveness of female employees as they pass male employees' desks;

- ✪ continued sexual jokes and innuendos;

- ✪ demands for sexual favors from subordinates;

- ✪ unwelcomed sexual propositions or flirtation;

✪ unwelcomed physical contact; and,

✪ whistling or leering at members of the opposite sex.

In 1993, the United States Supreme Court ruled that an employee can make a claim for sexual harassment even without proof of a specific injury. However, lower federal courts in more recent cases have dismissed cases where no specific injury was shown. These new cases may indicate that the pendulum has stopped moving toward expanded rights for the employee.

On the other hand, another recent case ruled that an employer can be liable for the harassment of an employee by a supervisor—even if the employer was unaware of the supervisor's conduct—if the employer did not have a system in place to allow complaints against harassment. This area of law is still developing, but to avoid a possible lawsuit, you should be aware of the things that could potentially cause liability and avoid them.

Some things a business can do to protect against claims of sexual harassment include the following.

✪ Distribute a written policy against all kinds of sexual harassment to all employees.

✪ Encourage employees to report all incidents of sexual harassment.

✪ Ensure there is no retaliation against those who complain.

✪ Make clear that your policy is zero tolerance.

✪ Explain that sexual harassment includes both requests for sexual favors and a work environment that some employees may consider hostile.

✦   Allow employees to report harassment to someone other than their immediate supervisor, in case that person is involved in the harassment.

✦   Promise as much confidentiality as possible to complainants.

Florida Law

Florida's Civil Rights Act also prohibits sexual harassment. (Fla. Stat., Ch. 760.) It applies to employers with fifteen or more employees for each working day in each of twenty or more calendar weeks in the current or preceding calendar year.

The law requires employers to post notices as required by the Florida Commission on Human Relations, and allows victims to either file complaints with the commission or to sue in civil court for damages, including punitive damages.

Common Law

Although both the federal and Florida civil rights laws only apply to businesses with fifteen or more employees, it is possible for an employee to sue for sexual harassment in civil court. However, this is difficult and expensive, and would only be worthwhile where there were substantial damages.

WAGE AND HOUR LAWS

The *Fair Labor Standards Act* (FLSA) applies to all employers who are engaged in *interstate commerce* or in the production of goods for interstate commerce (anything that will cross the state line), and all employees of hospitals, schools, residential facilities for the disabled or aged, or public agencies. It also applies to all employees of enterprises that gross $500,000 or more per year.

While many small businesses might not think they are engaged in interstate commerce, the laws have been interpreted so broadly that nearly any use of the mails, interstate telephone service, or other interstate services, however minor, is enough to bring a business under the law.

Minimum Wage

The federal wage and hour laws are contained in the *Federal Fair Labor Standards Act*. In 1996, Congress passed and President

Clinton signed legislation raising the minimum wage to $5.15 an hour beginning September 1, 1997.

In certain circumstances, a wage of $4.25 may be paid to employees under 20 years of age for a ninety-day training period.

For employees who regularly receive more than $30 a month in tips, the minimum wage is $2.13 per hour. If the employee's tips do not bring him or her up to the full $5.15 minimum wage, then the employer must make up the difference.

Florida Law   In 2004, voters amended the Florida Constitution to provide a minimum wage of $6.15, which is raised each year by the Florida Agency for Workforce Innovation to cover inflation. The minimum wage set for 2006 is $6.40. The new wage for each year is set each fall. For tipped employees, the minimum wage that must be paid by the employer is $3.38.

Florida's other law regarding wages or hours is one regarding a day's work. (Fla. Stat. Sec. 448.01.) Unless provided otherwise in a written agreement, ten hours a day is a legal day's work. An employee is entitled to *extra pay* for all work in excess of ten hours. However, this law would only affect those few businesses to which the federal laws do not apply.

Exempt Employees   While nearly all businesses are covered, certain employees are exempt from the FLSA. Exempt employees include those who are considered executives, administrators, managers, professionals, computer professionals, and outside salespeople.

Whether or not one of these exceptions applies to a particular employee is a complicated legal question. Thousands of court cases have been decided on this issue, but they have given no clear answers. In one case, a person could be determined to be exempt because of his or her duties, but in another, a person with the same duties could be found not exempt.

One thing that is clear is that the determination is made on the employee's function, and not just the job title. You cannot make a secretary exempt by calling him or her a manager, if most of his or her duties are clerical. For more information, see the Department of Labor website **www.dol.gov/esa/whd/flsa** or contact their offices at:

Ft. Lauderdale: 954-356-6896
Jacksonville: 904-232-2489
Miami: 305-598-6607
Orlando: 407-648-6471
Tampa: 813-288-1242

On the Internet you can obtain information on the Department of Labor's *Employment Law Guide* at **www.dol.gov/asp/programs/guide/main.htm**.

Overtime The general rule is that employees who work more than forty hours a week must be paid time-and-a-half for hours worked over forty. However, there are many exemptions to this general rule based on salary and position. These exceptions were completely revised in 2004, and an explanation of the changes, including a tutorial video, are available at **www.dol.gov/esa**. For answers to questions about the law, call the Department of Labor at 866-4-USA-DOL (866-487-2365).

PENSION AND BENEFIT LAWS

There are no laws requiring small businesses to provide any types of special benefits to employees. Such benefits are given to attract and keep good employees. With pension plans, the main concern is if you do start one, it must comply with federal tax laws.

There are no federal or Florida laws that require employees be given holidays off. You can require them to work Thanksgiving and Christmas, and can dock their pay or fire them for failing to show up. Of course, you will not have much luck keeping employees with such a policy.

Holidays Most companies give full-time employees a certain number of paid holidays, such as: New Year's Day (January 1); Memorial Day (last Monday in May); Fourth of July; Labor Day (first Monday in September); Thanksgiving (fourth Thursday in November); and Christmas (December 25). Some employers include other holidays such as Martin Luther King, Jr.'s birthday (January 15); President's Day; and Columbus Day. If one of the holidays falls on a Saturday or Sunday, many employers give the preceding Friday or following Monday off.

Florida law says that legal holidays include all of those in the previous paragraph (except President's Day), as well as Robert E. Lee's birthday (January 19); Abraham Lincoln's birthday (February 12); Susan B. Anthony's birthday (February 15); George Washington's birthday (February 22); Good Friday (varies); Pascua Florida Day (April 2); Confederate Memorial Day (April 26); Jefferson Davis' birthday (June 3); Flag Day (June 14); Columbus Day and Farmers' Day (second Monday in October); Veterans' Day (November 11); and General Election Day (varies).

However, the fact that these are designated state holidays does not mean anything. In fact, not even the state government is closed on all of these days.

Sick Days
There is no federal or Florida law mandating that an employee be paid for time that he or she is home sick. The situation seems to be that the larger the company, the more paid sick leave is allowed. Part-time workers rarely get sick leave, and small business sick leave is usually limited for the simple reason that they cannot afford to pay for time that employees do not work.

Some small companies have an official policy of no paid sick leave, but when an important employee misses a day because he or she is clearly sick, it is paid.

Breaks
There are no federal or Florida laws requiring coffee breaks or lunch breaks. However, it is common sense that employees will be more productive if they have reasonable breaks for nourishment or to use the toilet facilities.

Pension Plans and Retirement Accounts
Few small new businesses can afford to provide pension plans for their employees. The first concern of a small business is usually how the owner can shelter income in a pension plan without having to set up a pension plan for an employee. Under most pension plans, this is not allowed.

IRA. Any individual can put up to $4,000 ($5,000 if age 50 or over) in an Individual Retirement Account (IRA). Unless the person, or his or her spouse, is covered by a company pension plan and has income over a certain amount, the amount put into the account is fully tax deductible.

Roth IRA. Contributions to a Roth IRA are not tax deductible, but when the money is taken out, it is not taxable. People who expect to still have taxable income when they withdraw from their IRA can benefit from these.

SEP IRA, SAR-SEP IRA, SIMPLE IRA. With these types of retirement accounts, a person can put a much greater amount into a retirement plan and deduct it from their taxable income. Employees must also be covered by such plans, but certain employees are exempt, so it is sometimes possible to use these for the owners alone. The best source for more information is a mutual fund company (such as Vanguard, Fidelity, or Dreyfus) or a local bank, which can set up the plan and provide you with all of the rules. These have an advantage over qualified plans (discussed below) since they do not have the high annual fees.

Qualified Retirement Plans. Qualified retirement plans are 401(k) plans, Keogh plans, and corporate retirement plans. These are covered by the *Employee Retirement Income Security Act* (ERISA), which is a complicated law meant to protect employee pension plans. Congress did not want employees who contributed to pension plans all their lives ending up with nothing if the plan went bankrupt. The law is so complicated and the penalties so severe that some companies are cancelling their pension plans, and applications for new plans are a fraction of what they were previously. However, many banks and mutual funds have created *canned plans*, which can be used instead of drafting one from scratch. Still, the fees for administering them are steep. Check with a bank or mutual fund for details.

FAMILY AND MEDICAL LEAVE LAW

To assist business owners in deciding what type of leave to offer their employees, Congress passed the *Family and Medical Leave Act of*

1993 (FMLA). This law requires an employee to be given up to twelve weeks of unpaid leave when:

✪   the employee or employee's spouse has a child;

✪   the employee adopts a child or takes in a foster child;

✪   the employee needs to care for an ill spouse, child, or parent; or,

✪   the employee becomes seriously ill.

The law only applies to employers with fifty or more employees. Also, the top 10% of an employer's salaried employees can be denied this leave because of the disruption in business their loss could cause.

Florida Law   There is no Florida law requiring family or medical leave.

CHILD LABOR LAWS

The *Federal Fair Labor Standards Act* also contains rules regarding the hiring of children. The basic rules are that children under 16 years old may not be hired at all except in a few jobs, such as acting and newspaper delivery, and those under 18 may not be hired for dangerous jobs. Children may not work more than three hours a day or eighteen hours a week in a school week, or more than eight hours a day or forty hours a week in a non-school week. If you plan to hire children, you should check the Federal Fair Labor Standards Act, which is in United States Code (U.S.C.), Title 29, and the related regulations, which are in the Code of Federal Regulations (C.F.R.), Title 29.

Florida Law   Florida also has a set of child labor laws.

Child labor. (Fla. Stat. Sec. 450.021.) The following rules apply to child labor in Florida, in addition to federal laws.

✪   Minors of any age may work as pages in the legislature, in the entertainment industry, and in domestic or farm work for their parents. Children working for their parents may not do so during school hours.

- No child 10 years of age or younger may engage in the sale and distribution of newspapers or the street trades.

- No child under 14 years of age may be employed in any gainful occupation at any time except as described above.

- No person under 18 years of age may work where alcoholic beverages are sold at retail, unless excepted by Florida's Division of Alcoholic Beverages and Tobacco. (Fla. Stat. Sec. 562.13.)

Hazardous occupations. (Fla. Stat. Sec. 450.061.) No child under 16 years of age may work in the following occupations or use the following equipment:

- power-driven machinery (except mowers with blades of forty inches or less);

- oiling or cleaning machines;

- working in freezers or meat coolers;

- using meat or vegetable slicers;

- power-driven laundry or dry cleaning machinery;

- door-to-door sales of subscriptions or products, except for merchandise of nonprofit organizations;

- spray painting;

- operating a motor vehicle;

- any manufacturing using industrial machines;

- manufacturing or transportation of explosive or flammable materials;

- logging; and,

- alligator wrestling.

No person under the age of 18 may work in the following occupations or use this equipment:

- ✪   in or around explosives;

- ✪   logging or sawmilling;

- ✪   in or around toxic substances, corrosives, and pesticides;

- ✪   firefighting;

- ✪   slaughtering, meat packing, processing, or rendering;

- ✪   electrical work;

- ✪   operating or assisting to operate tractors over twenty PTO horsepower, forklifts, earth-moving equipment, any harvesting, planting, or plowing machinery, or any moving machinery;

- ✪   any scaffolding, roofs, or ladders above six feet;

- ✪   wrecking, demolition, or excavation;

- ✪   mining occupations;

- ✪   operation of power-driven bakery, metal forming, woodworking, paper products, printing, or hoisting machines; and,

- ✪   manufacturing of brick, tile, or similar materials.

Poster. (Fla. Stat. Sec. 450.045(2).) Anyone employing a minor must display a poster explaining the Florida and federal child labor laws. (This is a good source of information for employers as well.) It is available on their website at **www.myflorida.com/dbpr/pro/farm/ compliance/childlabor/poster.shtml**.

Proof of child's age. (Fla. Stat. Sec. 450.045.) A person who employs a child must keep on file proof of the child's age, such as a photocopy of a birth certificate, driver's license, school-age certificate, passport, or visa.

Children's hours. (Fla. Stat. Sec. 450.081.) In addition to the requirements above, no child 17 years of age or younger may work more than six consecutive days in one week. Such children must have a meal break of at least thirty minutes after four hours of work. No child 16 or 17 years of age may work more than thirty hours in a week or more than eight hours in a day when the following day is a school day. No such child may work before 6:30 a.m. or after 11 p.m., and may not work during school hours except in a vocational educational program.

No child 15 years of age or younger may work before 7:00 a.m. or after 7:00 p.m. when school is scheduled the next day. No such child shall work more than fifteen hours a week or more than three hours in a day prior to a school day, except in a vocational education program.

However, these rules do not apply during holiday and summer vacations, or to 16- or 17-year-old graduates, students with school-authorized exemptions, students with economic hardships, children in domestic work in private homes, children working for their parents, or pages working for the legislature.

Child labor law waivers. The Division of Labor, Employment, and Training of the Department of Labor and Employment Security may grant a waiver of the child labor law.

IMMIGRATION LAWS

There are strict penalties for any business that hires aliens who are not eligible to work. You must verify both the identity and the employment eligibility of anyone you hire by using the **EMPLOYMENT ELIGIBILITY VERIFICATION (FORM I-9)**. (see form 4, p.243.) Both you and the employee must fill out the form, and you must check an employee's identification cards or papers. Fines for hiring illegal aliens range from $250 to $2,000 for the first offense and up to $10,000 for the third offense. Failure to maintain the proper paperwork may result in a fine of up to $1,000. The law does not apply to independent contractors with whom you may contract, and it does not penalize you if the employee used fake identification.

There are also penalties that apply to employers of four or more persons for discriminating against eligible applicants because they appear foreign or because of their national origin or citizenship status.

Appendix C has a list of acceptable documentation, a blank form, and instructions. (see form 4, p.243.) The blank form can also be downloaded at **http://uscis.gov/graphics/formsfee/forms/i-9.htm**.

For more information, call 800-357-2099. For the *Handbook for Employers and Instructions for Completing Form I-9,* check the *United States Citizenship and Immigration Services* (USCIS) website at **http://uscis.gov**.

Foreign employees. If you wish to hire employees who are foreign citizens and are not able to provide the proper documentation, they must first obtain a work visa from USCIS.

Work visas for foreigners are not easy to get. Millions of people around the globe would like to come to the U.S. to work, but the laws are designed to keep most of them out to protect the jobs of American citizens.

Whether or not a person can get a work visa depends on whether there is a shortage of U.S. workers available to fill the job. For jobs requiring few or no skills, it is practically impossible to get a visa. For highly skilled jobs, such as nurses and physical therapists, and for those of exceptional ability, such as Nobel Prize winners and Olympic medalists, obtaining a visa is fairly easy.

There are several types of visas, and different rules for different countries. For example, NAFTA has made it easier for some types of workers to enter the U.S. from Canada and Mexico. For some positions, the shortage of workers is assumed by the USCIS. For others, a business must first advertise a position available in the United States. Only after no qualified persons apply can it hire someone from another country.

The visa system is complicated and subject to regular change. If you wish to hire a foreign worker, you should consult with an immigration specialist or a book on the subject.

Florida Law   Florida Statutes Section 448.09 makes it illegal to hire aliens who are not legally authorized to work.

HIRING OFF THE BOOKS

Because of the taxes, insurance, and red tape involved with hiring employees, some new businesses hire people *off the books*. They pay them in cash and never admit they are employees. While the cash paid in wages would not be deductible, they consider this a smaller cost than compliance. Some even use off the books receipts to cover it.

Except when your spouse or child is giving you some temporary help, this is a terrible idea. Hiring people off the books can result in civil fines, loss of insurance coverage, and even criminal penalties. When engaged in dangerous work, like roofing or using power tools, you are risking millions of dollars in potential liability if a worker is killed or seriously injured. It may be more costly and time-consuming to comply with the employment laws, but if you are concerned with long-term growth with less risk, it is the wiser way to go.

FEDERAL CONTRACTS

Companies that do work for the federal government are subject to several laws.

The *Davis-Bacon Act* requires contractors engaged in U.S. government construction projects to pay wages and benefits that are equal to or better than the prevailing wages in the area.

The *McNamara-O'Hara Service Contract Act* sets wages and other labor standards for contractors furnishing services to agencies of the U.S. government.

The *Walsh-Healey Public Contracts Act* requires the Department of Labor to settle disputes regarding manufacturers supplying products to the U.S. government.

MISCELLANEOUS LAWS

In addition to the broad categories of laws affecting businesses, there are several other federal and state laws that you should be familiar with.

Federal Law

Federal law regulates affirmative action, layoffs, unions, and informational posters.

Affirmative action. In most cases, the federal government does not tell employers who they must hire. The only situation in which a small business would need to comply with affirmative action requirements would be if it accepted federal contracts or subcontracts. These requirements could include hiring minorities or veterans of the conflict in Vietnam.

Layoffs. Companies with 100 or more full-time employees at one location are subject to the *Worker Adjustment and Retraining Notification Act*. This law requires a sixty-day notification prior to certain layoffs and has other strict provisions.

Unions. The *National Labor Relations Act of 1935* gives employees the right to organize a union or to join one. (29 U.S.C. Secs. 151 et seq.) There are things employers can do to protect themselves, but you should consult a labor attorney or a book on the subject before taking action that might be illegal and result in fines.

Poster laws. Poster laws require certain posters to be displayed to inform employees of their rights. Not all businesses are required to display all posters, but the following list should be of help.

- ✪ All employers must display the wage and hour poster available from the U.S. Department of Labor at **www.dol.gov/esa**.

- ✪ Employers with fifteen or more employees for twenty weeks of the year must display the sex, race, religion, and ethnic discrimination poster, as well as the age discrimination poster available from the EEOC at **www.eeoc.gov/publications.html**.

- ✪ Employers with federal contracts or subcontracts of $10,000 or more must display the sex, race, religion, and ethnic discrimination poster, plus a poster regarding Vietnam Era Veterans (available from the local federal contracting office).

✪ Employers with government contracts subject to the *Service Contract Act* or the *Public Contracts Act* must display a notice to employees working on government contracts available from the Employment Standards Division at **www.dol.gov/esa/whd**.

Florida Law Florida law regulates threats of discharge, wrongful combination against workers, seating for employees, payment for labor, direct deposit, and migrant and farm labor.

Threat of discharge for failing to trade with particular firm. (Fla. Stat. Sec. 448.03.) It is a misdemeanor for an employer to require an employee to deal with or not to deal with any particular firm or person (in the employee's personal affairs), or to discharge or threaten to discharge an employee for such a reason.

Wrongful combination against workers. (Fla. Stat. Sec. 448.045.) It is a first-degree criminal misdemeanor for two or more persons to conspire to deny a person work, cause the discharge of a person in a firm, or threaten to injure the life, property, or business of any person for this purpose.

Seats. (Fla. Stat., Sec. 448.05.) It is a second-degree misdemeanor to fail to provide a seat for an employee or to fail to allow an employee to make reasonable use of the seat when such use will not interfere with the requirements of the employment.

Devices used as payment for labor. (Fla. Stat., Ch. 532.) If any person issues coupons, tokens, or other devices for payment of labor, he or she is liable for payment in cash of the full face value on or before the thirtieth day after issuance, no matter what other restrictions are printed on the device. Anyone violating this rule will be liable for the full value, interest, and 10% of the amount as well as attorney's fees.

Checks and drafts. Any payment for labor by check, draft, note, memorandum, or other acknowledgment of indebtedness must be payable in cash on demand, without discount, at some established place of business within the state. The name and address of the place of business where it is payable must be on the instrument, and at the time of issuance and for thirty days thereafter, there must be sufficient funds to cover it.

Direct deposit. The rules for checks and drafts do not prohibit direct deposit of funds, but a payor of wages may not fire an employee for refusing to have his or her wages directly deposited. A violation of this rule can result in an employee having his or her attorney's fees paid by the violator in an enforcement action.

Migrant and farm labor. Employers who hire migrant or farm labor should read Florida Statutes Sections 450.181 through 450.38.

Advertising and Promotion Laws

Because of the unscrupulous and deceptive advertising techniques of some companies, as well as the multitude of con artists trying to steal from innocent consumers, numerous federal and state statutes have been enacted that make it unlawful to use improper advertising and promotional techniques in soliciting business.

ADVERTISING LAWS AND RULES

The federal government regulates advertising through the *Federal Trade Commission* (FTC). The rules are contained in the *Code of Federal Regulations* (C.F.R.). You can find these rules in most law libraries and many public libraries. If you plan on doing any advertising that you think may be questionable, you might want to check the rules. As you read the rules, you will probably think of many violations you see every day.

Federal rules do not apply to every business, and small businesses that operate only within the state and do not use the postal service may be exempt. However, many of the federal rules have been adopted into law by the State of Florida. Therefore, a violation could be prosecuted by the state rather than the federal government.

Some of the important rules are summarized in this section. If you wish to learn more details about the rules, you should obtain copies from your library.

Deceptive Pricing

(C.F.R., Title 16, Ch. I, Part 233.) When prices are being compared, it is required that actual and not inflated prices are used. For example, if an object would usually be sold for $7, you should not first offer it for $10 and then start offering it at 30% off. It is considered misleading to suggest that a discount from list price is a bargain if the item is seldom actually sold at list price. If most surrounding stores sell an item for $7, it is considered misleading to say it has a retail value of $10, even if there are some stores elsewhere selling it at that price.

Bait Advertising

(C.F.R., Title 16, Ch. I, Part 238.) Bait advertising is placing an ad when you do not really want the respondents to buy the product offered, but want them to switch to another item.

Use of "Free," "Half-Off," and Similar Words

(C.F.R., Title 16, Ch. I, Part 251.) Use of words such as "free," "1¢ sale," and the like must not be misleading. This means that the regular price must not include a mark-up to cover the free item. The seller must expect to sell the product without the free item at some time in the future.

Substantiation of Claims

(C.F.R., Title 16; Federal Regulations (F.R.), Title 48, Page 10471 (1983).) The FTC requires that advertisers be able to substantiate their claims. Some information on this policy is contained on the Internet at **www.ftc.gov/bcp/guides/ad3subst.htm**.

Endorsements

(C.F.R., Title 16, Ch. I, Part 255.) This rule forbids endorsements that are misleading. An example is a quote from a film review that is used in such a way as to change the substance of the review. It is not necessary to use the exact words of the person endorsing the product, as long as the opinion is not distorted. If a product is changed, an endorsement that does not apply to the new version cannot be used. For some items, such as drugs, claims cannot be used without scientific proof. Endorsements by organizations cannot be used unless one is sure that the membership holds the same opinion.

Unfairness   (15 U.S.C. Section 45.) Any advertising practices that can be deemed to be *unfair* are forbidden by the FTC. An explanation of this policy is located on the Internet at **www.ftc.gov/bcp/policystmt/ ad-unfair.htm**.

Negative Option Plans   (C.F.R., Title 16, Ch. I, Part 425.) When a seller uses a sales system in which the buyer must notify the seller if he or she does not want the goods, the seller must provide the buyer with a form to decline the sale and at least ten days in which to decline. Bonus merchandise must be shipped promptly, and the seller must promptly terminate shipment for any who so request after completion of the contract.

Laser Eye Surgery   (15 U.S.C. Sections 45, 52–57.) Under the laws governing deceptive advertising, the FTC and the FDA are regulating the advertising of laser eye surgery. Anyone involved in this area should obtain a copy of these rules. They are located on the Internet at **www.ftc.gov/ bcp/guides/eyecare2.htm**.

Food and Dietary Supplements   (21 U.S.C. Section 343.) Under the *Nutritional Labeling Education Act of 1990*, the FTC and the FDA regulate the packaging and advertising of food and dietary products. Anyone involved in this area should obtain a copy of these rules. They are located on the Internet at **www.ftc.gov/bcp/menu-health.htm**.

Jewelry and Precious Metals   (F.R., Title 61, Page 27212.) The FTC has numerous rules governing the sale and advertising of jewelry and precious metals. Anyone in this business should obtain a copy of these rules. They are located on the Internet at **www.ftc.gov/bcp/guides/jewel-gd.htm**.

Florida Laws   Most of Florida's advertising laws are included with the criminal statutes. Violation of the first three below is a misdemeanor, and a second offense is punishable with a fine of up to $10,000.

Misleading advertising. (Fla. Stat. Sec. 817.41.) It is illegal to use advertising that is *misleading*, or to use words like *wholesale* or *below cost* unless the goods are actually at or below the retailer's net cost. If demanded by a consumer, a retailer must provide to the Better Business Bureau, the Chamber of Commerce, or the State Attorney's office proof of the cost, and must help that person figure out the net cost. Retailers may not advertise items at a special price unless they have reasonable quantities or state in the ad the quantity available (unless they give rain checks). A customer may sue a business under this law and receive attorney's fees, court costs, actual damages, and punitive damages.

False information. (Fla. Stat. Sec. 817.411.) No advertisement may state that an item or investment is insured when it is not.

Insurance advertising. (Fla. Stat. Sec. 817.47.) Insurance advertising is covered exclusively by insurance laws.

Names and photographs. (Fla. Stat. Sec. 540.08). It is unlawful to use, for trade or advertising purposes, the name or likeness of any person who has not been dead at least forty years without the permission of the person, or his or her agent or heirs. This does not apply to a picture of people in public who are not identified.

INTERNET SALES LAWS

There are not yet specific laws governing Internet transactions that are different from laws governing other transactions. The FTC feels that its current rules regarding deceptive advertising, substantiation, disclaimers, refunds, and related matters must be followed by Internet businesses, and that consumers are adequately protected by them. See the first three pages of this chapter and Chapter 10 for that information.

For some specific guidelines on Internet advertising, see the FTC's site at **www.ftc.gov/bcp/conline/pubs/buspubs/ruleroad.htm**.

EMAIL ADVERTISING

The *Controlling the Assault of Non-Solicited Pornography And Marketing Act of 2003* (CANSPAM) has put numerous controls on how you can use email to solicit business for your company. It requires unsolicited commercial email messages to be labeled, and the message must include opt-out instructions and the sender's physical address. Some of the prohibited activities under the Act are:

○ false or misleading information in an email;

○ deceptive subject heading;

○ failure to include a functioning return address;

○ mailing to someone who has asked not to receive solicitations;

○ failure to include a valid postal address;

○ omitting an opt-out procedure;

○ failure to clearly mark the email as advertising; and,

○ including sexual material without adequate warnings.

Some of the provisions contain criminal penalties as well as civil fines.

For more information on the CANSPAM Act, see **www.gigalaw.com/ canspam**. For text of the Act plus other spam laws around the world, see **www.spamlaws.com**.

Florida   Florida also has enacted laws regarding email advertising. The *Electronic Mail Communications Act* applies to unsolicited commercial electronic mail. (Fla. Stat. Secs. 668.60–668.6075.) The intent of the law is to protect the public and legitimate businesses from deceptive and unsolicited commercial electronic mail.

The law states that a person may not use a computer located in Florida or send a message to a computer in Florida that:

○ uses a third party's Internet domain name without permission of the third party;

○ contains falsified or missing routing information;

○ contains false or misleading information in the subject line; or,

○ contains a computer virus.

Violating this statute can be deemed an unfair and deceptive trade practice, and civil damages may be claimed. A person prevailing in an action filed under this law is entitled to:

- ✪ an injunction to enjoin future violations;

- ✪ damages equal to any actual damage proven, or liquidated damages of $500 for each unsolicited commercial electronic mail message; and,

- ✪ attorney's fees and other litigation costs.

HOME SOLICITATION LAWS

The Federal Trade Commission has rules governing door-to-door sales. In any such sale, it is a deceptive trade practice to fail to furnish a receipt explaining the sale (in the language of the presentation), as is failure to give notice that there is a right to back out of the contract within three days, known as a *right of rescission*. The notice must be supplied in duplicate, must be in at least 10-point type, and must be captioned either "Notice of Right to Cancel" or "Notice of Cancellation." The notice must be worded as the example on page 141 illustrates.

NOTICE OF CANCELLATION

_____
Date

YOU MAY CANCEL THIS TRANSACTION, WITHOUT ANY PENALTY OR OBLIGATION, WITHIN THREE BUSINESS DAYS FROM THE ABOVE DATE.

IF YOU CANCEL, ANY PROPERTY TRADED IN, ANY PAYMENTS MADE BY YOU UNDER THE CONTRACT OR SALE, AND ANY NEGOTIABLE INSTRUMENT EXECUTED BY YOU WILL BE RETURNED TO YOU WITHIN 10 BUSINESS DAYS FOLLOWING RECEIPT BY THE SELLER OF YOUR CANCELLATION NOTICE, AND ANY SECURITY INTEREST ARISING OUT OF THE TRANS-ACTION WILL BE CANCELLED.

IF YOU CANCEL, YOU MUST MAKE AVAILABLE TO THE SELLER AT YOUR RESIDENCE, IN SUBSTANTIALLY AS GOOD CONDITION AS WHEN RECEIVED, ANY GOODS DELIVERED TO YOU UNDER THIS CONTRACT OR SALE; OR YOU MAY, IF YOU WISH, COMPLY WITH THE INSTRUCTIONS OF THE SELLER REGARDING THE RETURN SHIPMENT OF THE GOODS AT THE SELLER'S EXPENSE AND RISK.

IF YOU DO MAKE THE GOODS AVAILABLE TO THE SELLER AND THE SELLER DOES NOT PICK THEM UP WITHIN 20 DAYS OF THE DATE OF YOUR NOTICE OF CANCELLATION, YOU MAY RETAIN OR DISPOSE OF THE GOODS WITHOUT ANY FURTHER OBLIGATION. IF YOU FAIL TO MAKE THE GOODS AVAILABLE TO THE SELLER, OR IF YOU AGREE TO RETURN THE GOODS AND FAIL TO DO SO, THEN YOU REMAIN LIABLE FOR PER-FORMANCE OF ALL OBLIGATIONS UNDER THE CONTRACT.

TO CANCEL THIS TRANSACTION, MAIL OR DELIVER A SIGNED AND DATED COPY OF THIS CANCELLATION NOTICE OR ANY OTHER WRITTEN NOTICE, OR SEND A TELEGRAM, TO _____(name of seller), AT _____(address of seller's place of business) NOT LATER THAN MIDNIGHT OF _____ (date).

I HEREBY CANCEL THIS TRANSACTION.

_____   _____
(Buyer's signature)   (Date)

The seller must complete the notice and orally inform the buyer of the right to cancel. He or she cannot misrepresent the right to cancel, assign the contract until the fifth business day, or include a confession of judgment in the contract. For more specific details, see the rules contained in the Code of Federal Regulations, Title 16, Chapter I, Part 429.

Florida Law   Florida Statutes Sections 501.021 through 501.055 are titled *Home Solicitation Sales*, but the definition of such sales is much broader. These sections actually cover all transactions that are:

- consumer transactions (sale, rental, lease);

- over $25 (including all charges, interest, etc.);

- solicited other than at the seller's regular place of business;

- consummated other than at the seller's regular place of business; and,

- unsolicited telephone sales.

Sales at trade shows are included under the law, but it does not include sales at fairs; sales from a purchaser's request for specific goods; sales by motor vehicle dealers at a place open to the public or to a designated group; sales of insurance; and, sales of farm equipment or machinery.

Right to cancel. Any such described sale may be cancelled by the buyer by written notice, in any form, postmarked any time before midnight of the third business day after the sales day. Business days do not include Sunday, New Year's Day, Washington's Birthday, Memorial Day, Independence Day, Labor Day, Columbus Day, Veteran's Day, Thanksgiving Day, and Christmas Day.

Written agreement. Every such sale must be in writing and contain the buyer's signature, the date the buyer signed, and the notice on page 143.

BUYER'S RIGHT TO CANCEL

This is a home solicitation sale, and if you do not want the goods or services, you may cancel this agreement by providing written notice to the Seller in person, by telegram, or by mail. This notice must indicate that you do not want the goods or services, and must be delivered or postmarked before midnight of the third business day after you sign this agreement. If you cancel this agreement, the Seller may not keep all or part of any cash down payment.

Refund. The refund must be made to the buyer within ten days. If it is not, the seller may be subject to criminal and civil penalties.

Buyer's duty. Within a reasonable time after cancellation and demand by seller, a buyer must return any goods received under the contract unless the seller fails to refund the buyer's deposit as required. If the seller has not made demand within forty days, the buyer may keep the goods. If the seller does not refund the buyer's deposit, the buyer may retain possession of the goods and has a lien on them for the amount due. The buyer must take reasonable care of the goods in his or her possession, but does not have to deliver them to the seller at any place other than the buyer's residence.

Seller's duty. All businesses conducting solicitation sales must:

❂ ensure that all employees have the required permits;

❂ provide identification to salespeople for face-to-face sales, which includes the seller's name, description, and signature; the name, address, and phone number of the company; and, the name, address, and signature of the seller's supervisor; and,

❂ direct sales agents to leave a business card, contract, or receipt with the buyer, including the following information: name, address, and phone number of the company and of the sales agent, and the buyer's Right to Cancel Notice (described above).

In telephone solicitations, the name, address, and phone number of the company must be clearly disclosed on sales materials and contracts sent to the buyer.

Prohibitions. In conducting home solicitations, no person shall:

- ✪ misrepresent terms of the sale;

- ✪ misrepresent seller's affiliation with the company;

- ✪ misrepresent reasons for solicitation (such as contests or handicaps that are not true);

- ✪ imply the contract is noncancelable; or,

- ✪ misrepresent anything else.

TELEPHONE SOLICITATION LAWS

Telephone solicitations are governed by the *Telephone Consumer Protection Act* (47 U.S.C. Sec. 227) and the Federal Communications Commission rules implementing the Act (C.F.R., Title 47, Sec. 64.1200). Violators of the act can be sued for $500 damages by consumers and can be fined $10,000 by the FCC. Some of the requirements under the law include the following.

- ✪ Calls can only be made between 8 a.m. and 9 p.m.

- ✪ Solicitors must keep a *do not call* list and honor requests not to call.

- ✪ There must be a written policy that the parties called are told the name of the caller, the caller's business name and phone number or address, that the call is a sales call, and the nature of the goods or services.

- ✪ Personnel must be trained in the policies.

- ✪ Recorded messages cannot be used to call residences.

In 2003, the FCC introduced the national *Do Not Call Registry*, in which individuals could register their telephone numbers and prohibit certain telephone solicitors from calling the registered numbers. Once a person registers a telephone number, it remains on the registry for five years. Telemarketing firms can receive heavy fines for violating the registry statute, with fines ranging up to $11,000 per violation. Not all telephone solicitations are barred, however. The following solicitors may still contact a person whose telephone number has been entered in the registry:

- calls from companies with which the registered person has a prior business relationship;

- calls for which the recipient has given written consent;

- calls that do not include advertisements; and,

- calls from charitable organizations.

It is illegal under the Act to send advertising faxes to anyone who has not consented to receiving such faxes or is not an existing customer.

Florida Law   The telephone solicitation law, found in Florida Statutes Section 501.059, applies to any transaction involving real or personal property normally used primarily for personal, family, or household purposes. It includes cemetery lots and time-shares. It does not apply to calls to businesses. Penalties for violations include a fine of up to $10,000, attorney's fees, and court costs. The law contains these main provisions.

Identification. Any person who makes a telephone solicitation call must identify him- or herself by true first and last name, and the name of the business represented, immediately upon making contact.

Prohibition. No solicitation calls may be made to any person who is listed in a quarterly directory published by the Division of Consumer Services of the Florida Department of Agriculture and Consumer Services. The fee for a listing in the directory is $10 for the first year and $5 for each additional year. Businesses may purchase a copy of this directory from the Division.

Enforceability. A contract agreed to after a telephone solicitation is not enforceable unless the seller obtains a signed contract from the buyer that accurately describes the goods; contains the name, address, and phone number of the seller; contains in bold, conspicuous type the clause, "You are not obligated to pay any money unless you sign this contract and return it to the seller"; includes all oral representations made by the seller; and, complies with all applicable laws and rules. However, this rule does not apply to contractual sales that are regulated by other sections of Florida Statutes, to telephone companies, securities or financial services, or cable television companies.

Credit cards. A merchant (except a charity or newspaper) may not charge an amount to a person's credit card for a sale procured through a telephone solicitation until the merchant receives a signed contract from the customer, unless:

✪ the customer has first visited a permanent place of business where the merchant has the goods on display;

✪ the customer may receive a full refund by giving notice of cancellation within seven days, and the refund will be processed within thirty days; or,

✪ the consumer made the purchase pursuant to television, radio, or print advertising or a brochure, sample, or catalog that contains the name, address, and telephone number of the merchant, a description of the goods or services being sold, and any conditions of the offer.

This law does not apply to calls to persons who have made contact with the businesses, or to newspapers or charities. Also exempt are real estate agents who make calls in response to yard signs or other ads by property owners.

Automatic dialing. (Fla. Stat. Sec. 501.059(7).) Except in limited circumstances, it is forbidden to use any machine for automatic dialing or playing a recorded message. An automatic dialing system may be used with live messages if:

- ✪ the calls are made only to persons who have requested information;

- ✪ the dialing is screened to exclude persons who are on the *no solicitation calls* list;

- ✪ the dialing is screened to exclude people who have unlisted numbers; or,

- ✪ the calls concern goods or services previously ordered or purchased.

There are both civil and criminal penalties for violation of this law.

Fax advertising. (Fla. Stat. Sec. 365.1657.) It is illegal to send unsolicited advertising materials by fax within the state of Florida.

PRICING, WEIGHTS, AND LABELING
All food products are required to have labels displaying information on the product's nutritional values, such as calories, fat, and protein. For most products, the label must be in the required format so that consumers can easily compare products. However, if such a format will not fit on the product label, the information may be in another format that is easily readable.

Federal rules require metric measurement be included on products. Under these rules, metric measures do not have to be the first measurement on the container, but they must be included. Food items that are packaged as they are sold (such as delicatessen items) do not have to contain metric labels.

Florida Law Under Florida Statutes, Chapter 531, it is a second-degree misdemeanor (meaning a fine of up to $500 and up to sixty days in jail) to violate any of the following rules (administrative penalties start at $1,000 for the first violation).

Misrepresenting quantity. No person shall misrepresent the quantity of goods offered for sale or goods purchased.

Misrepresenting price. No person shall misrepresent the price of any commodity, or represent the price in any manner calculated to confuse. When a price includes a fraction of a cent, all elements of the fraction must be prominently displayed.

Method of sale. Generally, commodities in liquid form must be sold by liquid measure or weight. Those not sold in liquid form must be sold only by weight, area, or volume, or by count, as long as the method of sale provides accurate quantity information.

Bulk sale. Bulk sales of over $20 must be accompanied by a delivery ticket containing the following information:

- ✪   the name and address of the seller and buyer;

- ✪   date delivered;

- ✪   net quantity delivered and net quantity for basis of price, if this differs from quantity delivered;

- ✪   identity of the commodity in commercially practicable terms, including representations made in connection with the sale; and,

- ✪   the count of individually wrapped packages, if there are more than one of such packages.

Information required on packages. Generally, all packages of commodities for sale must bear a conspicuous statement of:

- ✪   identity of commodity (unless it can be identified through wrapper);

- ✪   net quantity of contents in terms of weight, measure, or count; and,

- ✪   for goods sold other than where they are packed, the name and place of business of the manufacturer, packer, or distributor.

Declarations of unit price on random packages. In addition to the bulk sales requirements, when goods are offered in packages of different weights, with the price stated on them, the price per single unit of weight must also be stated.

Advertising packages for sale. When a packaged commodity is advertised for sale with a price stated, the quantity must also be conspicuously stated.

PRICE GOUGING

It is a misdemeanor to charge unconscionable prices for essential commodities after a state of emergency has been declared by the governor. Essential commodities include those items that are important during an emergency, such as food, water, ice, lumber, and chemicals. Also included are unconscionable prices for labor and lodging. Besides the criminal penalties, a violator may be fined up to $25,000 per day. (Fla. Stats. Secs. 501.160 and 501.164.)

DECEPTIVE PRACTICES

If a business engages in practices that may be regarded as deceptive or unfair in a consumer transaction, it may be subject to the following penalties under Florida law. (Florida Statutes Sections 501.201 to 501.213.)

- ✪ The State Attorney or the Department of Legal Affairs may bring court action for injunctions, damages to consumers, and fines of up to $10,000 for each violation. If the victim is a senior citizen or a handicapped person, the fine may be up to $15,000 plus restitution.

- ✪ A consumer may bring a suit for damages plus attorney's fees.

No damages can be recovered against a retailer who acted in good faith in repeating claims of a manufacturer or wholesaler, and did not know he or she was in violation of this law.

REFUNDS

If a retail establishment has a policy of no refunds or exchanges, a notice of such policy must be posted at the point of sale. If no notice is posted, a seller must grant a refund to purchasers requesting one within seven days of purchase and producing proof of purchase. However, the merchandise must be unused and in the original packaging (Fla. Stat. Sec. 501.142). This rule does not apply to food that cannot be resold by a merchant because of a law or regulation, perishables, goods that are custom-made or altered, or goods that cannot be resold.

If a seller uses any type of receipt on delivery of a packaged item in which the buyer is requested or required to agree in writing that the goods are satisfactory, the statement must also contain the following notice. (Fla. Stat. Sec. 501.141.)

BUYER'S RIGHT TO CANCEL

If the goods you have received are not in satisfactory condition or operation, you may cancel this statement of satisfaction by mailing a notice to the Seller. This notice must indicate that you do not want the goods in the condition in which they were delivered and must be postmarked before midnight of the fifth business day after you sign.

Payment and Collection

Depending on the business you are in, you may be paid by cash, checks, credit cards, or some sort of financing arrangement, such as a promissory note or mortgage. Both state and federal laws affect the type of payments you collect, and failure to follow the laws can cost you considerably.

CASH

Cash is probably the easiest form of payment and it is subject to few restrictions. The most important one is that you keep an accurate accounting of your cash transactions and that you report all of your cash income on your tax return. Recent efforts to stop the drug trade have resulted in some serious penalties for failing to report cash transactions and for money laundering. The laws are so sweeping that even if you deal in cash in an ordinary business, you may violate the law and face huge fines and imprisonment.

The most important law to be concerned with is the one requiring the filing of the *Report of Cash Payments over $10,000* (IRS form 8300). (A copy of form 8300 can be found at **www.irs.gov**.) If one person pays you with $10,000 or more in cash, you are required to file this form. A transaction does not have to happen in one day. If a person brings you smaller amounts of cash that add up to $10,000 and the government can construe them as one transaction, then the form must be filed. Under this law, *cash* also includes travelers' checks and money orders, but not cashiers' checks or bank checks.

CHECKS

It is important to accept checks in your business. While there is a small percentage that will be bad, most checks will be good, and you will be able to accommodate more customers. To avoid having problems with checks, you should abide by the rules discussed in this section.

A business may not require a customer to provide a credit card number or expiration date in order to pay by or cash a check. (Fla. Stat. Sec. 832.075.) The business can request to see a card to establish that the customer is creditworthy or for additional identification, and can record the type of credit card and issuing company. The business cannot record the number of the card. The penalty for a violation is a fine of $250 for the first violation and $1,000 for each subsequent violation.

Bad Checks   Florida has a fairly effective bad check collection process. If you follow the rules, you will probably be able to collect on a bad check. Some counties even have special divisions of the sheriff's department that actively help you collect on bad checks.

The first rule is that you must be able to identify the person who gave you the check. To do this, you should require identification and write down the sources of identification on the face of the check. Another rule is that you cannot accept post-dated checks. Also, you must send a demand to the person by certified mail that they pay the amount of the check plus a penalty of $25 to $40, depending on the value the check was written for, or 5% of the face amount of the check, whichever is greater. The notice is contained in the Florida Statutes. (Fla. Stat. Sec. 832.07.)

Refunds after   A popular scam is for a person to purchase something by using a
Cashing Check   check and then come back the next day demanding a refund. After

making the refund, the business discovers the initial payment check bounced. Do not make refunds until checks clear.

CREDIT CARDS

In our buy now, pay later society, charge cards can add greatly to your sales potential, especially with large, discretionary purchases. For MasterCard, Visa, and Discover, the fees businesses must pay to accept these cards are about 2%, and this amount is easily paid for by the extra purchases that the cards allow. American Express charges 4% to 5%. (You may decide this is not worth paying, since almost everyone who has an American Express card also has another card.)

For businesses that have a retail outlet, there is usually no problem getting merchant status. Most commercial banks can handle it. Discover can also set you up to accept their card as well as MasterCard and Visa, and they will wire the money into your bank account daily.

For mail order businesses, especially those operating out of the home, it is much harder to get merchant status because of the number of scams in which large amounts are charged, no products are shipped, and the company folds. Today, things are a little better. Some companies are even soliciting merchants. However, beware of those that charge exorbitant fees (such as $5 or $10 per order for "processing"). American Express will accept mail order companies operating out of the home. However, not as many people have their cards as others.

Some companies open a small storefront (or share one) to get merchant status, then process mostly mail orders. The processors usually do not want to accept you if you will do more than 50% mail order business; but if you do not have many complaints, you may be allowed to process mostly mail orders. Whatever you do, keep your charge customers happy so that they do not complain.

You might be tempted to try to run your charges through another business. This may be all right if you actually sell your products through the other businesses, but if you run your business charges through that account, the other business may lose its merchant status. People who bought a book by mail from you and then find a charge on their statement from a florist shop will probably call the credit card company saying that they never bought anything from the florist shop. If you have too many of these, the account will be closed.

A new money-making scheme by the credit card companies is to offer business credit cards that the merchants are charged a higher fee for accepting. To make these more profitable, the credit card companies are telling customers they are not allowed to use their personal credit cards for business purposes. To keep your processing fees down, you can tell your customers you prefer personal, not business, credit cards.

FINANCING LAWS

Some businesses can more easily make sales if they finance the purchases themselves. If the business has enough capital to do this, it can earn extra profits on the financing terms. Nonetheless, because of abuses, many consumer protection laws have been passed by both the federal and state governments.

Regulation Z   Two important federal laws regarding financing are called the *Truth in Lending Act* and the *Fair Credit Billing Act*. These are implemented by what is called *Regulation Z* (commonly known as *Reg. Z*), issued by the Board of Governors of the Federal Reserve System. (1 C.F.R., Vol. 12, p. 226.) This is a very complicated law, and some have said that no business can be sure to be in compliance with it.

The regulation covers all transactions in which four conditions are met:

1.   credit is offered;

2   the offering of credit is regularly done;

3.   there is a finance charge for the credit or there is a written agreement with more than four payments; and,

4.   the credit is for personal, family, or household purposes.

It also covers credit card transactions where only the first two conditions are met. It applies to leases if the consumer ends up paying the full value and keeping the item leased. It does not apply to the following transactions:

✪ transactions with businesses or agricultural purposes;

✪ transactions with organizations such as corporations or the government;

✪ transactions of over $25,000 that are not secured by the consumer's dwelling;

✪ credit involving public utilities;

✪ credit involving securities or commodities; and,

✪ home fuel budget plans.

The way for a small business to avoid Reg. Z violations is to avoid transactions that meet the conditions or to make sure all transactions fall under the exceptions. For many businesses, this is easy. Instead of extending credit to customers, accept credit cards and let the credit card company extend the credit. However, if your customers usually do not have credit cards or if you are in a business that often extends credit, such as used car sales, you should consult a lawyer knowledgeable about Reg. Z or get a copy for yourself at **www.cardreport.com/laws/tila/tila.html**.

Florida Law   Florida also has laws regarding financing arrangements. Anyone engaged in retail installment-selling must be licensed by the Florida Department of Banking and Finance. The law specifies what size type must be used in printed contracts, what notices must be included in them, and many other details. Anyone engaged in installment sales in Florida should carefully review the latest versions of the following statutes.

✪ Florida Consumer Finance Act (Fla. Stat. Secs. 516.001–.36)

✪ Motor Vehicle Sales Finance (Fla. Stat., Ch. 520, Part I)

- Retail Installment Sales (Fla. Stat., Ch. 520, Part II)

- Installment Sales Finance (Fla. Stat., Ch. 520, Part III)

- Home Improvement Sales and Finance (Fla. Stat., Ch. 520, Part IV)

- Department Regulation of Sales and Finance (Fla. Stat., Ch. 520, Part V)

- Rental-Purchase Agreement Act (Fla. Stat. Secs. 559.9231–.9241)

In addition to these acts, Florida forbids discrimination based upon sex, marital status, or race in the areas of loaning money, granting credit, or providing equal pay for equal services performed. (Fla. Stat. Sec. 725.07.) Discrimination is forbidden in the financing of residential real estate based upon race, color, national origin, sex, handicap, familial status, or religion. (Fla. Stat. Sec. 760.25.)

USURY

Usury is the charging of an illegally high rate of interest. In Florida, if you have a written agreement, the maximum rate of interest you may charge is 18%, except on loans of over $500,000, on which the maximum rate is 25%. (Fla. Stat., Ch. 687.) If there is no written agreement as to the rate of interest, the rate is set by law. Some businesses, such as banks, are excluded from this law.

The penalty for charging in excess of the legal rate is that the borrower does not have to pay any interest and the lender has to repay double the amounts received.

Anyone charging or receiving interest at a rate of over 25% but less than 45% is guilty of a misdemeanor, and anyone charging or receiving interest of 45% or greater is guilty of a felony. The borrower may also sue for damages, costs, punitive damages, and attorney's fees.

COLLECTIONS

The *Fair Debt Collection Practices Act of 1977* bans the use of deception, harassment, and other unreasonable acts in the collection of debts. It has strict requirements whenever someone is collecting a debt for someone else. If you are in the collection business, you must get a copy of this law.

The Federal Trade Commission has issued some rules that prohibit deceptive representations, such as pretending to be in the motion picture industry, the government, or a credit bureau, or using questionnaires that do not say that they are for the purpose of collecting a debt. (C.F.R., Title 16, Ch. I, Part 237.)

Florida Law   The *Consumer Collection Practices Law* applies to debts owed by persons (not corporations) for transactions that were for personal, family, or household purposes. (Fla. Stat. Sec. 559.57.) The law forbids:

✪   simulating a law enforcement officer or government agency;

✪   using or threatening force or violence;

✪   threatening to disclose the debt to others without explaining that the fact that there is a dispute over the debt will also be disclosed;

✪   contacting or threatening to contact a debtor's employer prior to obtaining a final judgment, unless the debtor has given permission in writing or unless the debtor has agreed in writing as to the debt, after the debt goes to collection;

✪   disclosing information affecting the debtor's reputation to persons outside the debtor's family who do not have a legitimate business need for the information;

✪   disclosing information affecting the debtor's reputation, knowing the information to be false;

✪   disclosing information about a disputed debt without disclosing the dispute;

✪   willfully harassing the debtor or his or her family;

✪   using profane, obscene, vulgar, or willfully abusive language with the debtor or his or her family;

✪   attempting to collect a debt that is not legitimate;

✪   claiming a legal right, knowing that this right does not exist;

✪   using communication that looks like it is from a court, government, or attorney if it is not;

✪   pretending to be an attorney by using an attorney's stationery or forms;

✪   orally pretending to be an attorney or associated with an attorney;

✪   advertising or threatening to advertise sale of a claim unless under court order or as assignee;

✪   publishing or posting a *deadbeat* list;

✪   refusing to identify one's self or employer when requested by a debtor;

✪   mailing any communication to a debtor that contains embarrassing words on the outside of the envelope; and,

✪   communicating with a debtor between 9 p.m. and 8 a.m. without prior consent of the debtor.

A debtor who is a victim of any of the above violations may sue the creditor for actual damages or $500 (whichever is greater), costs, and attorney's fees, and in some cases, punitive damages. (If a debtor wrongly brings a suit, he or she may have to pay the creditor's attorney's fees and court costs.)

The Division of Consumer Services also investigates complaints by debtors of violations of this law. The agency may issue warnings, reprimands, revocation of licensing, and fines. The state attorney may seek criminal penalties and injunctions for certain violations.

Business Relations Law

At both the federal and state levels, there exist many laws regarding how businesses relate to one another. Some of the more important ones are discussed in this chapter.

THE UNIFORM COMMERCIAL CODE

The *Uniform Commercial Code* (UCC) is a set of laws regulating numerous aspects of doing business. A national group drafted this set of uniform laws to avoid having a patchwork of different laws around the fifty states. Although some states modified some sections of the laws, the code is basically the same in most of the states. In Florida, the UCC is contained in Chapters 670 to 680 of the Florida Statutes. Each chapter is concerned with a different aspect of commercial relations, such as sales, warranties, bank deposits, commercial paper, and bulk transfers.

Businesses that wish to know their rights in all types of transactions should obtain a copy of the UCC and become familiar with it. It is especially useful in transactions between merchants. However, the meaning is not always clear from reading the statutes.

COMMERCIAL DISCRIMINATION

The *Robinson-Patman Act of 1936* prohibits businesses from injuring competition by offering the same goods at different prices to different buyers. This means that the large chain stores should not be getting a better price than your small shop. It also requires that promotional allowances must be made on proportionally the same terms to all buyers.

As a small business, you may be a victim of Robinson-Patman Act violation, but fighting a much larger company in court would probably be too expensive for you. Your best bet, if an actual violation has occurred, would be to see if you could get the government to prosecute it. For more information on what constitutes a violation, see the Federal Trade Commission and the Department of Justice's joint site at **www.ftc.gov/bc/compguide/index.htm**.

Florida Law It is unlawful for anyone who is engaged in the production, manufacture, sale, or distribution of any article, product, thing of value, service, or output of a service trade, to attempt to destroy the business of a competitor through discrimination between different sections, communities, or cities, by selling at a lower rate in one section. (Fla. Stat. Sec. 542.18.) The law also provides that:

- it is not unlawful to discriminate in prices in a good faith effort to meet competition;

- complaints may be made to a State Attorney or to the Department of State in Tallahassee; and,

- violation is a first-degree misdemeanor punishable by a fine of up to $1,000 or a year in prison.

RESTRAINING TRADE

One of the earliest federal laws affecting business is the *Sherman Antitrust Act of 1890*. The purpose of the law was to protect competition in the marketplace by prohibiting monopolies.

Examples of some things that are prohibited are:

✪   agreements between competitors to sell at the same prices;

✪   agreements between competitors on how much will be sold or produced;

✪   agreements between competitors to divide up a market;

✪   refusing to sell one product without a second product; or,

✪   exchanging information among competitors, which results in similarity of prices.

As a small business, you will probably not be in a position to violate the Sherman Act, but you should be aware of it if a larger competitor tries to put you out of business. Fighting a much larger company in court would probably be too expensive for you, but if an actual violation has occurred, you might be able to get the government to prosecute it. For more information on what constitutes a violation, see the website by the Federal Trade Commission and the Department of Justice at **www.ftc.gov/bc/compguide**.

Florida Law   It is unlawful to have any contract, combination, or conspiracy to restrain trade or to monopolize, attempt to monopolize, or combine or conspire with any other person to monopolize, any part of trade or commerce. (Fla. Stat. Sec. 542.19.)

✪   The penalty for any violation is up to $100,000 for a natural person and up to $1,000,000 for a company.

✪   Anyone knowingly violating or knowingly aiding or advising a violation can be guilty of a felony and sentenced to up to three years in prison in addition to the fines.

✪   A person whose business is hurt by a violation can seek an injunction to prohibit violations and may collect triple damages in a suit against a violator, along with costs and attorney's fees.

COMMERCIAL BRIBERY

In 1990, the Florida legislature created a new felony called *commercial bribery*. (Fla. Stat. Secs. 838.15 and 838.16.) Commercial bribery is defined as soliciting, accepting, or agreeing to accept a benefit with intent to violate a law. It applies to agents, employees, trustees, guardians, fiduciaries, lawyers, physicians, accountants, appraisers, or other professional advisors, arbitrators, or officers, directors, managers, partners or others in control of an organization. Commercial bribery is committed by anyone on the other side of the above-described transaction.

In 1995, the Florida Supreme Court ruled that the law was unconstitutional because it was too vague. The court noted that the law could even be used to convict a head waiter who gave someone a better table for a tip. The law is still in the Florida statutes, but in light of the court case, it would not be enforceable until revised by the legislature.

INTELLECTUAL PROPERTY PROTECTION

As a business owner, you should know enough about intellectual property law to protect your own creations and to keep from violating the rights of others. Intellectual property is the product of human creativity, such as writings, designs, inventions, melodies, and processes. They are things that can be stolen without being physically taken. For example, if you write a book, someone can steal the words from your book without stealing a physical copy of it.

As the Internet grows, intellectual property is becoming more valuable. Business owners should take the action necessary to protect their companies' intellectual property. Additionally, business owners should know intellectual property law to be sure that they do not violate the rights of others. Even an unknowing violation of the law can result in stiff fines and penalties.

The following are the types of intellectual property and the ways to protect them.

Patent   A *patent* is protection given to new and useful inventions, discoveries, and designs. To be entitled to a patent, a work must be completely new and unobvious. A patent is granted to the first inventor who files for the patent. Once an invention is patented, no one else can make use of that invention, even if they discover it independently after a lifetime of research. A patent protects an invention for seventeen years; for designs, it is protected for three and one-half, seven, or fourteen years. Patents cannot be renewed. The patent application must clearly explain how to make the invention so that when the patent expires, others will be able to freely make and use the invention. Patents are registered with the *United States Patent and Trademark Office* (PTO). Examples of things that would be patentable would be mechanical devices or new drug formulas.

In recent years, patents have been used to protect computer programs and things such as business methods, including Amazon's one-click ordering. Few cases challenging these patents have gotten through the court system, so it is too early to tell if they will hold up. About half the patents that reach the Supreme Court are held to be invalid.

Copyright

A *copyright* is protection given to original works of authorship, such as written works, musical works, visual works, performance works, or computer software programs. A copyright exists from the moment of creation, but one cannot register a copyright until it has been fixed in tangible form. Also, one cannot copyright titles, names, or slogans. A copyright currently gives the author and his or her heirs exclusive right to the work for the life of the author plus seventy years.

Copyrights first registered before 1978 last for ninety-five years. (This was previously seventy-five years, but was extended twenty years to match the European system.) Copyrights are registered with the Register of Copyrights at the Library of Congress. Examples of works that would be copyrightable are books, paintings, songs, poems, plays, drawings, and films.

Trademark

A *trademark* is protection given to a name or symbol used to distinguish one person's goods or services from those of others. It can consist of letters, numerals, packaging, labeling, musical notes, colors, or a combination of these. If a trademark is used on services as opposed to goods, it is called a *service mark*.

A trademark lasts indefinitely if it is used continuously and renewed properly. Trademarks are registered with the United States Patent and Trademark Office and with individual states. (This is explained further in Chapter 3.) Examples of trademarks are the Chrysler name on automobiles, the red border on TIME magazine, and the shape of the Coca-Cola bottle.

Trade Secret

A *trade secret* is some information or process that provides a commercial advantage that is protected by keeping it a secret. Examples of trade secrets may be a list of successful distributors, the formula for Coca-Cola, or some unique source code in a computer program. Trade secrets are not registered anywhere—they are protected by the fact that they are not disclosed. They are protected only for as long as they are kept secret. If you independently discover the formula for Coca-Cola tomorrow, you can freely market it (but you cannot use the trademark "Coca-Cola" on your product to market it).

Florida law. Florida has passed the *Uniform Trade Secrets Act*, which protects trade secrets from appropriation by other businesses. (Fla. Stat., Ch. 688.) It provides for injunctions, damages, and attorney's fees for violation of the act.

There are numerous other Florida laws dealing with trade secrets. If you have some concerns about trade secrets in your business you should check the index to Florida Statutes under "trade secrets."

Unprotected Creations

Some things just cannot be protected—such things as ideas, systems, and discoveries are not allowed any protection under any law. If you have a great idea, such as selling packets of hangover medicine in bars, you cannot stop others from doing the same thing. If you invent a new medicine, you can patent it; if you pick a distinctive name for it, you can register it as a trademark; if you create a unique picture or instructions for the package, you can copyright them. However, you cannot stop others from using your basic business idea of marketing hangover medicine in bars.

Notice the subtle differences between the protective systems available. If you invent something two days after someone else does, you cannot even use it yourself if the other person has patented it. However, if you write the same poem as someone else and neither of you copied the other, both of you can copyright the poem. If you patent something, you can have the exclusive rights to it for the term of the patent, but you must disclose how others can make it after the patent expires. However, if you keep it a trade secret, you have exclusive rights as long as no one learns the secret.

Endless Laws

The state of Florida and the federal government have numerous laws and rules that apply to every aspect of every type of business. There are even laws governing such things as fence posts, hosiery, rabbit raising, refund policies, frozen desserts, and advertising. Every business is affected by at least one of these laws.

Some activities are covered by both state and federal laws. In such cases, you must obey the stricter of the rules. In addition, more than one agency of the state or federal government may have rules governing your business. Each of these may have the power to investigate violations and impose fines or other penalties.

Penalties for violations of these laws can range from a warning to a criminal fine and even jail time. In some cases, employees can sue for damages. Recently, employees have been given awards of millions of dollars from employers who violated the law. Since ignorance of the law is no excuse, it is your duty to learn which laws apply to your business, or to risk these penalties.

Very few people in business know the laws that apply to their businesses. If you take the time to learn them, you can become an expert in your field, and avoid problems with regulators. You can also fight back if one of your competitors uses some illegal method to compete with you.

The laws and rules that affect the most businesses are explained in this section. Following that is a list of more specialized laws. You should read through this list and see which ones may apply to your business. Then, go to your public library or law library and read them. Some may not apply to your phase of the business, but if any of them do apply, you should make copies to keep on hand.

No one could possibly know all the rules that affect business, much less comply with them all. (The Interstate Commerce Commission alone has 40 trillion rates on its books telling the transportation industry what it should charge!) However, if you keep up with the important rules, you will stay out of trouble and have more chance of success.

FEDERAL LAWS

The federal laws that are most likely to affect small businesses are rules of the Federal Trade Commission (FTC). The FTC has some rules that affect many businesses, such as the rules about labeling, warranties, and mail order sales. Other rules affect only certain industries.

If you sell goods by mail, you should send for the FTC's booklet, *A Business Guide to the Federal Trade Commission's Mail Order Rule*. If you are going to be involved in a certain industry, such as those listed in this section, or using warranties or your own labeling, you should ask for their latest information on the subject. The address is:

Federal Trade Commission
600 Pennsylvania Avenue, NW
Washington, DC 20580

The rules of the FTC are contained in the Code of Federal Regulations (C.F.R.). Some of the industries covered are the following.

Industry	**Part**
Adhesive Compositions	235
Aerosol Products Used for Frosting Cocktail Glasses	417
Automobiles (New car fuel economy advertising)	259
Barber Equipment and Supplies	248
Binoculars	402
Business Opportunities and Franchises	436
Cigarettes	408
Decorative Wall Paneling	243
Dog and Cat Food	241
Dry Cell Batteries	403
Extension Ladders	418
Fallout Shelters	229
Feather and Down Products	253
Fiber Glass Curtains	413
Food (Games of Chance)	419
Funerals	453
Gasoline (Octane posting)	306
Gasoline	419
Greeting Cards	244
Home Entertainment Amplifiers	432
Home Insulation	460
Hosiery	22
Household Furniture	250
Jewelry	23
Ladies' Handbags	247
Law Books	256
Light Bulbs	409
Luggage and Related Products	24
Mail Order Insurance	234
Mail Order Merchandise	435
Men's and Boys' Tailored Clothing	412
Metallic Watch Band	19
Mirrors	21
Nursery	18
Ophthalmic Practices	456
Photographic Film and Film Processing	242
Private Vocational and Home Study Schools	254
Radiation Monitoring Instruments	232
Retail Food Stores (Advertising)	424
Shell Homes	230
Shoes	231
Sleeping Bags	400
Tablecloths and Related Products	404
Television Sets	410
Textile Wearing Apparel	423
Textiles	236
Tires	228
Used Automobile Parts	20
Used Lubricating Oil	406
Used Motor Vehicles	455
Waist Belts	405
Watches	245
Wigs and Hairpieces	252

Some other federal laws that affect businesses are as follows.

- ✪ *Alcohol Administration Act*

- ✪ *Child Protection and Toy Safety Act*

- ✪ *Clean Water Act*

- ✪ *Comprehensive Smokeless Tobacco Health Education Act*

- ✪ *Consumer Credit Protection Act*

- ✪ *Consumer Product Safety Act*

- ✪ *Energy Policy and Conservation Act*

- ✪ *Environmental Pesticide Control Act of 1972*

- ✪ *Fair Credit Reporting Act*

- ✪ *Fair Packaging and Labeling Act (1966)*

- ✪ *Flammable Fabrics Act*

- ✪ *Food, Drug, and Cosmetic Act*

- ✪ *Fur Products Labeling Act*

- ✪ *Hazardous Substances Act*

- ✪ *Hobby Protection Act*

- ✪ *Insecticide, Fungicide, and Rodenticide Act*

- ✪ *Magnuson-Moss Warranty Act*

- ✪ *Poison Prevention Packaging Act of 1970*

- ✪ *Solid Waste Disposal Act*

- *Textile Fiber Products Identification Act*

- *Toxic Substance Control Act*

- *Wool Products Labeling Act*

- *Nutrition Labeling and Education Act of 1990*

- *Food Safety Enforcement Enhancement Act of 1997*

FLORIDA LAWS

Florida has numerous laws regulating specific types of businesses or certain activities of businesses. The following is a list of those laws that are most likely to affect small businesses. If you are running a type of business that is not mentioned here, or using some sales technique that could come under government regulation, you should check the indexes to the Florida Statutes (Fla. Stat.) and the Florida Administrative Code (Fla. Admin. Code). Since these indexes are not well done, you should look up every possible synonym or related word to be sure not to miss anything.

Adoption agencies	Fla. Stat., Ch. 63
Adult congregate living facilities	Fla. Stat. Secs. 400.401–.454
Adult day care facilities	Fla. Stat. Secs. 400.55–.564
Adult foster home care	Fla. Stat. Secs. 400.616–.702
Air conditioning	Fla. Admin. Code, Chs. 2–14
Aircraft, pilots, and airports	Fla. Stat., Ch. 330
Alcoholic beverages	Fla. Stat., Chs. 561-565,
	Fla. Admin. Code, Ch. 61A
Ambulance service contracts	Fla. Stat., Ch. 638
Anatomical matter	Fla. Stat., Ch. 873
Animals	Fla. Stat. Secs. 585, 877.14; 877.16,
	Fla. Admin. Code, Ch. 5C
Antifreeze	Fla. Stat. Secs. 501.91-.923
Aquaculture	Fla. Stat., Ch. 597
Art and craft material	Fla. Stat. Sec. 501.124
Auctions	Fla. Stat., Ch. 559, Part III
Automobile racing	Fla. Stat., Ch. 549

Bail bondsmen	Fla. Stat., Ch. 648
Banking	Fla. Admin. Code, Ch. 3
Boiler safety	Fla. Stat., Ch. 554
Bottles and boxes, markings	Fla. Stat., Ch. 506
Boxing and fighting	Fla. Stat., Ch. 548,
	Fla. Admin. Code, Ch. 61K1
Brake fluid	Fla. Stat., Ch. 526
Budget planning	Fla. Stat., Ch. 559, Part II
Buildings, radon resistance stds.	Fla. Stat., Ch. 553
Burial contracts	Fla. Stat., Ch. 639
Business opportunities	Fla. Stat., Ch. 559, Part VII,
	Fla. Admin. Code, Chs. 5J-10
Cemeteries	Fla. Stat. Secs. 497, 817.35
Charitable solicitation	Fla. Stat., Ch. 496
Citrus	Fla. Stat., Ch. 600–601
Collections	Fla. Stat., Ch. 559 Part V
Commissions merchants	Fla. Stat., Ch. 522
Condominiums	Fla. Stat., Ch. 718,
	Fla. Admin. Code, Chs. 2-16; 61B
Construction	Fla. Admin. Code, Ch. 61G4
Consumer finance	Fla. Stat., Ch. 516
Cooperatives	Fla. Stat., Ch. 719
Cosmetics	Fla. Stat., Chs. 500, 544
Counseling and psychotherapy	Fla. Stat., Ch. 491
Crash parts	Fla. Stat. Secs. 501.30–.34
Credit cards	Fla. Stat. Secs. 501.011–.0117
Credit service organizations	Fla. Stat., Ch. 817, Part III
Dairies	Fla. Stat., Ch. 502,
	Fla. Admin. Code, Ch. 5D
Dance studios	Fla. Stat. Secs. 205.1969; 501.143,
	Fla. Admin. Code, Ch. 5J-8
Desserts, frozen	Fla. Stat., Ch. 503
Dog racing and horse racing	Fla. Stat., Ch. 550
Drinking water	Fla. Stat. Secs. 403.850–.864
Driving schools	Fla. Stat., Ch. 488
Drugs	Fla. Stat., Chs. 499; 500; 544; 893
Eggs and poultry	Fla. Stat., Ch. 583
Electrical	Fla. Stat., Ch. 553
Electronic repair	Fla. Admin. Code, Chs. 2–28

Elevators, Escalators	Fla. Stat., Ch. 399,
	Fla. Admin. Code, Ch. 61C-5
Energy conservation standards	Fla. Stat., Ch. 553
Equity exchanges	Fla. Stat., Ch. 519
Explosives	Fla. Stat., Ch. 552
Factory-built housing	Fla. Stat., Ch. 553
Fence posts	Fla. Stat. Sec. 501.90
Fences and livestock at large	Fla. Stat., Ch. 588
Fiduciary funds	Fla. Stat., Ch. 518
Fireworks	Fla. Stat., Ch. 791
Food	Fla. Stat., Chs. 500, 544
Franchises	Fla. Stat. Sec. 817.416,
	Fla. Admin. Code, Chs. 2–17
Frontons	Fla. Stat., Ch. 551
Fruits and vegetables	Fla. Stat., Ch. 504,
	Fla. Admin. Code, Ch. 5G; 5H
Fuels, liquid	Fla. Stat., Ch. 526
Future consumer services	Fla. Admin. Code, Chs. 2–18
Gambling and lotteries	Fla. Stat., Ch. 849
Gas, liquefied petroleum	Fla. Stat., Ch. 527,
	Fla. Admin. Code, Chs. 2–20; 4B
Gasoline and oil	Fla. Stat., Ch. 525
Glass	Fla. Stat., Ch. 553
Hazardous substances	Fla. Stat. Secs. 501.061–.121
Hazardous waste amnesty	Fla. Stat. Sec. 403.7264
Health care	Fla. Stat., Chs. 381;
	383-85; 390-92; 395; 400,
	Fla. Admin. Code, Ch. 7G
Health studios	Fla. Stat. Sec. 501.012,
	Fla. Admin. Code, Ch. 5J-4
Home health agencies	Fla. Stat. Secs. 401.461–.505
Home improvement sales and fin.	Fla. Stat. Secs. 520.60–.98
Home solicitation sales	Fla. Stat., Ch. 501,
	Fla. Admin. Code, Ch. 5J-2
Honey	Fla. Stat., Ch. 586
Horse sales, shows, exhibitions	Fla. Stat., Ch. 535
Hospices	Fla. Stat. Secs. 400.601–.614
Hotels	Fla. Stat., Ch. 509,
	Fla. Admin. Code, Ch. 61C
Household products	Fla. Stat., Ch. 499

Housing codes, state minimum	Fla. Stat., Ch. 553
Identification cards	Fla. Stat. Sec. 877.18
Insurance and service plans	Fla. Stat., Chs. 624-651; 865.02, Fla. Admin. Code, Ch. 4
Invention development	Fla. Stat. Sec. 501.136
Land sales	Fla. Stat., Ch. 498, Fla. Admin. Code, Ch. 61B
Lasers and nonionizing radiation	Fla. Stat. Sec. 501.122
Lead acid batteries	Fla. Stat. Sec. 403.718
Legal services	Fla. Stat. Secs. 877.01–.02
Linen suppliers	Fla. Stat. Secs. 865.10
Liquor	Fla. Stat., Chs. 561-568
Livestock	Fla. Stat. Secs. 534; 877.05–.06
Lodging	Fla. Admin. Code, Ch. 61C
Marketing establishments	Fla. Stat. Sec. 877.061
Meats	Fla. Stat., Ch. 544
Mental health	Fla. Stat., Ch. 394
Metal recyclers	Fla. Stat., Ch. 538
Milk and milk products	Fla. Stat., Ch. 502, Fla. Admin. Code, Ch. 5D
Mining waste	Fla. Stat., Ch. 533
Mobile homes	Fla. Stat., Ch. 723, Fla. Admin. Code, Chs. 2-12; 61B
Money orders	Fla. Stat., Ch. 560
Motion pictures	Fla. Stat. Sec. 501.138
Motor vehicle lemon law	Fla. Stat., Ch. 681, Fla. Admin. Code, Chs. 2–30
Motor vehicles	Fla. Stat. Secs. 520.01–.13; Ch. 545; Ch. 559, Part VIII, Fla. Admin. Code, Chs. 5J-11, 5J-12
Multilevel marketing	Fla. Admin. Code, Chs. 2–17
Naval stores	Fla. Stat., Ch. 523
Newsprint	Fla. Stat. Sec. 403.7195
Nursing homes	Fla. Stat. Secs. 400.011–.332
Obscene literature	Fla. Stat., Ch. 847
Occupational therapists	Fla. Stat., Ch. 468, Fla. Admin. Code, Ch. 61F6
Oil	Fla. Stat. Secs. 403.75–.769
Outdoor advertising	Fla. Stat., Ch. 479
Outdoor theatres	Fla. Stat., Ch. 555

Pari-mutuel wagering	Fla. Admin. Code, Ch. 61D
Peanut marketing	Fla. Stat., Ch. 573, Part VI
Pest control	Fla. Stat., Ch. 487
Photos of admission parks	Fla. Stat. Sec. 540.09
Plants and nurseries	Fla. Stat., Ch. 573, Part II; 575-581; 865.05, Fla. Admin. Code, Ch. 5B
Plumbing	Fla. Stat., Ch. 553
Private investigators	Fla. Stat., Ch. 493
Prostitution	Fla. Stat., Ch. 796
Pyramid schemes	Fla. Admin. Code, Chs. 2–17
Radiation	Fla. Stat., Ch. 404
Radio and television repairs	Fla. Stat. Sec. 817.53
Real estate sales	Fla. Stat. Secs. 501.1375; 877.10, Fla. Admin. Code, Chs. 2–13
Rental housing	Fla. Stat., Ch. 83, Fla. Admin. Code, Chs. 2-11
Restaurants	Fla. Stat., Ch. 509, Fla. Admin. Code, Ch. 7C
Sanitarians	Fla. Stat. Sec. 381.0101
Secondhand dealers	Fla. Stat., Ch. 538
Securities transactions	Fla. Stat., Ch. 517, Fla. Admin. Code, Ch. 3E
Soybean marketing	Fla. Stat., Ch. 573, Part IV
Swimming and bathing places	Fla. Stat., Ch. 514
Syrup	Fla. Stat. Sec. 865.07
Telegraph and cable companies	Fla. Stat., Ch. 363
Telemarketing	Fla. Stat., Ch. 501, Fla. Admin. Code, Chs. 5J-6
Telephone companies	Fla. Stat., Ch. 364
Television picture tubes	Fla. Stat. Secs. 817.559–.56
Term papers, dissertations	Fla. Stat. Sec. 877.17
Thermal efficiency standards	Fla. Stat., Ch. 553
Timber and lumber	Fla. Stat., Ch. 536
Time-shares	Fla. Stat., Ch. 721, Fla. Admin. Code, Chs. 2–23
Tires	Fla. Stat. Sec . 403.718
Tobacco	Fla. Stat., Ch. 573, Part V; 574; 865.08, Fla. Admin. Code, Ch. 7A
Tourist attraction	Fla. Stat. Sec. 817.55

Tourist camps	Fla. Stat., Ch. 513
Travel services	Fla. Stat., Ch. 559, Part IX; 817.554, Fla. Admin. Code, Ch. 5J-3, 5J-9
Sound and film, copying	Fla. Stat., Ch. 540
Viticulture	Fla. Stat., Ch. 599
Watches, used	Fla. Stat. Sec. 501.925
Watermelon marketing	Fla. Stat., Ch. 573, Part III
Weapons and firearms	Fla. Stat., Ch. 790
Yacht or ship brokers	Fla. Stat., Ch. 326, Fla. Admin. Code, Chs. 61B-60

Bookkeeping and Accounting

It is beyond the scope of this book to explain all the intricacies of setting up a business's bookkeeping and accounting systems. However, it is important to realize that if you do not set up an understandable bookkeeping system, your business will undoubtedly fail.

Without accurate records of where your income is coming from and where it is going, you will be unable to increase your profits, lower your expenses, obtain needed financing, or make the right decisions in all areas of your business. The time to decide how you will handle your bookkeeping is when you open your business—not a year later when it is tax time.

INITIAL BOOKKEEPING

If you do not understand business taxation, you should pick up a good book on the subject as well as the IRS tax guide for your type of business (proprietorship, partnership, corporation, or limited liability company).

The IRS tax book for small businesses is Publication 334, *Tax Guide for Small Businesses*. There are also instruction booklets for each type of business form, including Schedule C for proprietorships, Form 1120 or 1120S for C corporations and S corporations, and 1165 for partnerships and businesses that are taxed like partnerships (LLCs, LLPs).

Keep in mind that the IRS does not give you the best advice for saving on taxes and does not give you the other side of contested issues. For that, you need a private tax guide or advisor.

The most important thing to do is to set up your bookkeeping so that you can easily fill out your monthly, quarterly, and annual tax returns. The best way to do this is to get copies of the returns—not the totals that you will need to supply—and set up your bookkeeping system to group those totals.

For example, for a sole proprietorship, you will use Schedule C to report business income and expenses to the IRS at the end of the year. Use the categories on that form to sort your expenses. To make your job especially easy, every time you pay a bill, put the category number on the check.

ACCOUNTANTS

Most likely, your new business will not be able to afford hiring an accountant right away to handle your books. Do not be discouraged—doing them yourself will force you to learn about business accounting and taxation. The worst way to run a business is to know nothing about the tax laws and turn everything over to an accountant at the end of the year to find out what is due.

You should know the basics of tax law before making basic decisions, such as whether to buy or rent equipment or premises. You should understand accounting so you can time your financial affairs appropriately. If your business needs to buy supplies, inventory, or equipment, and provides goods or services throughout the year, you need to at least have a basic understanding of the system within which you are working.

Once you can afford an accountant, you should weigh the cost against your time and the risk that you will make an error. Even if you think you know enough to do your own corporate tax return, you should still take it to an accountant one year to see if you have been missing any deductions. You might decide that the money saved is worth the cost of the accountant's services.

COMPUTER PROGRAMS

Today, every business should keep its books by computer. There are inexpensive programs, such as Quicken, that can instantly provide you with reports of your income and expenses, as well as the right figures to plug into your tax returns.

Most programs even offer a tax program each year that will take all of your information and print it out on the current year's tax forms.

TAX TIPS

The following are a few tax tips for small businesses that will help you save money.

- ✪ Usually, when you buy equipment for a business, you must amortize the cost over several years. That is, you do not deduct it all when you buy it, but instead, take, say, 25% of the cost off your taxes each year for four years. (The time is determined by the theoretical usefulness of the item.) However, small businesses are allowed to write off the entire cost of a limited amount of items under Internal Revenue Code (I.R.C.) Sec. 179. If you have income to shelter, use it.

- ✪ Owners of S corporations do not have to pay Social Security or Medicare taxes on the part of their profits that is not considered salary. As long as you pay yourself a reasonable salary, other money you take out is not subject to these taxes.

✪   You should not neglect to deposit withholding taxes for your own salary or profits. Besides being a large sum to come up with at once in April, there are penalties that must be paid for failure to do so.

✪   Do not fail to keep track of and remit your employees' withholding. You will be personally liable for them even if you are a corporation.

✪   If you keep track of the use of your car for business, you can deduct 44.5¢ per mile (this may go up or down each year—check with the IRS for current rates). If you use your car for business a considerable amount of the time, you may be able to depreciate it.

✪   If your business is a corporation and if you designate the stock as Section 1244 stock, then if the business fails you are able to get a much better deduction for the loss.

✪   By setting up a retirement plan, you can exempt up to 20% of your salary from income tax. However, do not use money you might need later. There are penalties for taking it out of the retirement plan.

✪   When you buy things that will be resold or made into products that will be resold, you do not have to pay sales taxes on those purchases.

chapter 18

Paying Federal Taxes

As we all know, the federal government levies many different types of taxes on individuals and businesses. It is very important that you consult an accountant or attorney to properly comply with and take advantage of the incredibly complex federal tax code and regulations. This chapter discusses several of the most important federal taxes that will most likely affect your new business.

INCOME TAX

The manner in which each type of business pays taxes is as follows.

Proprietorship   A proprietor reports profits and expenses on Schedule C attached to the usual Form 1040, and pays tax on all of the net income of the business. Each quarter, Form ES-1040 must be filed along with payment of one-quarter of the amount of income tax and Social Security taxes estimated to be due for the year.

Partnership   The partnership files a return showing the income and expenses, but pays no tax. Each partner is given a form showing his or her share of the profits or losses, and reports these on Schedule E of Form 1040.

Each quarter, Form ES-1040 must be filed by each partner along with payment of one-quarter of the amount of income tax and Social Security taxes estimated to be due for the year.

C Corporation

A regular corporation is a separate taxpayer, and pays tax on its profits after deducting all expenses, including officers' salaries. If dividends are distributed, they are paid out of after-tax dollars, and the shareholders pay tax a second time when they receive the dividends. If a corporation needs to accumulate money for investment, it may be able to do so at lower tax rates than the shareholders. However, if all profits will be distributed to shareholders, the double-taxation may be excessive unless all income is paid as salaries. C corporations file Form 1120.

S Corporation

A small corporation has the option of being taxed like a partnership. If Form 2553 is filed by the corporation and accepted by the Internal Revenue Service, the S corporation will only file an informational return listing profits and expenses. Then, each shareholder will be taxed on a proportional share of the profits (or be able to deduct a proportional share of the losses). Unless a corporation will make a large profit that will not be distributed, S status is usually best in the beginning. An S corporation files Form 1120S and distributes Form K-1 to each shareholder. If any money is taken out by a shareholder that is not listed as wages subject to withholding, then the shareholder will usually have to file Form ES-1040 each quarter along with payment of the estimated withholding on the withdrawals.

Limited Liability Companies and Partnerships

Limited liability companies and professional limited liability companies are allowed by the IRS to elect to be taxed either as a partnership or a corporation. To make this election, you file Form 8832, *Entity Classification Election,* with the IRS.

Tax Workshops and Booklets

The IRS conducts workshops to inform businesses about the tax laws. (Do not expect an in-depth study of the loopholes.) For more information, call or write to the IRS at the following addresses. If you prefer to just read the manual for the workshop, which is IRS Publication 1066, you can download it from their website at **www.irs.gov**.

City	Street Address	Telephone
Daytona Beach/ Holly Hill	921 North Nova Road Daytona Beach, FL 32117	386-258-4105
Fort Myers	2891 Center Pointe Drive Fort Myers, FL 33916	941-936-3956
Gainesville	104 North Main Street Gainesville, FL 32601	352-395-6197
Jacksonville	550 Water Street Jacksonville, FL 32202	904-665-1040
Lakeland	124 South Tennessee Avenue Lakeland, FL 33801	863-688-2066
Maitland/Orlando	850 Trafalgar Court Maitland, FL 32751	407-660-5830
Melbourne	129 West Hibiscus Boulevard Melbourne, FL 32901	321-674-0047
Miami	51 S.W. First Avenue Miami, FL 33130	305-982-5077
Ocala	3300 S.W. 34th Avenue Ocala, FL 34475	352-401-0010
Panama City	651-F West 14th Street Panama City, FL 32401	850-769-1684
Pensacola	125 West Romana Street Pensacola, FL 32501	850-435-8468
Plantation/ Fort Lauderdale	7850 S.W. Sixth Court Plantation, FL 33324	954-423-7300
Port St. Lucie	7410 South US 1 Port St. Lucie, FL 34952	772-340-5606
Sarasota	2201 Cantu Court Sarasota, FL 34232	941-371-1710
Saint Petersburg	9450 Koger Boulevard Saint Petersburg, FL 33702	727-570-5552
Tampa	3848 West Columbus Drive Tampa, FL 33607	813-348-1831
Tallahassee	227 North Bronough Street Tallahassee, FL 32301	850-942-8995
West Palm Beach	1700 Palm Beach Lakes Boulevard West Palm Beach, FL 33401	561-616-2002

WITHHOLDING, SOCIAL SECURITY, AND MEDICARE TAXES

If you need basic information on business tax returns, the IRS publishes a rather large booklet that answers most questions and is available free of charge. Call or write them and ask for Publication No. 334. If you have any questions, look up their toll-free number in the phone book under "United States Government/Internal Revenue Service." If you want more creative answers and tax saving information, you should find a good local accountant. To get started, you will need to be familiar with the following:

- ✪ Employer Identification Number;

- ✪ Employee's Withholding Allowance Certificate;

- ✪ Federal tax deposit coupons;

- ✪ Electronic filing;

- ✪ Estimated Tax Payment Voucher;

- ✪ Employer's quarterly tax return;

- ✪ Wage and Tax Statement;

- ✪ Form 1099 Miscellaneous; and,

- ✪ Earned Income Credit.

Employer Identification Number

If you are a sole proprietor with no employees, you can use your Social Security number for your business. If you are a corporation, a partnership, or a proprietorship with employees, you must obtain an employer identification number. This is done by filing the **APPLICATION FOR EMPLOYER IDENTIFICATION NUMBER (IRS FORM SS-4)**. (see form 5, p.247.) It usually takes a week or two to receive. You will need this number to open bank accounts for the business, so you should file this form a soon as you decide to go into business. The blank form with instructions is in Appendix C.

Employee's Withholding Allowance Certificate

You must have each employee fill out an **EMPLOYEE'S WITHHOLDING ALLOWANCE CERTIFICATE (IRS FORM W-4)** to calculate the amount of federal taxes to be deducted and to obtain their Social Security numbers. (see form 7, p.261.) (The number of allowances on this form is used with IRS Circular E, Publication 15, to figure out the exact deductions.)

Federal Tax Deposit Coupons

After taking withholdings from employees' wages, you must deposit them at a bank that is authorized to accept such funds. If at the end of any month you have over $1,000 in withheld taxes, including your contribution to FICA (Social Security and Medicare), you must make a deposit prior to the 15th of the following month. If on the 3rd, 7th, 11th, 15th, 19th, 22nd, or 25th of any month you have over $3,000 in withheld taxes, you must make a deposit within three banking days.

Electronic Filing

Each year, the IRS requires a few more forms to be filed electronically or over the telephone. When you receive your paper filing forms from the IRS, they will include your options for filing electronically or by telephone. In some cases, electronic filing may save time, but if your business is small and most of your numbers are zeros, it may be faster to mail in the paper forms.

Estimated Tax Payment Voucher

Sole proprietors and partners usually take draws from their businesses without the formality of withholding. However, they are still required to make deposits of income and FICA taxes each quarter. If more than $500 is due in April on a person's 1040 form, then not enough money was withheld each quarter and a penalty is assessed, unless the person falls into an exception. The quarterly withholding is submitted on form 1040-ES on January 15th, April 15th, June 15th, and September 15th each year. If these days fall on a weekend, the due date is the following Monday. The worksheet with **ESTIMATED TAX PAYMENT VOUCHER (FORM 1040-ES)** can be used to determine the amount to pay.

NOTE: *One of the exceptions to the rule is that if you withhold the same amount as last year's tax bill, then you do not have to pay a penalty. This is usually a lot easier than filling out the 1040-ES worksheet.*

Employer's Quarterly Tax Return

Each quarter, you must file Form 941, reporting your federal withholding and FICA taxes. If you owe more than $1,000 at the end of a quarter, you are required to make a deposit at the end of any month that you have $1,000 in withholding. The deposits are made to the Federal Reserve Bank or an authorized financial institution on Form 501. Most banks are authorized to accept deposits. If you owe more than $3,000 for any month, you must make a deposit at any point in the month in which you owe $3,000. After you file Form SS-4, the 941 forms will be sent to you automatically if you checked the box saying that you expect to have employees.

Wage and Tax Statement

At the end of each year, you are required to issue a W-2 Form to each employee. This form shows the amount of wages paid to the employee during the year, as well as the amounts withheld for taxes, Social Security, Medicare, and other purposes.

Form 1099 Miscellaneous

If you pay at least $600 to a person other than an employee (such as independent contractors), you are required to file a Form 1099-MISC for that person. Along with the 1099s, you must file a Form 1096, which is a summary sheet of all the 1099s you issued.

Many people are not aware of this law and fail to file these forms, but they are required for such things as services, royalties, rents, awards, and prizes that you pay to individuals (but not corporations). The rules for this are quite complicated, so you should either obtain Package 1099 from the IRS or consult your accountant.

Earned Income Credit

Persons who are not liable to pay income tax may have the right to a check from the government because of the Earned Income Credit. You are required to notify your employees of this. You can satisfy this requirement with one of the following:

✪   a W-2 Form with the notice on the back;

✪   a substitute for the W-2 Form with the notice on it;

✪   a copy of Notice 797; or,

✪   a written statement with the wording from Notice 797.

A Notice 797 can be downloaded from the IRS website at **www.irs.gov/pub/irs-pdf/n797.pdf**.

EXCISE TAXES

Excise taxes are taxes on certain activities or items. Some of the things that are subject to federal excise taxes are tobacco and alcohol, gasoline, tires and inner tubes, some trucks and trailers, firearms, ammunition, bows, arrows, fishing equipment, the use of highway vehicles of over 55,000 pounds, aircraft, wagering, telephone and tele-type services, coal, hazardous wastes, and vaccines. If you are involved with any of these, you should obtain from the IRS publica-tion No. 510, *Information on Excise Taxes*.

UNEMPLOYMENT COMPENSATION TAX

You must pay federal unemployment taxes if you paid wages of $1,500 in any quarter, or if you had at least one employee for twenty calendar weeks. The federal tax amount is 0.8% of the first $7,000 of wages paid each employee. If more than $100 is due by the end of any quarter (if you paid $12,500 in wages for the quarter), then Form 508 must be filed with an authorized financial institution or the Federal Reserve Bank in your area. You will receive Form 508 when you obtain your employer identification number.

For more information on unemployment compensation in Florida, write to:

Division of Unemployment Compensation
107 East Madison Street
Tallahassee, FL 32399

At the end of each year, you must file Form 940 or Form 940EZ. This is your annual report of federal unemployment taxes. You will receive an original form from the IRS.

Paying Florida Taxes

In addition to the federal taxes a Florida business must pay, the State of Florida imposes several of its own.

SALES AND USE TAXES

If you will be selling or renting goods or services at retail, you must collect Florida Sales and Use Tax. Some services, such as doctors and attorney's fees and newspaper advertising, are not taxed, but most others are. If you have any doubt, check with the Florida Department of Revenue.

First, you must obtain a tax number by filling out the **APPLICATION TO COLLECT AND/OR REPORT TAX IN FLORIDA (DR-1)** and paying a $5 fee. (see form 8, p.263.) A sample, filled-in copy of the form is in Appendix B on page 221. Some information for filling out the form and a blank form are in Appendix C. (see form 8, p.263.) For more details about the tax, you should obtain the booklet, *Sales and Use Tax Registration Handbook for Business Operators*, from the Department of Revenue. Their website is at **www.myflorida.com/dor**. Their phone numbers are 800-352-3671 (Florida only) and 850-488-6800.

The **Sales and Use Tax Returns (DR-15CS)** are due for each month on the 20th of the following month. (see form 9, p.271.) You are allowed to deduct 2.5% of the tax as your reimbursement for collecting the tax. Rest assured the amount will never be near enough to compensate for the work. In some cases, if your sales are very limited (under $100 a quarter), you may be allowed to file returns quarterly or semi-annually.

Once you file your *Application for Sales and Use Tax Registration*, you will have to start filing monthly returns whether you have any sales or not. If you do not file the return, even if you had no sales, then you must pay a $5 penalty. If you do not expect to have any sales for the first few months while you are setting up your business, you probably should wait before sending in the registration. Otherwise, you may forget to file the returns marked with zeros and end up paying the penalties.

One reason to get a tax number early is to exempt your purchases from tax. When you buy a product that you will resell, or use as part of a product that you will sell, you are exempt from paying tax on it. To get the exemption, you need to submit a copy of your Annual Resale Certificate for Sales Tax (form DR-13). This form comes with your booklet of tax coupons each year.

If you will only be selling items wholesale or out of state, you might think that you would not need a tax number or to submit returns, but you will need to be registered to obtain the tax number to exempt your purchases.

If you have any sales before you get your monthly tax return forms, you should calculate the tax anyway and submit the tax before the 20th of the following month. Otherwise, you will be charged a penalty even if it was not your fault that they did not send you the forms.

You should be aware that the Florida Department of Revenue has not been very well-organized in the past. They have sometimes given incorrect tax information, failed to send out refunds when due, taken a year to send refunds, and failed to send out forms on time or to the correct address. This is improving, but be sure to stay on top of your state tax situation.

After you obtain your tax number, you will be required to collect sales tax on all purchases. In some cases, new businesses are required to post a bond to ensure taxes are paid.

Selling to Tax Exempt Purchasers

You are required to collect sales and use taxes for all sales you make unless you have documentation on file proving that a purchase was exempt from the tax. A purchaser who claims to be exempt should give you a signed copy of their form DR-13. Each year, you need to obtain a copy of their new form DR-13.

UNEMPLOYMENT COMPENSATION TAX

You are not liable to pay unemployment compensation taxes until you had an employee work part of a day in any twenty calendar weeks or paid $1,500 in wages in a quarter. However, once you reach that point, you are liable for all back taxes. The rate starts at 2.7%, but if your record is clear, it may drop to 0.1%. The tax is paid on the first $7,000 of wages of each employee.

If you had an employee work for twenty weeks, you should complete sections A, D, and H on **APPLICATION TO COLLECT AND/OR REPORT TAX IN FLORIDA (FORM DR-1)**. (see form 8, p.263.) You will be sent quarterly forms to complete and send in.

Some businesses try to keep taxes low by having all work done by independent contractors instead of employees. One thing to be aware of is that if a business has no employees for several quarters, the Florida unemployment tax rate doubles. A payment of a small wage to someone each quarter will avoid this problem.

TANGIBLE AND INTANGIBLE PROPERTY TAXES

The tangible property tax is a tax on all personal property used in a business and on inventory. It includes such things as dishes, machinery, furniture, tools, signs, carpeting, appliances, laboratory equipment, and just about everything else.

Property is taxed on its value January 1st. A return must be filed by April 1st listing the property of the business, and a tax bill is sent out in November, the same time as the real property tax bill.

A Truth in Millage (TRIM) Notice is sent out in August by the county tax assessor, letting taxpayers know the assessed value of their property and the tax rate that will apply. If you feel there is an error in the valuation of your property, you may discuss it with an appraiser or file a petition for review.

It is not unusual to see the assessed value of personal property remain the same or even go up over the years while the actual value depreciates greatly. Filing a petition protesting the assessment occasionally helps, but for the small amount of money involved, it is usually not worth it. For the property assessors, this is the easiest way to collect taxes that are not due.

Intangible Property Tax

The intangible property tax is a tax on the value of such things as promissory notes, mortgages, accounts receivable, stocks, bonds, and mutual funds. The tax is $\frac{1}{10}$ of 1% ($1 per $1,000) of the value of the property on January 1st. The tax must be paid by individuals as well as businesses, but individuals have an exemption on the first $20,000 ($40,000 for married couples filing jointly).

The tax applies to all intangibles owned on January 1st and must be paid by June 30th. There is a discount of 1% per month for paying early (up to a maximum of 4% for paying in February).

The tax does not apply to deposits in banks, but it does apply to money market mutual funds. (For large amounts, some people save taxes by transferring the funds from a mutual fund to a bank just before January 1st, and then back again after the 1st. The tax does not apply to promissory notes secured by mortgages on real property or to IRA accounts.)

A corporation can pay the tax on its own tax held by stockholders in lieu of them paying it. The advantage is that the corporation can deduct the tax as a business expense. The shareholders can deduct the tax only if they itemize deduction. However, they get a $20,000 exclusion, which may eliminate the tax completely.

INCOME TAX

Florida does have an income tax. It only applies to C corporations and entities that elect to be taxed as corporations under federal law. Prior to 1998, limited liability companies were subject to the corporate income tax, but now they can elect partnership taxation. The tax is 5.5% of the Florida net income.

NOTE: *Professional service corporations that do not elect S status must pay the tax.*

Occasionally, there is a proposal to extend this tax to S corporations. It has not yet passed, but it may if there is another budget crisis. Most proposals exempt small S corporations.

Forms and instructions can be obtained from the Department of Revenue's website **www.myflorida.com/dor** or by calling 800-352-3671 (FL only) or 850-488-6800.

EXCISE TAXES

Florida imposes taxes on the following businesses:

- wholesale tobacco dealers and tobacco vending machine operators (contact the Division of Alcoholic Beverages and Tobacco of the Department of Business Regulation);

- alcohol manufacturers and distributors (contact the Division of Alcoholic Beverages and Tobacco of the Department of Business Regulation);

- mineral, oil, and gas producers (contact the Department of Revenue); and,

- motor fuel dealers (contact the Department of Revenue).

Out-of-State Taxes

As a Florida business, if you operate your business outside of the borders of the state of Florida, you not only have to comply with Florida and federal tax laws, but also with the laws of the states and other countries in which you do business. This can prove to be very complicated.

STATE SALES TAXES

In 1992, the United States Supreme Court struck a blow for the rights of small businesses by ruling that state tax authorities cannot force them to collect sales taxes on interstate mail orders (*Quill Corporation v. North Dakota*). Unfortunately, the court left open the possibility that Congress could allow interstate taxation of mail order sales, and since then several bills have been introduced that would do so.

At present, companies are only required to collect sales taxes for states in which they *do business*. Exactly what business is enough to trigger taxation is a legal question, and some states try to define it as broadly as possible.

If you have an office in a state, you are doing business there, and any goods shipped to consumers in that state are subject to sales taxes. If you have a full-time employee working in the state much of the year, many states will consider you doing business there. In some states, attending a two-day trade show is enough business to trigger taxation for the entire year for every order shipped to the state. One loophole that often works is to be represented at shows by persons who are not your employees.

Because the laws are different in each state, you will have to do some research on a state-by-state basis to find out how much business you can do in a state without being subject to their taxation. You can request a state's rules from its department of revenue, but keep in mind that what a department of revenue wants the law to be is not always what the courts will rule that it is.

BUSINESS TAXES

Be wary of being subject to a state's income or other business taxes. For example, California charges every company doing business in the state a minimum $800 a year fee and charges income tax on a portion of the company's worldwide income. Doing a small amount of business in the state is clearly not worth getting mired in California taxation. For this reason, some trade shows have been moved from the state. This has resulted in a review of the tax policies and some *safe-harbor* guidelines to advise companies on what they can do without becoming subject to taxation.

Write to the department of revenue of any state with which you have business contacts to see what might trigger your taxation.

INTERNET TAXES

State revenue departments are eager to tax commerce on the Internet. Theories have already been proposed that websites available to state residents mean a company is doing business in a state. Fortunately, Congress has passed a moratorium on taxation of Internet business.

CANADIAN TAXES

The Canadian government expects American companies that sell goods by mail order to Canadians to collect taxes for them and file returns with Revenue Canada, their tax department. Those companies that receive an occasional unsolicited order are not expected to register, and Canadian customers who order things from the U.S. pay the tax plus a $5 fee upon receipt of the goods. Companies that solicit Canadian orders are expected to be registered if their worldwide income is $30,000 or more per year. In some cases, a company may be required to post a bond and to pay for the cost of Canadian auditors visiting its premises and auditing its books. For these reasons, you may notice that some companies decline to accept orders from Canada.

The End...
and the Beginning

If you have read through this whole book, you know more about the rules and laws for operating a Florida business than most people in business today. However, after learning about all the governmental regulations, you may become discouraged. You are probably wondering how you can keep track of all the laws and how you will have any time left to make money after complying with the laws. It is not that bad. People are starting businesses every day and they are making money—lots of money.

With this book as your guide, you should be able to navigate business law and make your own business thrive.

Congratulations on deciding to start a business in Florida! If you have any unusual experiences along the way, drop us a line at the following address. The information may be useful for a future book.

Sphinx Publishing
P.O. Box 4410
Naperville, IL 60567-4410

Glossary

A

acceptance. Agreeing to the terms of an offer and creating a contract.

affirmative action. Hiring an employee to achieve a balance in the workplace, and avoid existing or continuing discrimination based on minority status.

alien. A person who is not a citizen of the country.

articles of incorporation. The document that sets forth the organization of a corporation.

B

bait advertising. Offering a product for sale with the intention of selling another product.

bulk sales. Selling substantially all of a company's inventory.

C

C corporation. A corporation that pays taxes on its profits.

collections. The collection of money owed to a business.

common law. Laws that are determined in court cases rather than statutes.

consideration. The exchange of value or promises in a contract.

contract. An agreement between two or more parties.

copyright. Legal protection given to original works of authorship.

corporation. An artificial person that is set up to conduct a business owned by shareholders, and run by officers and directors.

D

deceptive pricing. Pricing goods or services in a manner intended to deceive the customers.

discrimination. The choosing among various options based on their characteristics. It is illegal to use discriminatory hiring practices.

domain name. The address of a website.

E

employee. Person who works for another under that person's control and direction.

endorsements. Positive statements about goods or services.

excise tax. A tax paid on the sale or consumption of goods or services.

express warranty. A specific guarantee of a product or service.

F

fictitious name. A name used by a business that is not its personal or legal name.

G

general partnership. A business that is owned by two or more persons.

goods. Items of personal property.

guarantee. A promise of quality of a good or service.

I

implied warranty. A guarantee of a product or service that is not specifically made, but can be implied from the circumstances of the sale.

independent contractor. Person who works for another as a separate business, not as an employee.

intangible property. Personal property that does not have physical presence, such as the ownership interest in a corporation.

intellectual property. Legal rights to the products of the mind, such as writings, musical compositions, formulas, and designs.

L

liability. The legal responsibility to pay for an injury.

limited liability company. An entity recognized as a legal person that is set up to conduct a business owned and run by members.

limited liability partnership. An entity recognized as a legal person that is set up to conduct a business owned and run by members that is set up for professionals, such as attorneys or doctors.

limited partnership. A business that is owned by two or more persons, of which one or more is liable for the debts of the business, and one or more has no liability for the debts.

limited warranty. A guarantee covering certain aspects of a good or service.

M

merchant. A person who is in business.

merchant's firm offer. An offer by a business made under specific terms.

N

nonprofit corporation. An entity recognized as a legal person that is set up to run an operation in which none of the profits are distributed to controlling members.

O

occupational license. A government-issued permit to transact business.

offer. A proposal to enter into a contract.

overtime. Hours worked in excess of forty hours in one week, or eight hours in one day.

P

partnership. A business formed by two or more persons.

patent. Protection given to inventions, discoveries, and designs.

personal property. Any type of property other than land and the structures attached to it.

pierce the corporate veil. When a court ignores the structure of a corporation and holds its owners responsible for its debts or liabilities.

professional association. An entity recognized as a legal person that is set up to conduct a business of professionals, such as attorneys or doctors.

proprietorship. A business that is owned by one person.

R

real property. Land and the structures attached to it.

resident alien. A person who is not a citizen of a country, but who may legally reside and work there.

S

S corporation. A corporation in which the profits are taxed to the shareholders.

sale on approval. Selling an item with the agreement that it may be brought back and the sale cancelled.

sale or return. An agreement whereby goods are to be purchased or returned to the vendor.

securities. Interests in a business, such as stocks or bonds.

sexual harassment. Activity that causes an employee to feel or be sexually threatened.

shares. Units of stock in a corporation.

statute of frauds. Law that requires certain contracts to be in writing.

stock. Ownership interests in a corporation.

sublease. An agreement to rent premises from an existing tenant.

T

tangible property. Physical personal property, such as desks and tables.

trade secret. Commercially valuable information or process that is protected by being kept a secret.

trademark. A name or symbol used to identify the source of goods or services.

U

unemployment compensation. Payments to a former employee who was terminated from a job for a reason not based on his or her fault.

usury. Charging an interest rate higher than that allowed by law.

W

withholding. Money taken out of an employee's salary and remitted to the government.

workers' compensation. Insurance program to cover injuries or deaths of employees.

Business Start-Up Checklist

- ❏ Make your plan
    - ❏ Obtain and read all relevant publications on your type of business
    - ❏ Obtain and read all laws and regulations affecting your business
    - ❏ Calculate whether your plan will produce a profit
    - ❏ Plan your sources of capital
    - ❏ Plan your sources of goods or services
    - ❏ Plan your marketing efforts
- ❏ Choose your business name
    - ❏ Check other business names and trademarks
    - ❏ Register your name, trademark, etc.
- ❏ Choose the business form
    - ❏ Prepare and file organizational papers
    - ❏ Prepare and file fictitious name if necessary
- ❏ Choose the location
    - ❏ Check competitors
    - ❏ Check zoning
- ❏ Obtain necessary licenses
    - ❏ City
    - ❏ County
    - ❏ State
    - ❏ Federal

❑ Choose a bank
   ❑ Checking
   ❑ Credit card processing
   ❑ Loans
❑ Obtain necessary insurance
   ❑ Automobile
   ❑ Hazard
   ❑ Health
   ❑ Liability
   ❑ Life/Disability
   ❑ Workers' Compensation
❑ File necessary federal tax registrations
❑ File necessary state tax registrations
❑ Set up a bookkeeping system
❑ Plan your hiring
   ❑ Obtain required posters
   ❑ Obtain or prepare employment application
   ❑ Obtain new hire tax forms
   ❑ Prepare employment policies
   ❑ Determine compliance with health and safety laws
❑ Plan your opening
   ❑ Obtain all necessary equipment and supplies
   ❑ Obtain all necessary inventory
   ❑ Do all necessary marketing and publicity
   ❑ Obtain all necessary forms and agreements
   ❑ Prepare your company policies on refunds, exchanges, returns, and so on

Sample, Filled-in Forms

The following forms are selected filled-in forms for demonstration purposes. They have a corresponding blank form in Appendix C. The form numbers in this appendix correspond to the form numbers in Appendix C. If you need instructions for these forms as you follow how they are filled out, they can be found in Appendix C, or in the pages in the chapters that discuss those forms.

APPLICATION FOR REGISTRATION OF FICTITIOUS NAME

Note: Acknowledgements/certificates will be sent to the address in Section 1 only.

Section 1

1. Krebbs Company
   Fictitious Name to be Registered (see instructions if name includes "Corp" or "Inc")

   100 Maynard Drive

   Mailing Address of Business
   Jacksonville   FL   32100
   City   State   Zip Code

3. Florida County of principal place of business: _____

   Bradford
   (see instructions if more than one county)

This space for office use only

Section 2

A. Owner(s) of Fictitious Name If Individual(s): (Use an attachment if necessary):

1. Krebbs   Darron   T
   Last   First   M.I.
   761 Ivy Grey Lane
   Address
   Jacksonville   FL   32100
   City   State   Zip Code

2. _____
   Last   First   M.I.
   _____
   Address
   _____
   City   State   Zip Code

B. Owner(s) of Fictitious Name If other than an individual: (Use attachment if necessary):

1. _____
   Entity Name
   _____
   Address
   _____
   City   State   Zip Code
   Florida Registration Number _____
   FEI Number: 410 00 300
   ☐ Applied for   ☐ Not Applicable

2. _____
   Entity Name
   _____
   Address
   _____
   City   State   Zip Code
   Florida Registration Number _____
   FEI Number: _____
   ☐ Applied for   ☐ Not Applicable

Section 3

I (we) the undersigned, being the sole (all the) party(ies) owning interest in the above fictitious name, certify that the information indicated on this form is true and accurate. In accordance with Section 865.09, F.S., I (we) understand that the signature(s) below shall have the same legal effect as if made under oath. (At Least One Signature Required)

Darron Krebbs   *Jan. 2, 2007*
Signature of Owner   Date

_____
Signature of Owner   Date

Phone Number: 904-594-1111

Phone Number: _____

Section 4

FOR CANCELLATION COMPLETE SECTION 4 ONLY:
FOR FICTITIOUS NAME OR OWNERSHIP CHANGE COMPLETE SECTIONS 1 THROUGH 4:

I (we) the undersigned, hereby cancel the fictitious name _____

_____, which was registered on _____ and was assigned

registration number _____

_____
Signature of Owner   Date

_____
Signature of Owner   Date

Mark the applicable boxes   ☐ Certificate of Status — $10   ☐ Certified Copy — $30
NON-REFUNDABLE PROCESSING FEE: $50

Single   CR4E001 (11/03)

Instructions for Completing Application for Registration of Fictitious Name

Section 1:   **Line 1:** Enter the name as you wish it to be registered. A fictitious name may <u>not</u> contain the words "Corporation" or "Incorporated," or the abbreviations "Corp." or "Inc.," unless the person or business for which the name is registered is incorporated or has obtained a certificate of authority to transact business in this state pursuant to chapter 607 or chapter 617 Florida Statutes. Corporations are not required to file under their exact corporate name.

Line 2: Enter the mailing address of the business. This address does not have to be the principal place of business and can be directed to anyone's attention. DO NOT USE AN ADDRESS THAT IS NOT YET OCCUPIED. ALL FUTURE MAILINGS AND ANY CERTIFICATION REQUESTED ON THIS REGISTRATION FORM WILL BE SENT TO THE ADDRESS IN SECTION 1. An address may be changed at any future date with no charge by simply writing the Division.

Line 3: Enter the name of the county in Florida where the principal place of business of the fictitious name is located. If there is more than one county, list all applicable counties or state "multiple".

Section 2:   **Part A:** Complete if the owner(s) of the fictitious name are individuals. The individual's name and address must be provided.

Part B: Complete if the owner(s) are not individuals. Examples are a corporation, limited partnership, joint venture, general partnership, trusts, fictitious name, etc. Provide the name of the owner, their address, their registration number as registered with the Division of Corporations, and the Federal Employer Identification (FEI) number. An FEI number must be provided or the appropriate box must be checked.

Owners listed in Part B must be registered with the Division of Corporations or provide documentation as to why they are not required to register. Examples would be Federally Chartered Corporations, or Legislatively created entities.

Additional owners may be listed on an attached page as long as all of the information requested in Part A or Part B is provided.

Section 3:   Only one signature is required. It is preferred that a daytime phone number be provided in order to contact the applicant if there are any questions about the application. Since the Department indexes fictitious names on a central database available on the internet, it is no longer required to advertise the intention to register a fictitious name.

Section 4:   **TO CANCEL A REGISTRATION ON FILE:** Provide fictitious name, date filed, and registration number of the fictitious name to be cancelled.

TO CHANGE OWNERSHIP OF A REGISTRATION: Complete section 4 to cancel the original registration. Complete sections 1 through 3 to re-register the fictitious name listing the new owner(s). An owner's signature is required in both sections 3 and 4.

TO CHANGE THE NAME OF A REGISTRATION: Complete section 4 to cancel the original registration. Complete sections 1 through 3 to re-register the new fictitious name. An owner's signature is required in both sections 3 and 4.

An acknowledgement letter will be mailed once the fictitious name registration has been filed.

If you wish to receive a certificate of status and/or certified copy at the time of filing of this registration, check the appropriate box at the bottom of the form. PLEASE NOTE: Acknowledgments/certificates will be sent to the address in Section 1. If a certificate of status is requested, an additional $10 is due. If a certified copy is requested, an additional $30 is due.

The registration and reregistration will be in effect until December 31 of the fifth year.

Send completed application with appropriate fees in the enclosed envelope to:

Fictitious Name Registration
PO Box 1300
Tallahassee, FL 32302-1300

Internet Address:
http://www.sunbiz.org

The fee for registering a fictitious name is $50. Please make a separate check for each filing payable to the Department of State. Application must be typed or printed in ink and legible.

TRADEMARK/SERVICE MARK REGISTRATION GUIDELINES

I. GENERAL INFORMATION

Trade and Service Marks may be registered with the Florida Department of State pursuant to Chapter 495, Florida Statutes. Registration must be denied if a mark does not meet and comply with all of the requirements and provisions stipulated in Chapter 495, Florida Statutes. Marks are checked against other marks registered or reserved with this division and not against corporations, fictitious names or other entities. Rights to a name or mark are perfected by actual use in the ordinary pursuit of the specific endeavor; rights are not perfected by registration only, and the general rule of "FIRST IN USE, FIRST IN RIGHT" is applicable.

Our agency registers trade and service marks on a state level. If you need information concerning the federal registration of trademarks, service marks or patents, please contact the Commissioner of Patents and Trademarks in Washington, D. C. by calling 571-272-1000. If you need information concerning copyrights, contact the Copyright Office in Washington, D. C. by calling 202-707-3000. Although trade names are defined in Chapter 495, Florida Statutes, there is no provision for their registration.

If you wish to register a mark pursuant to Chapter 495, Florida Statutes, please submit one original and one photocopy of the Trade or Service Mark Registration application completed in its entirety, three specimens and a check made payable to the Florida Department of State for the appropriate amount. The application must be typed or neatly handwritten, signed and notarized.

The mark must be in use before it can be registered. If registering a trademark, the good(s) or product(s) must be on sale in the market place. If registering a service mark, you must be rendering the service(s) you are advertising. The mere advertising of future goods or services does not constitute use of a trade or service mark.

II. FEES AND CLASSES

The fee to register a mark is $87.50 per class. Please refer to section 495.111, Florida Statutes (attached), for a list of classes.

Should you need additional information concerning these classes or your classification, please contact the Registration Section by calling (850) 245-6051.

III. SPECIMENS

If your mark is a trademark, we will need specimens that are affixed to the good(s) or product(s). Some acceptable trademark specimens are: labels, decals, tags, wrappers, boxes, and containers. If your mark is a service mark, we will need specimens which reflect the type of service(s) being provided. Some acceptable service mark specimens are: business cards, brochures, flyers, and newspaper advertisements. If your mark is both a trade and service mark, you must submit three appropriate trademark specimens and three appropriate service mark specimens.

Do not submit photocopies, camera-ready copies, letterhead stationery, envelopes, invoices or matchbooks as specimens. Photographs of bulky specimens are acceptable if the mark to be registered and the good(s) or product(s) are clearly legible. We will not accept any specimens that have been altered or defaced in any way.

IV. APPLICATION

Part I.

#1 - You must list the complete name and business address of the applicant. Please indicate if the applicant is an individual, a corporation, a limited partnership, a general partnership, etc. Enter the domicile state, Florida registration number and Federal Employer Identification number if the applicant is other than an individual.

#2(a) - If a service mark, list the services the mark is used in connection with (i.e., restaurant services, real estate agency, insurance agency, etc.).

#2(b) - If a trademark, list the goods/products the mark is used in connection with (i.e., window cleaner, furniture polish, ladies sportswear, etc.).

#2(c) - List how the mark is being used. If a trademark, tell how the mark is applied to the goods (i.e., label, decal, engraving, imprinting on the goods or products themselves, etc.).

If a service mark, tell how the mark is used in advertising (i.e., brochures, business cards, newspaper advertisements, etc.).

#2(d) - List the applicable class(es). Please refer to section 495.111, F.S., (attached) for a list of these classes.

Part II

#1(a) - Enter the date the mark was first used anywhere.

#1(b) - Enter the date the mark was first used in Florida.

Part III

#1 - Enter the mark to be registered. If the mark includes a design, include a brief written description. If your mark is in another language, please provide this office with an English translation of your mark in this section.

#2 - Disclaimer - Your mark may include a word or design that must be disclaimed. All geographical terms and representations of cities, states or countries must be disclaimed (i.e., Miami, Orlando, Florida, the design of the state of Florida, the design of the United States of America, etc.). Commonly used words, including corporate suffixes, must also be disclaimed.

Signature Portion

Complete the signature paragraph accordingly. Please note the applicant's signature must be notarized.

V. TRADEMARK/SERVICE MARK SEARCH

Due to the amount of time it takes to conduct a thorough search of the records, this office does not provide trademark/service mark searches over the telephone. However, you may submit a written request. The request must specify the exact mark to be used and the good(s) or service(s) the mark is to be used in connection with. Please direct all requests to the Trademark Registration Section, Division of Corporations, P. O. Box 6327, Tallahassee, FL 32314.

VI. PROCESSING TIME

The application should be processed within two to five business days from the date of receipt. The processing time may be longer during our peak periods. All applications meeting the requirements of Chapter 495, F. S., on the initial examination will be filed as of the date of receipt. Applications received by courier are not handled on an expedited basis.

VII. COURIER ADDRESS AND MAILING ADDRESS

Mailing Address
Registration Section
Division of Corporations
P.O. Box 6327
Tallahassee, FL 32314

Street/Courier Address
Registration Section
Division of Corporations
Clifton Building
2661 Executive Center Circle
Tallahassee, FL 32301

Applications received via a courier service are not handled on an expedited basis.

VIII. QUESTIONS

If you have any questions concerning the registration of a mark, please contact the Trademark Registration Section by calling (850)245-6051 between the hours of 8 a.m. and 5:00 p.m. or writing to an address listed above.

495.111 Classification. -

(1) The following general classes of goods and services are established for convenience of administration of this chapter:

(a) Goods:

Class 1 Chemicals

Class 2 Paints

Class 3 Cosmetics and cleaning preparations

Class 4 Lubricants and fuels

Class 5 Pharmaceuticals

Class 6 Metal goods

Class 7 Machinery

Class 8 Hand tools

Class 9 Electrical and scientific apparatus

Class 10 Medical Apparatus

Class 11 Environmental control apparatus

Class 12 Vehicles

Class 13 Firearms

Class 14 Jewelry

Class 15 Musical instruments

Class 16 Paper goods and printed matter

Class 17 Rubber goods

Class 18 Leather goods

Class 19 Nonmetallic building materials

Class 20 Furniture and articles not otherwise classified

Class 21 Housewares and glass

Class 22 Cordage and fibers

Class 23 Yarns and threads

Class 24 Fabrics

Class 25 Clothing

Class 26 Fancy goods

Class 27 Floor coverings

Class 28 Toys and sporting goods

Class 29 Meats and processed foods

Class 30 Staple foods

Class 31 Natural agricultural products

Class 32 Light beverages

Class 33 Wines and spirits

Class 34 Smoker's articles

(b) Services:

Class 35 Advertising and business

Class 36 Insurance and financial

Class 37 Construction and repair

Class 38 Communication

Class 39 Transportation and storage

Class 40 Material treatment

Class 41 Education and entertainment

Class 42 Miscellaneous

COVER LETTER

TO: Registration Section
           Division of Corporations

SUBJECT: __crab logo_____
                          (Mark to be registered)

The enclosed Trademark/Service Mark Application, specimens and fee(s) are submitted for filing.

Please return all correspondence concerning this matter to the following:

__Darron Krebbs_____
                    (Name of Person)

__Krebbs Company_____
                    (Firm/Company)

__100 Maynard Drive_____
                    (Address)

__Jacksonville____FL_____32100_____
                (City/State and Zip Code)

For further information concerning this matter, please call:

__Darron Krebbs_____ at (__904__) __594-1111_____
        (Name of Person)   (Area Code & Daytime Telephone Number)

MAILING ADDRESS: **STREET/COURIER ADDRESS:**
Registration Section   Registration Section
Division of Corporations   Division of Corporations
P.O. Box 6327   Clifton Building
Tallahassee, FL 32314   2661 Executive Center Circle
                                        Tallahassee, FL 32301

APPLICATION FOR THE REGISTRATION OF A TRADEMARK OR SERVICE MARK
PURSUANT TO CHAPTER 495, FLORIDA STATUTES

TO: **Division of Corporations**
Post Office Box 6327
Tallahassee, FL 32314

Name & address to whom acknowledgment should be sent:

Krebbs Company/Darron Krebbs

100 Maynard Drive

Jacksonville   FL   32100

(904) 594-1111
Daytime Telephone number

PART I

1. (a) Applicant's name: Darron Krebbs/Krebbs Company

   (b) Applicant's business address: 100 Maynard Drive

   Jacksonville   FL   32100
   City/State/Zip

If different, Applicant's mailing address: 761 Ivy Grey Lane

   Jacksonville   FL   32100
   City/State/Zip

   (c) Applicant's telephone number: (904) 594-1111
   [X] Individual   [ ] Corporation   [ ] Joint Venture   [ ] Other:
   [ ] General Partnership   [ ] Limited Partnership   [ ] Union

If other than an individual,

(1) Florida registration/document number: _____ (2) Domicile State: _____

(3) Federal Employer Identification Number: _____

2. (a) If the mark to be registered is a service mark, the services in connection with which the mark is used: (i.e., furniture moving services, diaper services, house painting services, etc.)

_____

_____

   (b) If the mark to be registered is a trademark, the goods in connection with which the mark is used: (i.e., ladies sportswear, cat food, barbecue grills, shoe laces, etc.)

Wines and Spirits in Class 33

_____

   (c) The mode or manner in which the mark is used:(i.e., labels, decals, newspaper advertisements, brochures, etc.)

Labels are glued onto front of goods

_____

(Continued)

d) The class(es) in which goods or services fall:

__Class 33__

PART II
1. Date first used by the applicant, predecessor, or a related company (must include month, day and year):

(a) Date first used anywhere: __July 19, 2006__   (b) Date first used in Florida: __July 19, 2006__

PART III
1. The mark to be registered is: (If logo/design is included, please give brief written description which must be 25 words or less.)
   __Logo is small, crab-like figure holding a bunch of grapes in one claw and grains in the other.__

   __Claws are crossing his chest.__

English Translation_____

2. DISCLAIMER (if applicable)
NO CLAIM IS MADE TO THE EXCLUSIVE RIGHT TO USE THE TERM "_____
_____ " APART FROM THE MARK AS SHOWN.

I,_____Darron Krebbs_____, *being sworn, depose and say that I am the owner and the applicant herein, or that I am authorized to sign on behalf of the owner and applicant herein, and no other person except a related company has the right to use such mark in Florida either in the identical form or in such near resemblance as to be likely to deceive or confuse or to be mistaken therefor. I make this affidavit and verification on my/the applicant's behalf. I further acknowledge that I have read the application and know the contents thereof and that the facts stated herein are true and correct*

_____Darron Krebbs_____
Typed or printed name of applicant

_____*Darron Krebbs*_____
Applicant's signature
(List name and title)

STATE OF __Florida_____

COUNTY OF __Florida_____

On this __23rd__ day of __May_____ , __2007__ , __Darron Krebbs_____personally
appeared before me,
   ☐ who is personally known to me   ☐ whose identity I proved on the basis of _____
   __FL Dr. Lic. # K123-45-67-890__   .

(Seal)

_____*Joan Nichte*_____
Notary Public Signature

_____Joan Nichte_____
Notary's Printed Name

My Commission Expires: __Jan. 02, 2008_____

FEE: $87.50 per class

FLORIDA
DEPARTMENT OF REVENUE

APPLICATION TO COLLECT AND/OR REPORT TAX IN FLORIDA

DR-1
R. 07/05

Who must apply?

You may be required to register to collect, accrue, and remit the taxes or fees listed below if you are engaged in any of the activities listed beneath each tax or fee.

Sales Tax

Complete Sections A, B, and H	Pay $5 fee (in-state only)*

- Sales, leases, or licenses to use certain property or goods (tangible personal property).
- Sales and rentals/admissions, amusement machine receipts, or vending machine receipts for all taxable items.
- Repair or alteration of tangible personal property.
- Leases or licenses to use commercial real property (includes management companies).
- Rental of transient (six months or less) living or sleeping accommodations (includes management companies). A local tourist development tax (bed tax) may also apply. Contact the taxing authority in the county where the property is located.
- Sales or rental of self-propelled, power-drawn, or power-driven farm equipment.
- Sales of electric power or energy.
- Sales of prepaid telephone calling cards.
- Sales of commercial pest control services, nonresidential building cleaning services, commercial/residential burglary and security services, or detective services.
- Sales of secondhand goods. A secondhand dealer registration (Form DR-1S) may also be required.

*Note: If you are registering an in-state business or property location, you must submit a $5 fee with this application. Online registration is free.

Documentary Stamp Tax

Complete Sections A, F, and H	NO fee

- Entering into written financing agreements (five or more transactions per month).
- Making title loans.
- Self-financing dealers (buy here – pay here).
- Banks, mortgage companies, and consumer finance companies.
- Promissory notes.

Use Tax

Complete Sections A, B, and H	NO fee

- Any taxable purchases that were not taxed by the seller at the time of purchase.
- Repeated untaxed purchases through the Internet or from out-of-state vendors.
- Any purchases originally for resale, but later used or consumed by your business or for personal use.
- Use of dyed diesel fuel for off-road purposes.

Unemployment Tax

Complete Sections A, D, and H	NO fee

- Paid wages of $1,500 in any quarter or employed at least one worker for 20 weeks in a calendar year. (Payments made to corporate officers are wages.)
- Applicant is a governmental entity, Indian tribe or tribal unit.
- Hold a section 501(c)(3) exemption from federal income tax and employ four or more workers for 20 weeks in a calendar year.
- Agricultural employer with a $10,000 cash quarterly payroll, or who employs five or more workers for 20 weeks in a calendar year.
- Private home or college club that paid $1,000 cash in a quarter for domestic services.
- Acquired all or part of the organization, trade, business, or assets of a liable employer.
- Liable for federal unemployment taxes.
- Previously liable for unemployment tax in the State of Florida.

Gross Receipts Tax

Complete Sections A, E, and H	NO fee

- Sales of electric power or gas.

Register Online

It's FREE, fast, easy, and secure

You can file this application online, via the Department's Internet site at www.myflorida.com/dor/eservices/apps/register. **There is no fee for Internet registration.** See instructions, next page.

Communications Services Tax

Complete Sections A, G, and H	NO fee

- Sales of communications services (telephone, paging, certain facsimile services, videoconferencing).
- Sales of cable services.
- Sales of direct-to-home satellite services.
- Resellers (for example, pay telephones and prepaid calling arrangements).
- Seeking a direct pay permit.

Solid Waste Fees and Pollutants Tax

Complete Sections A, B, C, and H	Pay $30 fee (drycleaning only)*

- Sales of new tires for motor vehicles.
- Sales of new or remanufactured lead-acid batteries.
- Rental or lease of motor vehicles to others.
- Sales of dry-cleaning services (plants or drop-off facilities). *Note: You must submit a $30 fee with this application. Online registration is free.

How can I register online?

The DR-1 application is on the Department's web site at **www.myflorida.com/dor/eservices/apps/register**. An interactive wizard will guide you through an application from start to finish. Before you begin, gather specific information about your business activities, location, and beginning dates. **There are no fees for online registration.**

Sales and use tax certificate numbers will be issued within three business days of your online submission. After that time, you can return to the site and retrieve your certificate number.

How can I be sure that the information I submit online is secure?

The Department's Internet registration site uses 128-bit secure socket layer technology and has been certified by VeriSign, an industry leader in data security.

If a husband and wife jointly operate and own a business, what type of ownership must we indicate?

Normally, when a husband and wife jointly own and operate a business, the ownership is a "partnership." We suggest you contact the Internal Revenue Service for more information on partnership reporting requirements.

What will I receive from the Department once I register?

1. A *Certificate of Registration* or notification of liability for the tax(es) for which you registered.
2. Personalized returns or reports for filing, with instructions.

3. For active sales tax and communications services tax dealers, an *Annual Resale Certificate* will accompany the *Certificate of Registration.*

What is an *Annual Resale Certificate*?

The Department issues *Annual Resale Certificates* to active, registered sales tax dealers and communications services tax dealers. The *Annual Resale Certificate* allows businesses to make tax-exempt purchases from their suppliers, provided the item or service is purchased for resale. A copy of a current *Annual Resale Certificate* must be extended to the supplier; otherwise, tax must be paid on the transaction at the time of purchase. Tax Information Publication (TIP) 99A01-34 explains the resale provisions for sales and use tax. TIP 01BER-01 explains the resale provisions for communications services tax. Consult the Department's Internet site for further information. **Misuse of the *Annual Resale Certificate* will subject the user to penalties as provided by law.**

What are my responsibilities?

1. You must register for all taxes for which you are liable before beginning business activities, otherwise you may be subject to penalties. For more information, visit our Internet site or contact Taxpayer Services.
2. Complete and return this application to the Florida Department of Revenue with the applicable registration fee. IF MAILING, DO NOT SEND CASH. SEND CHECK OR MONEY ORDER.
3. Collect and/or report tax appropriately, maintain accurate records, post your certificate (if required), and file returns and reports timely. A return/report must be filed even if no tax is due.

4. Notify the Department if your address changes, your business entity or activity changes, you open additional locations, or you close your business.
5. Provide your certificate or account number on all returns, remittances, and correspondence.

What if my business has more than one location?

Sales tax: You must complete a separate application for each location. **Gross receipts tax on electric power or gas:** You have the option of registering all locations under one account number or separately registering each location. **Documentary stamp tax:** You must register each location where books and records are maintained. **Communications services tax and unemployment tax:** You must register each entity that has its own Federal Employer Identification Number (FEIN).
Solid waste fees and pollutants tax (rental car surcharge): You must register for each county where you have a rental location.

What if I am managing commercial or residential rental property for others?

For sales tax, commercial property managers must use this application; residential property managers may use Form DR-1C, *Application for Collective Registration for Rental of Living or Sleeping Accommodations*. Contact Central Registration at 850-488-9750 for assistance.

Are educational seminars offered?

Yes. To get a schedule of upcoming seminars or to register for one, visit us online at **www.myflorida.com/dor** or call the service center nearest you.

Before returning application, remove this page and retain for future reference.

FLORIDA DEPARTMENT OF REVENUE SERVICE CENTERS

CT—Central Time
ET—Eastern Time

Alachua Service Center
14107 US Highway 441 Ste 100
Alachua FL 32615-6390
386-418-4444 (ET)

Clearwater Service Center
Arbor Shoreline Office Park
19337 US Highway 19 N Ste 200
Clearwater FL 33764-3149
727-538-7400 (ET)

Cocoa Service Center
2428 Clearlake Rd Bldg M
Cocoa FL 32922-5731
321-504-0950 (ET)

Coral Springs Service Center
Florida Sunrise Tower
3111 N University Dr Ste 501
Coral Springs FL 33065-5090
954-346-3000 (ET)

Daytona Beach Service Center
1821 Business Park Blvd
Daytona Beach FL 32114-1230
386-274-6600 (ET)

Fort Myers Service Center
2295 Victoria Ave Ste 270
Fort Myers FL 33901-3871
239-338-2400 (ET)

Fort Pierce Service Center
Benton Building
337 N US Highway 1 Ste 207-B
Fort Pierce FL 34950-4255
772-429-2900 (ET)

Hollywood Service Center
Taft Office Complex
6565 Taft St Ste 300
Hollywood FL 33024-4044
954-967-1000 (ET)

Jacksonville Service Center
921 N Davis St A250
Jacksonville FL 32209-6829
904-359-6070 (ET)

Key West Service Center
3118 Flagler Ave
Key West FL 33040-4602
305-292-6725 (ET)

Lake City Service Center
1401 W US Highway 90 Ste 100
Lake City FL 32055-6123
386-758-0420 (ET)

Lakeland Service Center
230 S Florida Ave Ste 101
Lakeland FL 33801-4625
863-499-2260 (ET)

Leesburg Service Center
1415 S 14th St Ste 103
Leesburg FL 34748-6686
352-315-4470 (ET)

Maitland Service Center
Ste 160
2301 Maitland Center Parkway
Maitland FL 32751-4192
407-475-1200 (ET)

Marianna Service Center
4230 Lafayette St Ste D
Marianna FL 32446-8231
850-482-9518 (CT)

Miami Service Center
8175 NW 12th St Ste 119
Miami FL 33126-1828
305-470-5001 (ET)

Naples Service Center
3073 Horseshoe Dr S Ste 110
Naples FL 34104-6145
239-434-4858 (ET)

Orlando Service Center
AmSouth Bank Building
5401 S Kirkman Rd 5th Floor
Orlando FL 32819-7911
407-903-7350 (ET)

Panama City Service Center
703 W 15th St Ste A
Panama City FL 32401-2238
850-872-4165 (CT)

Pensacola Service Center
3670C N L St
Pensacola FL 32505-5217
850-595-5170 (CT)

Port Richey Service Center
6709 Ridge Rd Ste 300
Port Richey FL 34668-6842
727-841-4407 (ET)

Sarasota Service Center
Sarasota Main Plaza
1991 Main St Ste 240
Sarasota FL 34236-5940
941-361-6001 (ET)

Tallahassee Service Center
2410 Allen Rd
Tallahassee FL 32312-2603
850-488-9719 (ET)

Tampa Service Center
Ste 100
6302 E Martin Luther King Blvd
Tampa FL 33619-1166
813-744-6344 (ET)

West Palm Beach Service Center
2468 Metrocentre Blvd
West Palm Beach FL 33407-3105
561-640-2800 (ET)

Central Registration
5050 W Tennessee St
Tallahassee, FL 32399-0100
850-488-9750

Taxpayer Services
800-352-3671 or
850-488-6800
TDD: 800-367-8331

Internet Site
www.myflorida.com/dor

Tax Law Library
www.myflorida.com/dor/law

APPLICATION TO COLLECT AND/OR REPORT TAX IN FLORIDA
SECTION A — BUSINESS INFORMATION

DR-1
R. 07/05
Page 1

Please use BLACK or BLUE ink ONLY and type or print clearly.

Answer ALL questions in the section(s) that apply to your business.

1. This application is for (check all that apply):

✓	Tax Type	Fee Due	Complete Sections
	Sales and Use Tax	$5.00 *	A, B, H
	Use Tax Only	No fee	A, B, H
	Solid Waste Fees and Pollutants Tax	$30.00**	A, B, C, H
	Unemployment Tax	No fee	A, D, H
	Gross Receipts Tax on Electric Power and Gas	No fee	A, E, H
	Documentary Stamp Tax	No fee	A, F, H
	Communications Services Tax	No fee	A, G, H

*The $5 registration fee does not apply if:
• Your business location is outside the State of Florida.
• Your business is moving from one Florida county to another.
• You register online.

**The $30 registration fee applies to drycleaning only. There is no fee for online registration.

2. Indicate whether this is a new registration or a change to an existing registration:

New

A. ☐ New business entity   B. ☐ New business location   C. ☐ New tax obligation at existing location

Provide certificate number if you checked B or C:

☐☐ – ☐☐☐☐☐☐☐☐ – ☐

Beginning date of business activity:

1 1 / 1 0 / 2 0 0 6
month   day   year

Provide the date this business location or entity became or will become liable for Florida tax(es). Do not use your incorporation date unless that is the date your business became liable for tax. **If you have been in business longer than 30 days prior to registering, contact the DOR service center nearest you.**

Change

D. ☐ Change of county location (Business is moving from one Florida county to another)   E. ☐ Change of legal entity   F. ☐ Change of ownership

If you have checked Box D, E, or F, the Department will cancel your existing certificate(s) and issue a new one. Provide the certificate number(s) to be canceled. (Attach additional sheet if necessary.)

☐☐ – ☐☐☐☐☐☐☐☐ – ☐

If your business is relocating within the same county, do not use this application. Contact the Department to change your address.

This change is effective (enter date):

☐☐ / ☐☐ / ☐☐☐☐
month   day   year

Receipt Date Stamp

3. If this is a seasonal business (not open year-round), list the months of your open season.

Beginning date: ☐☐ / ☐☐ / ☐☐☐☐   Ending date: ☐☐ / ☐☐ / ☐☐☐☐
     month   day   year   month   day   year

** PLEASE TYPE OR PRINT CLEARLY **

4. Trade, fictitious (d/b/a), or location name:

Frankenfurter's Red Hots

Business telephone number:
305-867-5309

5. Legal name of corporation, partnership, or individual (last, first, middle):

Frankenfurter, Rocky

Owner telephone number:
305-555-5007

6. Complete physical address of business or real property. Home-based businesses and non-permanent flea market/craft show vendors must use their home addresses. Listing a post office box, private mailbox, or rural route number is not permitted.

1234 Bayshore Boulevard

Fax number:
305-555-5008

City/State/ZIP:
Miami, Florida 33940

County:
Dade County

7. Mail to the attention of:

Rocky Frankenfurter

Mailing address:
6950 S. Miami Avenue

City/State/ZIP:
Miami, Florida 33940

Would you like to receive correspondence via e-mail? ☒ Yes ☐ No

E-mail address:
Rocky@Frankenfurter.hot

8. If you have a **Consolidated Sales Tax Number** and want to include this business location, please complete the following:

_____   8 0 – ☐☐☐☐☐☐☐☐ – ☐

Consolidated registration name on record with the Florida Department of Revenue.
If you want to obtain a new consolidated number, contact the Department and request Form DR-1CON.

                                                         Consolidated registration number

9. Business Entity Identification Number. If an FEIN is not required for your business entity, the social security number of the owner will be accepted. If you are registering for unemployment tax, you **must** have an FEIN. Social security numbers are used by the Department as unique identifiers for the administration of Florida's tax laws. They are confidential under sections 119.0721 and 213.053, Florida Statutes, and are not subject to disclosure as public records.

a.   Federal Employer Identification Number (FEIN):   3 3 – 6 7 8 9 0 2 1
     or
b.   Social Security Number (SSN) of owner: ☐☐☐ – ☐☐ – ☐☐☐☐

(If you are required to have an FEIN, but have not yet been assigned one you may call the Internal Revenue Service at 800-829-4933 to request one.)

SECTION A — BUSINESS INFORMATION (CONT'D.)

10. Identify proprietors or owners, partners, officers, members, or trustees. Include the person whose social security number is listed under Question 9. **Without this information, processing of your application may be stopped.**

Name Title	Social security number and Driver license number and state	Home address City/State/ZIP	Telephone number
Rocky Frankenfurter, owner	200 44 1000	6950 S. Miami Ave., Miami, FL 33940	(305) 555-5007
			(___) ___ - ____
			(___) ___ - ____
			(___) ___ - ____

11. **Type of ownership** - Check the box next to the exact entity structure of your business.

[X] **Sole proprietorship** - An unincorporated business that is owned by one individual.

[ ] **Partnership** - The relationship existing between two or more entities or individuals who join to carry on a trade or business. This includes a business jointly owned/operated by a husband and wife.

Check one: [ ] General partnership [ ] Limited partnership [ ] Joint venture [ ] Married couple

[ ] **Corporation** - A person or group of people who incorporate by receiving a charter from their state's Secretary of State (includes professional service corporations).

Check one: [ ] C-corporation [ ] S-corporation [ ] Not-for-profit corporation

[ ] **Limited liability company** - Two or more entities (or individuals) who file articles of organization with their state's Secretary of State.

Check one: [ ] Single-member LLC [ ] Multi-member LLC

[ ] Check here if you elected to be treated as a corporation for federal income tax purposes.

[ ] **Business trust** - An entity created under an agreement of trust for the purpose of conducting a business for profit (includes real estate investment trusts).

[ ] **Non-business trust/Fiduciary** - An entity created by a grantor for the specific benefit of a designated entity or individual.

[ ] **Estate** - An entity that is created upon the death of an individual, consisting of that individual's real or personal property.

Date of death: _____

[ ] **Government agency** - A legal government body formed by governing constitutions, statutes, or rules.

[ ] **Indian tribe or Tribal unit** - Any Indian tribe, band, nation, or other organized group or community which is recognized as eligible for the special programs and services provided by the United States to Indians because of their status as Indians (includes any subdivision, subsidiary, or business enterprise wholly owned by such an Indian tribe).

12. If a partnership, corporation, or limited liability company, provide your fiscal year ending date: [ ][ ] / [ ][ ]   month   day

13. If incorporated, chartered or otherwise registered to do business in Florida, provide your document/registration number from the Florida Secretary of State:

_____

Provide the date of incorporation, charter, or authorization to do business in Florida: [ ][ ] / [ ][ ] / [ ][ ][ ][ ]   month   day   year

Note: If not incorporated, chartered or registered to do business in Florida, you may be required to do so. Call the Florida Department of State, Division of Corporations at 850-488-9000 for more information.

14. Is your business location rented from another party? Yes [ ] No [X]
If yes, and you **do not operate from your home,** provide the following information.

Owner or landlord's name _____ Telephone number _____

Address _____ City/State/ZIP _____

15.a. What is your primary business activity? Food and beverage salves _____

b. What are your taxable business activities? _____

SECTION B — SALES AND USE TAX ACTIVITY — $5 FEE (IN-STATE ONLY)

16. Does your business activity include (check all that apply):

a. ☒ Sales of property or goods at retail (to consumers)?

b. ☐ Sales of property or goods at wholesale (to registered dealers)?

c. ☐ Sales of secondhand goods?

d. ☐ Rental of commercial real property to individuals or businesses?

e. ☐ Rental of transient living or sleeping accommodations (for six months or less)?

f. ☐ Management of transient living or sleeping accommodations belonging to others?

g. ☐ Rental of equipment or other property or goods to individuals or businesses?

h. ☐ Renting/leasing motor vehicles to others?

i. ☐ Repair or alteration of tangible personal property?

j. ☐ Charging admission or membership fees?

k. ☐ Placing and operating coin-operated amusement machines at business locations belonging to others?

l. ☐ Placing and operating vending machines at business locations belonging to others?

m. ☐ Purchasing items to be included in a finished product assembled or manufactured for sale?

n. ☐ Providing any of the following services? (Check all that apply.)

n1. ☐ Pest control for nonresidential buildings

n2. ☐ Cleaning services for nonresidential buildings

n3. ☐ Detective services

n4. ☐ Protection services

n5. ☐ Security alarm system monitoring

o. ☐ Purchasing items that were not taxed by the seller at time of purchase (includes, but is not limited to, purchases through the Internet, from catalogs, or from out-of-state sellers)?

p. ☐ Using dyed diesel fuel for off-road purposes?

q. ☐ Operating vending machine(s) owned by you at your business location?

17. What products or services do you purchase for resale? _____

hot dogs, potatoes, buns, carbonated beverages

COIN-OPERATED AMUSEMENT MACHINES

18. Are coin-operated amusement machines being operated at your business location? If yes, answer question 19. .... ☐ Yes ☒ No

19. Do you have a written agreement that requires someone other than yourself to obtain amusement machine certificates for any of the machines at your location? If yes, provide their information below. .... ☐ Yes ☐ No

_____ _____ _____
Name   Address   Telephone number

Note: You must complete an *Application for Amusement Machine Certificate* (Form DR-18) if you answered YES to question 18 **and** NO to question 19.

CONTRACTORS

20. Do you improve real property as a contractor? If yes, answer questions 21-23... ☐ Yes ☒ No

21. Do you sell tangible personal property at retail?.. ☐ Yes ☐ No

22. Do you purchase materials or supplies from vendors located outside of Florida? .... ☐ Yes ☐ No

23. Do you fabricate or manufacture any building component at a location other than contract sites? .... ☐ Yes ☐ No

MOTOR FUEL

24. Do you sell any type of fuel or use off-road, dyed, diesel fuel? If yes, answer questions 25 and 26. .... ☐ Yes ☒ No

25. a. Do you make retail sales of gasoline, diesel fuel, or aviation fuel at posted retail prices? .... ☐ Yes ☐ No

b. If yes to #25a, does this business exist as a marina? .... ☐ Yes ☐ No

c. If yes to #25a, do you expect to sell more diesel fuel than gasoline?.. ☐ Yes ☐ No

d. If yes to #25a, provide your Florida Department of Environmental Protection facility identification number for this location. ☐☐☐☐☐☐

26. Do you use dyed diesel fuel for off-road purposes that was not taxed at the time of purchase?..................... ☐ Yes ☐ No

SECTION C — SOLID WASTE FEES AND POLLUTANTS TAX — $30 FEE FOR DRYCLEANING ONLY

27. Do you sell tires or batteries, or rent/lease motor vehicles to others? If yes, answer questions 28-30............... ☐ Yes ☒ No

28. Do you make retail sales of new tires for motorized vehicles (either separately or as a part of a vehicle)? .... ☐ Yes ☐ No

29. Do you make retail sales of new or remanufactured lead-acid batteries sold separately or as a component part of another product such as new automobiles, golf carts, boats, etc.?.. ☐ Yes ☐ No

30. Are you in the business of renting or leasing vehicles that transport fewer than nine passengers to individuals or businesses?... ☐ Yes ☐ No

31. Do you own or operate a dry-cleaning dry drop-off facility or plant in Florida?.. ☐ Yes ☐ No
If yes, enclose the $30 dry-cleaning registration fee.

32. Do you produce or import perchloroethylene?.. ☐ Yes ☐ No
If yes, you must complete an *Application for Florida License to Produce or Import Taxable Pollutants* (Form DR-166).

SECTION D — UNEMPLOYMENT TAX — NO FEE

DR-1
R. 07/05
Page 4

If you are registering an additional business location and are already registered with the Florida Department of Revenue for unemployment tax, you do not need to complete this section.

If you need to reactivate a previously assigned unemployment tax (UT) account number, enter your account number and complete items 33-41 below. Make sure that you have entered your FEIN on page 2, item 9.

33. Employer type (check all that apply):

☐ Regular (If a leasing company, attach copy of license.) ☐ Agricultural (citrus) ☐ Governmental entity ☐ Nonprofit organization (501(c)(3) letter must be attached)

☐ Domestic (household) ☐ Agricultural (non citrus) ☐ Agricultural crew chief ☐ Indian tribe / Tribal unit

34. Did your business pay federal unemployment tax in another state in the current or previous calendar year?.......................... ☐ Yes ☐ No

If yes, in which state(s) _____ Year(s) _____

35. Do you lease any of your employees? ☐ Yes ☐ No If yes, check whether all or part of your workforce is leased:.......... ☐ All ☐ Part

Name of leasing company_____ Date leasing began _____ UT account number_____

36. For the current calendar year, how many full or partial weeks have you employed workers? _____

For the previous year, how many full or partial weeks did you employ workers? _____

37. Provide the date that you first employed or will employ workers in Florida. ☐☐/☐☐/☐☐☐☐
   month   day   year

38. Does another party (accountant, bookkeeper, agent) maintain your payroll? .... ☐ Yes ☐ No
If yes, provide the following information.

Name of agent _____ Telephone number _____

Address _____ City/State/ZIP _____

39. Provide only your **Florida** gross payroll by calendar quarters. Estimate amounts if exact figures are not available.

	Qtr Ending 3/31	Qtr Ending 6/30	Qtr Ending 9/30	Qtr Ending 12/31
Current year	$	$	$	$
Previous year	$	$	$	$
Next previous year	$	$	$	$
Next previous year	$	$	$	$
Next previous year	$	$	$	$

40. Did you purchase this business from another entity or change your business structure in any way? .... ☐ Yes ☐ No

If **yes**, complete items **a** through **i** below, providing information about the former entity. Also, complete and submit a *Report to Determine Succession and Application for Transfer of Experience Rating Records* (Form UCS-1S) to the Department of Revenue. This form must be postmarked within 90 days of the acquisition date to be considered timely.

a. Legal name of former entity _____

b. FEIN _____ c. UT account number _____

d. Trade name (d/b/a) _____

e. Address _____

f. Date of purchase/change_____ g. Portion of business acquired: ☐ All ☐ Part ☐ Unknown

h. Was the business in operation at the time the purchase/change occurred? ☐ Yes ☐ No If no, provide date business closed. _____

i. Was there any common ownership, management, or control at the time the purchase/change occurred? ☐ Yes ☐ No

41. **List the locations and nature of business conducted in Florida. Use additional sheets if necessary.**

Address, city, and county of work site	Principal products / services	Number of employees
_____	_____	_____
_____	_____	_____

Do the above work sites provide support for any other units of the company? .... ☐ Yes ☐ No

If yes, the services are: ☐ administrative ☐ research ☐ other, specify _____

SECTION E — GROSS RECEIPTS TAX — NO FEE

42. Do you sell electrical power or gas? If yes, answer questions a and b below. .... ☐ Yes ☒ No
Do you sell:
   a. Electrical power? .... ☐ Yes ☐ No
   b. Natural or manufactured gas? .... ☐ Yes ☐ No

SECTION F — DOCUMENTARY STAMP TAX — NO FEE

43. Do you make sales, finalized by written agreements, that do not require recording by the
Clerk of the Court, but do require documentary stamp tax to be paid? If yes, answer questions 44-46 .... ☐ Yes ☒ No

44. Do you anticipate five or more transactions subject to documentary stamp tax per month? .... ☐ Yes ☐ No

45. Do you anticipate your average monthly documentary stamp tax remittance to be less than $80 per month? .... ☐ Yes ☐ No

46. Is this application being completed to register your **first** location to collect documentary stamp tax? .... ☐ Yes ☐ No
If no, and this application is for additional locations, please list name and address of each additional location.
(Attach additional sheets if needed.)

Location name _____   Telephone number _____

Physical address _____   City/State/ZIP _____

SECTION G — COMMUNICATIONS SERVICES TAX — NO FEE

47. Do you sell communications services? If yes, check the items below that apply .... ☐ Yes ☒ No
   a. Telephone service (local, long distance, or mobile) .... ☐ Yes ☐ No
   b. Paging service .... ☐ Yes ☐ No
   c. Facsimile (fax) service (not in the course of advertising or professional services) .... ☐ Yes ☐ No
   d. Cable service .... ☐ Yes ☐ No
   e. Direct-to-home satellite service .... ☐ Yes ☐ No
   f. Pay telephone service .... ☐ Yes ☐ No
   g. Reseller (only sales for resale; no sales to any retail customers) .... ☐ Yes ☐ No
   h. Other services; please describe: _____ ☐ Yes ☐ No

48. Do you purchase communications services to integrate into prepaid calling arrangements? .... ☐ Yes ☒ No

49. Are you applying for a direct pay permit for communications services? .... ☐ Yes ☒ No

50. Check the appropriate box(es) for the method(s) you **intend** to use for determining the local taxing jurisdictions in which service addresses for your customers are located. If you use multiple databases, check all that apply. If you **only** sell pay telephone or direct-to-home satellite services, provide prepaid calling arrangements, are a reseller, or are applying for a direct pay permit, skip questions 50 and 51.

   ☐ 1. An electronic database provided by the Department.

   ☐ 2a. A database developed by this company that will be certified. To apply for certification of your database, complete an *Application for Certification of Communications Services Database* (Form DR-700012).

   ☐ 2b. A database supplied by a vendor. Provide the vendor's name: _____

   ☐ 3. ZIP+4 and a methodology for assignment when ZIP codes overlap jurisdictions.

   ☐ 4. ZIP+4 that does not overlap jurisdictions. Example: a hotel located in one jurisdiction.

   ☒ 5. None of the above.

Two collection allowance rates are available.
- Dealers whose databases meet the criteria in items 1, 3, or 4 above are eligible for a .75 percent (.0075) collection allowance.
- Dealers whose databases meet the criteria in item 5 are eligible for a .25 percent (.0025) collection allowance.
- Dealers meeting the criteria in item 2a are eligible for a .25 percent (.0025) collection allowance until the database is certified. Upon certification, the dealer will receive the .75 percent (.0075) collection allowance.
- Dealers meeting the criteria in 2b are eligible for the .75 percent (.0075) collection allowance if the vendor's database has been certified. If not, the .25 percent collection allowance (.0025) will apply.

Dealers with multiple databases may need to file two separate returns in order to maximize their collection allowances.
- If all databases are certified or a ZIP+4 method is used, then the dealer is entitled to the .75 percent (.0075) collection allowance.
- If some databases are certified or a ZIP+4 method is used, and some are not, the dealer has two options for reporting the tax. One is to file a single return for all taxable sales from all databases and receive a .25 percent (.0025) collection allowance. The second option is to file two returns: one reporting taxable sales from certified databases (.75 percent allowance) and a separate return for the taxable sales from non-certified databases (.25 percent allowance).
- If no databases are certified, the dealer will receive a .25 percent (.0025) collection allowance on all tax collected.

51. **If you wish to be eligible for both collection allowances, check the box below to indicate that you will file two separate returns.**

   ☐ I will file two separate communications services tax returns in order to maximize my collection allowance.

52. Provide the name of the managerial representative who can answer questions regarding filed tax returns.

Name _____   Telephone _____

E-Mail Address _____   Street Address _____

SECTION H — APPLICANT DECLARATION AND SIGNATURE

DR-1
R. 07/05
Page 6

This application will not be accepted if not signed by the applicant.

If the applicant is a sole proprietorship, the proprietor or owner must sign; if a partnership, a partner must sign; if a corporation, an officer of the corporation authorized to sign on behalf of the corporation must sign; if a limited liability company, an authorized member or manager must sign; if a trust, a trustee must sign; if applicant is represented by an authorized agent for unemployment tax purposes, the agent may sign (attach executed power of attorney). **THE SIGNATURE OF ANY OTHER PERSON WILL NOT BE ACCEPTED.**

Please note that any person (including employees, corporate directors, corporate officers, etc.) who is required to collect, truthfully account for, and pay any taxes and willfully fails to do so shall be liable for penalties under the provisions of section 213.29, Florida Statutes. All information provided by the applicant is confidential as provided in s. 213.053, F.S., and is not subject to Florida Public Records Law (s. 119.07, F.S.).

Under penalties of perjury, I attest that I am authorized to sign on behalf of the business entity identified herein, and also declare that I have read the information provided on this application and that the facts stated in it are true to the best of my knowledge and belief.

SIGN HERE ➤ *Rocky Frankenfurter*

Title owner

Print name Rocky Frankenfurter

Date 01/01/07

Amount enclosed: $ _____

• **$5 fee** – Sales tax registration for business/property located in Florida.
• **$30 fee** – Solid waste registration for dry cleaners.

USE THIS CHECKLIST TO ENSURE FAST PROCESSING OF YOUR APPLICATION.

✓ Complete the application in its entirety.
✓ Make sure that you have provided your FEIN or SSN.
✓ Sign and date the application.
✓ Attach check or money order for appropriate registration fee amount. **DO NOT SEND CASH.**

✓ Mail to: **FLORIDA DEPARTMENT OF REVENUE
5050 W TENNESSEE ST
TALLAHASSEE FL 32399-0100**

You may also mail or deliver your application to any service center listed on the inside front cover.

FOR DOR USE ONLY

NAICS Code(s):

PM/Delivery	☐☐ / ☐☐ / ☐☐☐
B.P. No.	☐☐☐☐☐☐
UT Acct. No..	☐☐☐☐☐☐☐ - ☐

Contract Object (MO) ☐☐☐☐☐☐☐
Contract Object (LO) ☐☐☐☐☐☐☐
Contract Object (other) ☐☐☐☐☐☐☐

Blank Forms

The following forms may be removed from this book, photocopied, and used immediately. Some of the tax forms explained in this book are not included here, because you should use original returns provided by the IRS (940, 941) or the Florida Department of Revenue (quarterly unemployment compensation form).

These forms are included on the following pages:

TAX TIMETABLE

	Florida					Federal			
	Sales	Unemploy-ment	Tangible	Intangible	Corp. Income	Est. Payment	Annual Return	Form 941*	Misc.
JAN	20th	31st				15th		31st	940 31st W-2 508 1099
FEB	20th			28th 4% disc.					28th W-3
MAR	20th		31st	31st 3% disc.			15th Corp. & Partnership		
APR	20th	30th	1st	30th 2% disc.	1st	15th	15th Personal	30th	30th 508
MAY	20th			31st 1% disc.					
JUN	20th			30th tax due		15th			
JUL	20th	31st						31st	31st 508
AUG	20th								
SEP	20th					15th			
OCT.	20th	31st						31st	31st 508
NOV	20th								
DEC	20th								

* In addition to form 941, deposits must be made regularly if withholding exceeds $500 in any month

This page intentionally blank.

APPLICATION FOR REGISTRATION OF FICTITIOUS NAME

Note: Acknowledgements/certificates will be sent to the address in Section 1 only.

Section 1

1. _____
Fictitious Name to be Registered (see instructions if name includes "Corp" or "Inc")

_____

_____
Mailing Address of Business

_____
City   State   Zip Code

3. Florida County of principal place of business: _____

_____
(see instructions if more than one county)

This space for office use only

Section 2

A. Owner(s) of Fictitious Name If Individual(s): (Use an attachment if necessary):

1. _____   2. _____
Last   First   M.I.   Last   First   M.I.

_____   _____
Address   Address

_____   _____
City   State   Zip Code   City   State   Zip Code

B. Owner(s) of Fictitious Name If other than an individual: (Use attachment if necessary):

1. _____   2. _____
Entity Name   Entity Name

_____   _____
Address   Address

_____   _____
City   State   Zip Code   City   State   Zip Code

Florida Registration Number _____   Florida Registration Number _____

FEI Number: _____   FEI Number: _____

☐ Applied for   ☐ Not Applicable   ☐ Applied for   ☐ Not Applicable

Section 3

I (we) the undersigned, being the sole (all the) party(ies) owning interest in the above fictitious name, certify that the information indicated on this form is true and accurate. In accordance with Section 865.09, F.S., I (we) understand that the signature(s) below shall have the same legal effect as if made under oath. (At Least One Signature Required)

_____   _____
Signature of Owner   Date   Signature of Owner   Date

Phone Number: _____   Phone Number: _____

Section 4

FOR CANCELLATION COMPLETE SECTION 4 ONLY:
FOR FICTITIOUS NAME OR OWNERSHIP CHANGE COMPLETE SECTIONS 1 THROUGH 4:

I (we) the undersigned, hereby cancel the fictitious name _____

_____, which was registered on _____ and was assigned

registration number _____

_____   _____
Signature of Owner   Date   Signature of Owner   Date

Mark the applicable boxes   ☐ Certificate of Status — $10   ☐ Certified Copy — $30
NON-REFUNDABLE PROCESSING FEE: $50

Single   CR4E001 (11/03)

Instructions for Completing Application for Registration of Fictitious Name

Section 1:　**Line 1:** Enter the name as you wish it to be registered. A fictitious name may <u>not</u> contain the words "Corporation" or "Incorporated," or the abbreviations "Corp." or "Inc.," unless the person or business for which the name is registered is incorporated or has obtained a certificate of authority to transact business in this state pursuant to chapter 607 or chapter 617 Florida Statutes. Corporations are not required to file under their exact corporate name.

Line 2: Enter the mailing address of the business. This address does not have to be the principal place of business and can be directed to anyone's attention. DO NOT USE AN ADDRESS THAT IS NOT YET OCCUPIED. ALL FUTURE MAILINGS AND ANY CERTIFICATION REQUESTED ON THIS REGISTRATION FORM WILL BE SENT TO THE ADDRESS IN SECTION 1. An address may be changed at any future date with no charge by simply writing the Division.

Line 3: Enter the name of the county in Florida where the principal place of business of the fictitious name is located. If there is more than one county, list all applicable counties or state "multiple".

Section 2:　**Part A:** Complete if the owner(s) of the fictitious name are individuals. The individual's name and address must be provided.

Part B: Complete if the owner(s) are not individuals. Examples are a corporation, limited partnership, joint venture, general partnership, trusts, fictitious name, etc. Provide the name of the owner, their address, their registration number as registered with the Division of Corporations, and the Federal Employer Identification (FEI) number. An FEI number must be provided or the appropriate box must be checked.

Owners listed in Part B must be registered with the Division of Corporations or provide documentation as to why they are not required to register. Examples would be Federally Chartered Corporations or Legislatively created entities.

Additional owners may be listed on an attached page as long as all of the information requested in Part A or Part B is provided.

Section 3:　Only one signature is required. It is preferred that a daytime phone number be provided in order to contact the applicant if there are any questions about the application. Since the Department indexes fictitious names on a central database available on the internet, it is no longer required to advertise the intention to register a fictitious name.

Section 4:　**TO CANCEL A REGISTRATION ON FILE:** Provide fictitious name, date filed, and registration number of the fictitious name to be cancelled.

TO CHANGE OWNERSHIP OF A REGISTRATION: Complete section 4 to cancel the original registration. Complete sections 1 through 3 to re-register the fictitious name listing the new owner(s). An owner's signature is required in both sections 3 and 4.

TO CHANGE THE NAME OF A REGISTRATION: Complete section 4 to cancel the original registration. Complete sections 1 through 3 to re-register the new fictitious name. An owner's signature is required in both sections 3 and 4.

An acknowledgement letter will be mailed once the fictitious name registration has been filed.

If you wish to receive a certificate of status and/or certified copy at the time of filing of this registration, check the appropriate box at the bottom of the form. PLEASE NOTE: Acknowledgments/certificates will be sent to the address in Section 1. If a certificate of status is requested, an additional $10 is due. If a certified copy is requested, an additional $30 is due.

The registration and reregistration will be in effect until December 31 of the fifth year.

Send completed application with appropriate fees in the enclosed envelope to:

Fictitious Name Registration　　　　　　　　　　　　　　　Internet Address:
PO Box 1300　　　　　　　　　　　　　　　　　　　　　　http://www.sunbiz.org
Tallahassee, FL 32302-1300

The fee for registering a fictitious name is $50. Please make a separate check for each filing payable to the Department of State. Application must be typed or printed in ink and legible.

TRADEMARK/SERVICE MARK REGISTRATION GUIDELINES

I. GENERAL INFORMATION

Trade and Service Marks may be registered with the Florida Department of State pursuant to Chapter 495, Florida Statutes. Registration must be denied if a mark does not meet and comply with all of the requirements and provisions stipulated in Chapter 495, Florida Statutes. Marks are checked against other marks registered or reserved with this division and not against corporations, fictitious names or other entities. Rights to a name or mark are perfected by actual use in the ordinary pursuit of the specific endeavor; rights are not perfected by registration only, and the general rule of "FIRST IN USE, FIRST IN RIGHT" is applicable.

Our agency registers trade and service marks on a state level. If you need information concerning the federal registration of trademarks, service marks or patents, please contact the Commissioner of Patents and Trademarks in Washington, D. C. by calling 571-272-1000. If you need information concerning copyrights, contact the Copyright Office in Washington, D. C. by calling 202-707-3000. Although trade names are defined in Chapter 495, Florida Statutes, there is no provision for their registration.

If you wish to register a mark pursuant to Chapter 495, Florida Statutes, please submit one original and one photocopy of the Trade or Service Mark Registration application completed in its entirety, three specimens and a check made payable to the Florida Department of State for the appropriate amount. The application must be typed or neatly handwritten, signed and notarized.

The mark must be in use before it can be registered. If registering a trademark, the good(s) or product(s) must be on sale in the market place. If registering a service mark, you must be rendering the service(s) you are advertising. The mere advertising of future goods or services does not constitute use of a trade or service mark.

II. FEES AND CLASSES

The fee to register a mark is $87.50 per class. Please refer to section 495.111, Florida Statutes (attached), for a list of classes.

Should you need additional information concerning these classes or your classification, please contact the Registration Section by calling (850) 245-6051.

III. SPECIMENS

If your mark is a trademark, we will need specimens that are affixed to the good(s) or product(s). Some acceptable trademark specimens are: labels, decals, tags, wrappers, boxes, and containers. If your mark is a service mark, we will need specimens which reflect the type of service(s) being provided. Some acceptable service mark specimens are: business cards, brochures, flyers, and newspaper advertisements. If your mark is both a trade and service mark, you must submit three appropriate trademark specimens and three appropriate service mark specimens.

CR2E014 (8/05)

Do not submit photocopies, camera-ready copies, letterhead stationery, envelopes, invoices or matchbooks as specimens. Photographs of bulky specimens are acceptable if the mark to be registered and the good(s) or product(s) are clearly legible. We will not accept any specimens that have been altered or defaced in any way.

IV. APPLICATION

Part I.

#1 - You must list the complete name and business address of the applicant. Please indicate if the applicant is an individual, a corporation, a limited partnership, a general partnership, etc. Enter the domicile state, Florida registration number and Federal Employer Identification number if the applicant is other than an individual.

#2(a) - If a service mark, list the services the mark is used in connection with (i.e., restaurant services, real estate agency, insurance agency, etc.).

#2(b) - If a trademark, list the goods/products the mark is used in connection with (i.e., window cleaner, furniture polish, ladies sportswear, etc.).

#2(c) - List how the mark is being used. If a trademark, tell how the mark is applied to the goods (i.e., label, decal, engraving, imprinting on the goods or products themselves, etc.).

If a service mark, tell how the mark is used in advertising (i.e., brochures, business cards, newspaper advertisements, etc.).

#2(d) - List the applicable class(es). Please refer to section 495.111, F.S., (attached) for a list of these classes.

Part II

#1(a) - Enter the date the mark was first used anywhere.

#1(b) - Enter the date the mark was first used in Florida.

Part III

#1 - Enter the mark to be registered. If the mark includes a design, include a brief written description. If your mark is in another language, please provide this office with an English translation of your mark in this section.

#2 - Disclaimer - Your mark may include a word or design that must be disclaimed. All geographical terms and representations of cities, states or countries must be disclaimed (i.e., Miami, Orlando, Florida, the design of the state of Florida, the design of the United States of America, etc.). Commonly used words, including corporate suffixes, must also be disclaimed.

Signature Portion

Complete the signature paragraph accordingly. Please note the applicant's signature must be notarized.

V. TRADEMARK/SERVICE MARK SEARCH

Due to the amount of time it takes to conduct a thorough search of the records, this office does not provide trademark/service mark searches over the telephone. However, you may submit a written request. The request must specify the exact mark to be used and the good(s) or service(s) the mark is to be used in connection with. Please direct all requests to the Trademark Registration Section, Division of Corporations, P. O. Box 6327, Tallahassee, FL 32314.

VI. PROCESSING TIME

The application should be processed within two to five business days from the date of receipt. The processing time may be longer during our peak periods. All applications meeting the requirements of Chapter 495, F. S., on the initial examination will be filed as of the date of receipt. Applications received by courier are not handled on an expedited basis.

VII. COURIER ADDRESS AND MAILING ADDRESS

Mailing Address
Registration Section
Division of Corporations
P.O. Box 6327
Tallahassee, FL 32314

Street/Courier Address
Registration Section
Division of Corporations
Clifton Building
2661 Executive Center Circle
Tallahassee, FL 32301

Applications received via a courier service are not handled on an expedited basis.

VIII. QUESTIONS

If you have any questions concerning the registration of a mark, please contact the Trademark Registration Section by calling (850)245-6051 between the hours of 8 a.m. and 5:00 p.m. or writing to an address listed above.

495.111 Classification. -

(1) The following general classes of goods and services are established for convenience of administration of this chapter:

(a) Goods:

Class 1 Chemicals
Class 2 Paints
Class 3 Cosmetics and cleaning preparations
Class 4 Lubricants and fuels
Class 5 Pharmaceuticals
Class 6 Metal goods
Class 7 Machinery
Class 8 Hand tools
Class 9 Electrical and scientific apparatus
Class 10 Medical Apparatus
Class 11 Environmental control apparatus
Class 12 Vehicles
Class 13 Firearms
Class 14 Jewelry
Class 15 Musical instruments
Class 16 Paper goods and printed matter
Class 17 Rubber goods
Class 18 Leather goods
Class 19 Nonmetallic building materials
Class 20 Furniture and articles not otherwise classified
Class 21 Housewares and glass
Class 22 Cordage and fibers
Class 23 Yarns and threads
Class 24 Fabrics
Class 25 Clothing
Class 26 Fancy goods
Class 27 Floor coverings
Class 28 Toys and sporting goods
Class 29 Meats and processed foods
Class 30 Staple foods
Class 31 Natural agricultural products
Class 32 Light beverages
Class 33 Wines and spirits
Class 34 Smoker's articles

(b) Services:

Class 35 Advertising and business
Class 36 Insurance and financial
Class 37 Construction and repair
Class 38 Communication
Class 39 Transportation and storage
Class 40 Material treatment
Class 41 Education and entertainment
Class 42 Miscellaneous

COVER LETTER

TO: Registration Section
Division of Corporations

SUBJECT: _____
(Mark to be registered)

The enclosed Trademark/Service Mark Application, specimens and fee(s) are submitted for filing.

Please return all correspondence concerning this matter to the following:

_____
(Name of Person)

_____
(Firm/Company)

_____
(Address)

_____
(City/State and Zip Code)

For further information concerning this matter, please call:

_____ at (_____) _____._____
(Name of Person)   (Area Code & Daytime Telephone Number)

MAILING ADDRESS: **STREET/COURIER ADDRESS:**
Registration Section   Registration Section
Division of Corporations   Division of Corporations
P.O. Box 6327   Clifton Building
Tallahassee, FL 32314   2661 Executive Center Circle
                                                  Tallahassee, FL 32301

APPLICATION FOR THE REGISTRATION OF A TRADEMARK OR SERVICE MARK
PURSUANT TO CHAPTER 495, FLORIDA STATUTES

TO: **Division of Corporations**
Post Office Box 6327
Tallahassee, FL 32314

Name & address to whom acknowledgment should be sent:

_____

_____

_____

(_____) _____
Daytime Telephone number

PART I

1. (a) Applicant's name: _____

    (b) Applicant's business address: _____

_____
City/State/Zip

If different, Applicant's mailing address: _____

_____
City/State/Zip

    (c) Applicant's telephone number: (_____)_____

☐ Individual   ☐ Corporation   ☐ Joint Venture   ☐ Other:_____

☐ General Partnership   ☐ Limited Partnership   ☐ Union

If other than an individual,

(1) Florida registration/document number: _____ (2) Domicile State: _____

(3) Federal Employer Identification Number: _____

2. (a) If the mark to be registered is a service mark, the services in connection with which the mark is used:
    (i.e., furniture moving services, diaper services, house painting services, etc.)

_____

_____

_____

    (b) If the mark to be registered is a trademark, the goods in connection with which the mark is used:
    (i.e., ladies sportswear, cat food, barbecue grills, shoe laces, etc.)

_____

_____

_____

    (c) The mode or manner in which the mark is used:(i.e., labels, decals, newspaper advertisements, brochures, etc.)

_____

_____

_____

(Continued)

d) The class(es) in which goods or services fall:

_____

_____

PART II
1. Date first used by the applicant, predecessor, or a related company (must include month, day and year):

(a) Date first used anywhere: _____ (b) Date first used in Florida: _____

PART III
1. The mark to be registered is: (If logo/design is included, please give brief written description which must be 25 words or less.)

_____

_____

_____

English Translation_____

2. DISCLAIMER (if applicable)
NO CLAIM IS MADE TO THE EXCLUSIVE RIGHT TO USE THE TERM " _____
_____ " APART FROM THE MARK AS SHOWN.

I,_____, being sworn, depose and say that I am the owner and the applicant herein, or that I am authorized to sign on behalf of the owner and applicant herein, and no other person except a related company has the right to use such mark in Florida either in the identical form or in such near resemblance as to be likely to deceive or confuse or to be mistaken therefor. I make this affidavit and verification on my/the applicant's behalf. I further acknowledge that I have read the application and know the contents thereof and that the facts stated herein are true and correct

_____
Typed or printed name of applicant

_____
Applicant's signature
(List name and title)

STATE OF _____

COUNTY OF _____

On this _____ day of _____ , _____ , _____personally appeared before me,
☐ who is personally known to me   ☐ whose identity I proved on the basis of _____
_____.

(Seal)

_____
Notary Public Signature

_____
Notary's Printed Name

My Commission Expires:_____

FEE: $87.50 per class

This page intentionally blank.

Department of Homeland Security
U.S. Citizenship and Immigration Services

OMB No. 1615-0047; Expires 03/31/07

Employment Eligibility Verification

Please read instructions carefully before completing this form. The instructions must be available during completion of this form. **ANTI-DISCRIMINATION NOTICE:** It is illegal to discriminate against work eligible individuals. Employers CANNOT specify which document(s) they will accept from an employee. The refusal to hire an individual because of a future expiration date may also constitute illegal discrimination.

Section 1. Employee Information and Verification. To be completed and signed by employee at the time employment begins.

Print Name: Last	First	Middle Initial	Maiden Name

Address (Street Name and Number)	Apt. #	Date of Birth (month/day/year)

City	State	Zip Code	Social Security #

I am aware that federal law provides for imprisonment and/or fines for false statements or use of false documents in connection with the completion of this form.

I attest, under penalty of perjury, that I am (check one of the following):

☐ A citizen or national of the United States
☐ A Lawful Permanent Resident (Alien #) A _____
☐ An alien authorized to work until _____

(Alien # or Admission #) _____

Employee's Signature	Date (month/day/year)

Preparer and/or Translator Certification. *(To be completed and signed if Section 1 is prepared by a person other than the employee.) I attest, under penalty of perjury, that I have assisted in the completion of this form and that to the best of my knowledge the information is true and correct.*

Preparer's/Translator's Signature	Print Name

Address (Street Name and Number, City, State, Zip Code)	Date (month/day/year)

Section 2. Employer Review and Verification. To be completed and signed by employer. Examine one document from List A OR examine one document from List B and one from List C, as listed on the reverse of this form, and record the title, number and expiration date, if any, of the document(s).

List A	OR	List B	AND	List C
Document title: _____		_____		_____
Issuing authority: _____		_____		_____
Document #: _____		_____		_____
Expiration Date (if any): _____		_____		_____
Document #: _____				
Expiration Date (if any): _____				

CERTIFICATION - I attest, under penalty of perjury, that I have examined the document(s) presented by the above-named employee, that the above-listed document(s) appear to be genuine and to relate to the employee named, that the employee began employment on *(month/day/year)* _____ **and that to the best of my knowledge the employee is eligible to work in the United States. (State employment agencies may omit the date the employee began employment.)**

Signature of Employer or Authorized Representative	Print Name	Title

Business or Organization Name	Address (Street Name and Number, City, State, Zip Code)	Date (month/day/year)

Section 3. Updating and Reverification. To be completed and signed by employer.

A. New Name (if applicable)	B. Date of rehire (month/day/year) (if applicable)

C. If employee's previous grant of work authorization has expired, provide the information below for the document that establishes current employment eligibility.

Document Title: _____ Document #: _____ Expiration Date (if any): _____

I attest, under penalty of perjury, that to the best of my knowledge, this employee is eligible to work in the United States, and if the employee presented document(s), the document(s) I have examined appear to be genuine and to relate to the individual.

Signature of Employer or Authorized Representative	Date (month/day/year)

NOTE: This is the 1991 edition of the Form I-9 that has been rebranded with a current printing date to reflect the recent transition from the INS to DHS and its components.

Form I-9 (Rev. 05/31/05)Y Page 2

OMB No. 1615-0047; Expires 03/31/07

Department of Homeland Security
U.S. Citizenship and Immigration Services

Employment Eligibility Verification

INSTRUCTIONS
PLEASE READ ALL INSTRUCTIONS CAREFULLY BEFORE COMPLETING THIS FORM.

Anti-Discrimination Notice. It is illegal to discriminate against any individual (other than an alien not authorized to work in the U.S.) in hiring, discharging, or recruiting or referring for a fee because of that individual's national origin or citizenship status. It is illegal to discriminate against work eligible individuals. Employers **CANNOT** specify which document(s) they will accept from an employee. The refusal to hire an individual because of a future expiration date may also constitute illegal discrimination.

Section 1- Employee.
All employees, citizens and noncitizens, hired after November 6, 1986, must complete Section 1 of this form at the time of hire, which is the actual beginning of employment. **The employer is responsible for ensuring that Section 1 is timely and properly completed.**

Preparer/Translator Certification. The Preparer/Translator Certification must be completed if Section 1 is prepared by a person other than the employee. A preparer/translator may be used only when the employee is unable to complete Section 1 on his/her own. However, the employee must still sign Section 1 personally.

Section 2 - Employer.
For the purpose of completing this form, the term "employer" includes those recruiters and referrers for a fee who are agricultural associations, agricultural employers or farm labor contractors.

Employers must complete Section 2 by examining evidence of identity and employment eligibility within three (3) business days of the date employment begins. If employees are authorized to work, but are unable to present the required document(s) within three business days, they must present a receipt for the application of the document(s) within three business days and the actual document(s) within ninety (90) days. However, if employers hire individuals for a duration of less than three business days, Section 2 must be completed at the time employment begins. **Employers must record: 1)** document title; **2)** issuing authority; **3)** document number, **4)** expiration date, if any; and **5)** the date employment begins. Employers must sign and date the certification. Employees must present original documents. Employers may, but are not required to, photocopy the document(s) presented. These photocopies may only be used for the verification process and must be retained with the I-9. **However, employers are still responsible for completing the I-9.**

Section 3 - Updating and Reverification.
Employers must complete Section 3 when updating and/or reverifying the I-9. Employers must reverify employment eligibility of their employees on or before the expiration date recorded in Section 1. Employers **CANNOT** specify which document(s) they will accept from an employee.

- If an employee's name has changed at the time this form is being updated/reverified, complete Block A.

- If an employee is rehired within three (3) years of the date this form was originally completed and the employee is still eligible to be employed on the same basis as previously indicated on this form (updating), complete Block B and the signature block.

- If an employee is rehired within three (3) years of the date this form was originally completed and the employee's work authorization has expired **or** if a current employee's work authorization is about to expire (reverification), complete Block B and:

- examine any document that reflects that the employee is authorized to work in the U.S. (see List A **or** C),

- record the document title, document number and expiration date (if any) in Block C, and

- complete the signature block.

Photocopying and Retaining Form I-9. A blank I-9 may be reproduced, provided both sides are copied. The Instructions must be available to all employees completing this form. Employers must retain completed I-9s for three (3) years after the date of hire or one (1) year after the date employment ends, whichever is later.

For more detailed information, you may refer to the Department of Homeland Security (DHS) Handbook for Employers, (Form M-274). You may obtain the handbook at your local U.S. Citizenship and Immigration Services (USCIS) office.

Privacy Act Notice. The authority for collecting this information is the Immigration Reform and Control Act of 1986, Pub. L. 99-603 (8 USC 1324a).

This information is for employers to verify the eligibility of individuals for employment to preclude the unlawful hiring, or recruiting or referring for a fee, of aliens who are not authorized to work in the United States.

This information will be used by employers as a record of their basis for determining eligibility of an employee to work in the United States. The form will be kept by the employer and made available for inspection by officials of the U.S. Immigration and Customs Enforcement, Department of Labor and Office of Special Counsel for Immigration Related Unfair Employment Practices.

Submission of the information required in this form is voluntary. However, an individual may not begin employment unless this form is completed, since employers are subject to civil or criminal penalties if they do not comply with the Immigration Reform and Control Act of 1986.

Reporting Burden. We try to create forms and instructions that are accurate, can be easily understood and which impose the least possible burden on you to provide us with information. Often this is difficult because some immigration laws are very complex. Accordingly, the reporting burden for this collection of information is computed as follows: **1)** learning about this form, 5 minutes; **2)** completing the form, 5 minutes; and **3)** assembling and filing (recordkeeping) the form, 5 minutes, for an average of 15 minutes per response. If you have comments regarding the accuracy of this burden estimate, or suggestions for making this form simpler, you can write to U.S. Citizenship and Immigration Services, Regulatory Management Division, 111 Massachuetts Avenue, N.W., Washington, DC 20529. OMB No. 1615-0047.

NOTE: This is the 1991 edition of the Form I-9 that has been rebranded with a current printing date to reflect the recent transition from the INS to DHS and its components.

EMPLOYERS MUST RETAIN COMPLETED FORM I-9
PLEASE DO NOT MAIL COMPLETED FORM I-9 TO ICE OR USCIS

Form I-9 (Rev. 05/31/05)Y

LISTS OF ACCEPTABLE DOCUMENTS

LIST A		LIST B		LIST C
Documents that Establish Both Identity and Employment Eligibility	**OR**	**Documents that Establish Identity**	**AND**	**Documents that Establish Employment Eligibility**

LIST A — Documents that Establish Both Identity and Employment Eligibility

1. U.S. Passport (unexpired or expired)

2. Certificate of U.S. Citizenship *(Form N-560 or N-561)*

3. Certificate of Naturalization *(Form N-550 or N-570)*

4. Unexpired foreign passport, with *I-551 stamp or* attached *Form I-94* indicating unexpired employment authorization

5. Permanent Resident Card or Alien Registration Receipt Card with photograph *(Form I-151 or I-551)*

6. Unexpired Temporary Resident Card *(Form I-688)*

7. Unexpired Employment Authorization Card *(Form I-688A)*

8. Unexpired Reentry Permit *(Form I-327)*

9. Unexpired Refugee Travel Document *(Form I-571)*

10. Unexpired Employment Authorization Document issued by DHS that contains a photograph *(Form I-688B)*

LIST B — Documents that Establish Identity

1. Driver's license or ID card issued by a state or outlying possession of the United States provided it contains a photograph or information such as name, date of birth, gender, height, eye color and address

2. ID card issued by federal, state or local government agencies or entities, provided it contains a photograph or information such as name, date of birth, gender, height, eye color and address

3. School ID card with a photograph

4. Voter's registration card

5. U.S. Military card or draft record

6. Military dependent's ID card

7. U.S. Coast Guard Merchant Mariner Card

8. Native American tribal document

9. Driver's license issued by a Canadian government authority

For persons under age 18 who are unable to present a document listed above:

10. School record or report card

11. Clinic, doctor or hospital record

12. Day-care or nursery school record

LIST C — Documents that Establish Employment Eligibility

1. U.S. social security card issued by the Social Security Administration *(other than a card stating it is not valid for employment)*

2. Certification of Birth Abroad issued by the Department of State *(Form FS-545 or Form DS-1350)*

3. Original or certified copy of a birth certificate issued by a state, county, municipal authority or outlying possession of the United States bearing an official seal

4. Native American tribal document

5. U.S. Citizen ID Card *(Form I-197)*

6. ID Card for use of Resident Citizen in the United States *(Form I-179)*

7. Unexpired employment authorization document issued by DHS *(other than those listed under List A)*

Illustrations of many of these documents appear in Part 8 of the Handbook for Employers (M-274)

This page intentionally blank.

Form **SS-4**
(Rev. December 2001)
Department of the Treasury
Internal Revenue Service

Application for Employer Identification Number

(For use by employers, corporations, partnerships, trusts, estates, churches, government agencies, Indian tribal entities, certain individuals, and others.)

▶ See separate instructions for each line.   ▶ Keep a copy for your records.

EIN

OMB No. 1545-0003

Type or print clearly.

1 Legal name of entity (or individual) for whom the EIN is being requested

2 Trade name of business (if different from name on line 1)

3 Executor, trustee, "care of" name

4a Mailing address (room, apt., suite no. and street, or P.O. box)

5a Street address (if different) (Do not enter a P.O. box.)

4b City, state, and ZIP code

5b City, state, and ZIP code

6 County and state where principal business is located

7a Name of principal officer, general partner, grantor, owner, or trustor

7b SSN, ITIN, or EIN

8a **Type of entity** (check only one box)
- ☐ Sole proprietor (SSN) _____
- ☐ Partnership
- ☐ Corporation (enter form number to be filed) ▶ _____
- ☐ Personal service corp.
- ☐ Church or church-controlled organization
- ☐ Other nonprofit organization (specify) ▶ _____
- ☐ Other (specify) ▶
- ☐ Estate (SSN of decedent) _____
- ☐ Plan administrator (SSN) _____
- ☐ Trust (SSN of grantor) _____
- ☐ National Guard   ☐ State/local government
- ☐ Farmers' cooperative   ☐ Federal government/military
- ☐ REMIC   ☐ Indian tribal governments/enterprises
- Group Exemption Number (GEN) ▶ _____

8b If a corporation, name the state or foreign country (if applicable) where incorporated

State

Foreign country

9 **Reason for applying** (check only one box)
- ☐ Started new business (specify type) ▶ _____
- ☐ Hired employees (Check the box and see line 12.)
- ☐ Compliance with IRS withholding regulations
- ☐ Other (specify) ▶
- ☐ Banking purpose (specify purpose) ▶ _____
- ☐ Changed type of organization (specify new type) ▶ _____
- ☐ Purchased going business
- ☐ Created a trust (specify type) ▶ _____
- ☐ Created a pension plan (specify type) ▶ _____

10 Date business started or acquired (month, day, year)

11 Closing month of accounting year

12 First date wages or annuities were paid or will be paid (month, day, year). **Note:** *If applicant is a withholding agent, enter date income will first be paid to nonresident alien. (month, day, year)* . . . . ▶

13 Highest number of employees expected in the next 12 months. **Note:** *If the applicant does not expect to have any employees during the period, enter "-0-."* . . . . ▶

Agricultural	Household	Other

14 Check **one** box that best describes the principal activity of your business.
- ☐ Construction   ☐ Rental & leasing   ☐ Transportation & warehousing
- ☐ Real estate   ☐ Manufacturing   ☐ Finance & insurance
- ☐ Health care & social assistance   ☐ Wholesale–agent/broker
- ☐ Accommodation & food service   ☐ Wholesale–other   ☐ Retail
- ☐ Other (specify)

15 Indicate principal line of merchandise sold; specific construction work done; products produced; or services provided.

16a Has the applicant ever applied for an employer identification number for this or any other business? . . . .   ☐ Yes   ☐ No
Note: *If "Yes," please complete lines 16b and 16c.*

16b If you checked "Yes" on line 16a, give applicant's legal name and trade name shown on prior application if different from line 1 or 2 above.
Legal name ▶   Trade name ▶

16c Approximate date when, and city and state where, the application was filed. Enter previous employer identification number if known.
Approximate date when filed (mo., day, year)   City and state where filed   Previous EIN

Third Party Designee

Complete this section **only** if you want to authorize the named individual to receive the entity's EIN and answer questions about the completion of this form.

Designee's name

Designee's telephone number (include area code)
( )

Address and ZIP code

Designee's fax number (include area code)
( )

Under penalties of perjury, I declare that I have examined this application, and to the best of my knowledge and belief, it is true, correct, and complete.

Applicant's telephone number (include area code)
( )

Name and title (type or print clearly) ▶

Applicant's fax number (include area code)
( )

Signature ▶   Date ▶

For Privacy Act and Paperwork Reduction Act Notice, see separate instructions.   Cat. No. 16055N   Form **SS-4** (Rev. 12-2001)

Do I Need an EIN?

File Form SS-4 if the applicant entity does not already have an EIN but is required to show an EIN on any return, statement, or other document.[1] **See also the separate instructions for each line on Form SS-4.**

IF the applicant...	AND...	THEN...
Started a new business	Does not currently have (nor expect to have) employees	Complete lines 1, 2, 4a–6, 8a, and 9–16c.
Hired (or will hire) employees, including household employees	Does not already have an EIN	Complete lines 1, 2, 4a–6, 7a–b (if applicable), 8a, 8b (if applicable), and 9–16c.
Opened a bank account	Needs an EIN for banking purposes only	Complete lines 1–5b, 7a–b (if applicable), 8a, 9, and 16a–c.
Changed type of organization	Either the legal character of the organization or its ownership changed (e.g., you incorporate a sole proprietorship or form a partnership)[2]	Complete lines 1–16c (as applicable).
Purchased a going business[3]	Does not already have an EIN	Complete lines 1–16c (as applicable).
Created a trust	The trust is other than a grantor trust or an IRA trust[4]	Complete lines 1–16c (as applicable).
Created a pension plan as a plan administrator[5]	Needs an EIN for reporting purposes	Complete lines 1, 2, 4a–6, 8a, 9, and 16a–c.
Is a foreign person needing an EIN to comply with IRS withholding regulations	Needs an EIN to complete a Form W-8 (other than Form W-8ECI), avoid withholding on portfolio assets, or claim tax treaty benefits[6]	Complete lines 1–5b, 7a–b (SSN or ITIN optional), 8a–9, and 16a–c.
Is administering an estate	Needs an EIN to report estate income on Form 1041	Complete lines 1, 3, 4a–b, 8a, 9, and 16a–c.
Is a withholding agent for taxes on non-wage income paid to an alien (i.e., individual, corporation, or partnership, etc.)	Is an agent, broker, fiduciary, manager, tenant, or spouse who is required to file **Form 1042,** Annual Withholding Tax Return for U.S. Source Income of Foreign Persons	Complete lines 1, 2, 3 (if applicable), 4a–5b, 7a–b (if applicable), 8a, 9, and 16a–c.
Is a state or local agency	Serves as a tax reporting agent for public assistance recipients under Rev. Proc. 80-4, 1980-1 C.B. 581[7]	Complete lines 1, 2, 4a–5b, 8a, 9, and 16a–c.
Is a single-member LLC	Needs an EIN to file **Form 8832,** Classification Election, for filing employment tax returns, **or** for state reporting purposes[8]	Complete lines 1–16c (as applicable).
Is an S corporation	Needs an EIN to file **Form 2553,** Election by a Small Business Corporation[9]	Complete lines 1–16c (as applicable).

[1] For example, a sole proprietorship or self-employed farmer who establishes a qualified retirement plan, or is required to file excise, employment, alcohol, tobacco, or firearms returns, must have an EIN. **A partnership, corporation, REMIC (real estate mortgage investment conduit), nonprofit organization (church, club, etc.), or farmers' cooperative must use an EIN for any tax-related purpose even if the entity does not have employees.**

[2] However, **do not** apply for a new EIN if the existing entity only **(a)** changed its business name, **(b)** elected on Form 8832 to change the way it is taxed (or is covered by the default rules), or **(c)** terminated its partnership status because at least 50% of the total interests in partnership capital and profits were sold or exchanged within a 12-month period. (The EIN of the terminated partnership should continue to be used. See Regulations section 301.6109-1(d)(2)(iii).)

[3] Do not use the EIN of the prior business unless you became the "owner" of a corporation by acquiring its stock.

[4] However, IRA trusts that are required to file **Form 990-T,** Exempt Organization Business Income Tax Return, must have an EIN.

[5] A plan administrator is the person or group of persons specified as the administrator by the instrument under which the plan is operated.

[6] Entities applying to be a Qualified Intermediary (QI) need a QI-EIN even if they already have an EIN. **See Rev. Proc. 2000-12.**

[7] See also *Household employer* on page 4. (**Note:** State or local agencies may need an EIN for other reasons, e.g., hired employees.)

[8] Most LLCs **do not** need to file Form 8832. See **Limited liability company (LLC)** on page 4 for details on completing Form SS-4 for an LLC.

[9] An existing corporation that is electing or revoking S corporation status should use its previously-assigned EIN.

Instructions for Form SS-4

(Rev. September 2003)

Department of the Treasury
Internal Revenue Service

For use with Form SS-4 (Rev. December 2001)
Application for Employer Identification Number.
Section references are to the Internal Revenue Code unless otherwise noted.

General Instructions

Use these instructions to complete **Form SS-4,** Application for Employer Identification Number. Also see **Do I Need an EIN?** on page 2 of Form SS-4.

Purpose of Form

Use Form SS-4 to apply for an employer identification number (EIN). An EIN is a nine-digit number (for example, 12-3456789) assigned to sole proprietors, corporations, partnerships, estates, trusts, and other entities for tax filing and reporting purposes. The information you provide on this form will establish your business tax account.

*An EIN is for use in connection with your business activities only. Do **not** use your EIN in place of your social security number (SSN).*

Items To Note

Apply online. You can now apply for and receive an EIN online using the internet. See **How To Apply** below.

File only one Form SS-4. Generally, a sole proprietor should file only one Form SS-4 and needs only one EIN, regardless of the number of businesses operated as a sole proprietorship or trade names under which a business operates. However, if the proprietorship incorporates or enters into a partnership, a new EIN is required. Also, each corporation in an affiliated group must have its own EIN.

EIN applied for, but not received. If you do not have an EIN by the time a return is due, write "Applied For" and the date you applied in the space shown for the number. **Do not** show your SSN as an EIN on returns.

If you do not have an EIN by the time a tax deposit is due, send your payment to the Internal Revenue Service Center for your filing area as shown in the instructions for the form that you are filing. Make your check or money order payable to the "United States Treasury" and show your name (as shown on Form SS-4), address, type of tax, period covered, and date you applied for an EIN.

How To Apply

You can apply for an EIN online, by telephone, by fax, or by mail depending on how soon you need to use the EIN. Use only one method for each entity so you do not receive more than one EIN for an entity.

Online. You can receive your EIN by internet and use it immediately to file a return or make a payment. Go to the IRS website at **www.irs.gov/businesses** and click on **Employer ID Numbers** under **topics.**

Telephone. You can receive your EIN by telephone and use it immediately to file a return or make a payment. Call the IRS at **1-800-829-4933.** (International applicants must call 215-516-6999.) The hours of operation are 7:00 a.m. to 10:00 p.m. The person making the call must be authorized to sign the form or be an authorized designee. See **Signature** and **Third Party Designee** on page 6. Also see the **TIP** below.

If you are applying by telephone, it will be helpful to complete Form SS-4 before contacting the IRS. An IRS representative will use the information from the Form SS-4 to establish your account and assign you an EIN. Write the number you are given on the upper right corner of the form and sign and date it. Keep this copy for your records.

If requested by an IRS representative, mail or fax (facsimile) the signed Form SS-4 (including any Third Party Designee authorization) within 24 hours to the IRS address provided by the IRS representative.

*Taxpayer representatives can apply for an EIN on behalf of their client and request that the EIN be faxed to their **client** on the same day. **Note:** By using this procedure, you are authorizing the IRS to fax the EIN without a cover sheet.*

Fax. Under the Fax-TIN program, you can receive your EIN by fax within 4 business days. Complete and fax Form SS-4 to the IRS using the Fax-TIN number listed on page 2 for your state. A long-distance charge to callers outside of the local calling area will apply. Fax-TIN numbers can only be used to apply for an EIN. **The numbers may change without notice.** Fax-TIN is available 24 hours a day, 7 days a week.

Be sure to provide your fax number so the IRS can fax the EIN back to you. **Note:** By using this procedure, you are authorizing the IRS to fax the EIN without a cover sheet.

Mail. Complete Form SS-4 at least 4 to 5 weeks before you will need an EIN. Sign and date the application and mail it to the service center address for your state. You will receive your EIN in the mail in approximately 4 weeks. See also **Third Party Designee** on page 6.

Call 1-800-829-4933 to verify a number or to ask about the status of an application by mail.

Cat. No. 62736F

Where To Fax or File

If your principal business, office or agency, or legal residence in the case of an individual, is located in:	Call the Fax-TIN number shown or file with the "Internal Revenue Service Center" at:
Connecticut, Delaware, District of Columbia, Florida, Georgia, Maine, Maryland, Massachusetts, New Hampshire, New Jersey, New York, North Carolina, Ohio, Pennsylvania, Rhode Island, South Carolina, Vermont, Virginia, West Virginia	Attn: EIN Operation P. 0. Box 9003 Holtsville, NY 11742-9003 Fax-TIN 631-447-8960
Illinois, Indiana, Kentucky, Michigan	Attn: EIN Operation Cincinnati, OH 45999 Fax-TIN 859-669-5760
Alabama, Alaska, Arizona, Arkansas, California, Colorado, Hawaii, Idaho, Iowa, Kansas, Louisiana, Minnesota, Mississippi, Missouri, Montana, Nebraska, Nevada, New Mexico, North Dakota, Oklahoma, Oregon, Puerto Rico, South Dakota, Tennessee, Texas, Utah, Washington, Wisconsin, Wyoming	Attn: EIN Operation Philadelphia, PA 19255 Fax-TIN 215-516-3990
If you have no legal residence, principal place of business, or principal office or agency in any state:	Attn: EIN Operation Philadelphia, PA 19255 Telephone 215-516-6999 Fax-TIN 215-516-3990

How To Get Forms and Publications

Phone. You can order forms, instructions, and publications by phone 24 hours a day, 7 days a week. Call 1-800-TAX-FORM (1-800-829-3676). You should receive your order or notification of its status within 10 workdays.

Personal computer. With your personal computer and modem, you can get the forms and information you need using the IRS website at **www.irs.gov** or File Transfer Protocol at **ftp.irs.gov.**

CD-ROM. For small businesses, return preparers, or others who may frequently need tax forms or publications, a CD-ROM containing over 2,000 tax products (including many prior year forms) can be purchased from the National Technical Information Service (NTIS).

To order **Pub. 1796,** Federal Tax Products on CD-ROM, call **1-877-CDFORMS** (1-877-233-6767) toll free or connect to **www.irs.gov/cdorders.**

Tax Help for Your Business

IRS-sponsored Small Business Workshops provide information about your Federal and state tax obligations.

For information about workshops in your area, call 1-800-829-4933.

Related Forms and Publications

The following **forms** and **instructions** may be useful to filers of Form SS-4:
- **Form 990-T,** Exempt Organization Business Income Tax Return
- **Instructions for Form 990-T**
- **Schedule C (Form 1040),** Profit or Loss From Business
- **Schedule F (Form 1040),** Profit or Loss From Farming
- **Instructions for Form 1041 and Schedules A, B, D, G, I, J, and K-1,** U.S. Income Tax Return for Estates and Trusts
- **Form 1042,** Annual Withholding Tax Return for U.S. Source Income of Foreign Persons
- **Instructions for Form 1065,** U.S. Return of Partnership Income
- **Instructions for Form 1066,** U.S. Real Estate Mortgage Investment Conduit (REMIC) Income Tax Return
- **Instructions for Forms 1120 and 1120-A**
- **Form 2553,** Election by a Small Business Corporation
- **Form 2848,** Power of Attorney and Declaration of Representative
- **Form 8821,** Tax Information Authorization
- **Form 8832,** Entity Classification Election
  For more **information** about filing Form SS-4 and related issues, see:
- **Circular A,** Agricultural Employer's Tax Guide (Pub. 51)
- **Circular E,** Employer's Tax Guide (Pub. 15)
- **Pub. 538,** Accounting Periods and Methods
- **Pub. 542,** Corporations
- **Pub. 557,** Exempt Status for Your Organization
- **Pub. 583,** Starting a Business and Keeping Records
- **Pub. 966,** Electronic Choices for Paying ALL Your Federal Taxes
- **Pub. 1635,** Understanding Your EIN
- **Package 1023,** Application for Recognition of Exemption Under Section 501(c)(3) of the Internal Revenue Code
- **Package 1024,** Application for Recognition of Exemption Under Section 501(a)

Specific Instructions

Print or type all entries on Form SS-4. Follow the instructions for each line to expedite processing and to avoid unnecessary IRS requests for additional information. Enter "N/A" (nonapplicable) on the lines that do not apply.

Line 1—Legal name of entity (or individual) for whom the EIN is being requested. Enter the legal name of the entity (or individual) applying for the EIN exactly as it appears on the social security card, charter, or other applicable legal document.

Individuals. Enter your first name, middle initial, and last name. If you are a sole proprietor, enter your individual name, not your business name. Enter your business name on line 2. Do not use abbreviations or nicknames on line 1.

Trusts. Enter the name of the trust.

Estate of a decedent. Enter the name of the estate.

Partnerships. Enter the legal name of the partnership as it appears in the partnership agreement.

Corporations. Enter the corporate name as it appears in the corporation charter or other legal document creating it.

Plan administrators. Enter the name of the plan administrator. A plan administrator who already has an EIN should use that number.

Line 2—Trade name of business. Enter the trade name of the business if different from the legal name. The trade name is the "doing business as " (DBA) name.

 *Use the full legal name shown on line 1 on all tax returns filed for the entity. (However, if you enter a trade name on line 2 and choose to use the trade name instead of the legal name, enter the trade name on **all returns** you file.) To prevent processing delays and errors, **always** use the legal name only (or the trade name only) on **all** tax returns.*

Line 3—Executor, trustee, "care of" name. Trusts enter the name of the trustee. Estates enter the name of the executor, administrator, or other fiduciary. If the entity applying has a designated person to receive tax information, enter that person's name as the "care of" person. Enter the individual's first name, middle initial, and last name.

Lines 4a-b—Mailing address. Enter the mailing address for the entity's correspondence. If line 3 is completed, enter the address for the executor, trustee or "care of" person. Generally, this address will be used on all tax returns.

 *File **Form 8822,** Change of Address, to report any subsequent changes to the entity's mailing address.*

Lines 5a-b—Street address. Provide the entity's physical address **only** if different from its mailing address shown in lines 4a-b. **Do not** enter a P.O. box number here.

Line 6—County and state where principal business is located. Enter the entity's primary **physical** location.

Lines 7a-b—Name of principal officer, general partner, grantor, owner, or trustor. Enter the first name, middle initial, last name, and SSN of **(a)** the principal officer if the business is a corporation, **(b)** a general partner if a partnership, **(c)** the owner of an entity that is disregarded as separate from its owner (disregarded entities owned by a corporation enter the corporation's name and EIN), or **(d)** a grantor, owner, or trustor if a trust.

If the person in question is an **alien individual** with a previously assigned individual taxpayer identification number (ITIN), enter the ITIN in the space provided and submit a copy of an official identifying document. If

necessary, complete **Form W-7,** Application for IRS Individual Taxpayer Identification Number, to obtain an ITIN.

You are **required** to enter an SSN, ITIN, or EIN unless the only reason you are applying for an EIN is to make an entity classification election (see Regulations sections 301.7701-1 through 301.7701-3) and you are a nonresident alien with no effectively connected income from sources within the United States.

Line 8a—Type of entity. Check the box that best describes the type of entity applying for the EIN. If you are an alien individual with an ITIN previously assigned to you, enter the ITIN in place of a requested SSN.

 *This is not an election for a tax classification of an entity. See **Limited liability company (LLC)** on page 4.*

Other. If not specifically listed, check the "Other" box, enter the type of entity and the type of return, if any, that will be filed (for example, "Common Trust Fund, Form 1065" or "Created a Pension Plan"). Do not enter "N/A." If you are an alien individual applying for an EIN, see the **Lines 7a-b** instructions above.

● **Household employer.** If you are an individual, check the "Other" box and enter "Household Employer" and your SSN. If you are a state or local agency serving as a tax reporting agent for public assistance recipients who become household employers, check the "Other" box and enter "Household Employer Agent." If you are a trust that qualifies as a household employer, you do not need a separate EIN for reporting tax information relating to household employees; use the EIN of the trust.

● **QSub.** For a qualified subchapter S subsidiary (QSub) check the "Other" box and specify "QSub."

● **Withholding agent.** If you are a withholding agent required to file Form 1042, check the "Other" box and enter "Withholding Agent."

Sole proprietor. Check this box if you file Schedule C, C-EZ, or F (Form 1040) and have a qualified plan, or are required to file excise, employment, alcohol, tobacco, or firearms returns, or are a payer of gambling winnings. Enter your SSN (or ITIN) in the space provided. If you are a nonresident alien with no effectively connected income from sources within the United States, you do not need to enter an SSN or ITIN.

Corporation. This box is for any corporation **other than a personal service corporation.** If you check this box, enter the income tax form number to be filed by the entity in the space provided.

 *If you entered **"1120S"** after the "Corporation" checkbox, the corporation **must** file Form 2553 **no later than the 15th day of the 3rd month of the tax year the election is to take effect.** Until Form 2553 has been received and approved, you will be considered a Form 1120 filer. See the Instructions for Form 2553.*

Personal service corp. Check this box if the entity is a personal service corporation. An entity is a personal service corporation for a tax year only if:

-3-

• The principal activity of the entity during the testing period (prior tax year) for the tax year is the performance of personal services substantially by employee-owners, and

• The employee-owners own at least 10% of the fair market value of the outstanding stock in the entity on the last day of the testing period.

Personal services include performance of services in such fields as health, law, accounting, or consulting. For more information about personal service corporations, see the Instructions for Forms 1120 and 1120-A and Pub. 542.

Other nonprofit organization. Check this box if the nonprofit organization is other than a church or church-controlled organization and specify the type of nonprofit organization (for example, an educational organization).

 *If the organization also seeks tax-exempt status, you **must** file either Package 1023 or Package 1024. See Pub. 557 for more information.*

If the organization is covered by a group exemption letter, enter the four-digit **group exemption number (GEN).** (Do not confuse the GEN with the nine-digit EIN.) If you do not know the GEN, contact the parent organization. Get Pub. 557 for more information about group exemption numbers.

Plan administrator. If the plan administrator is an individual, enter the plan administrator's SSN in the space provided.

REMIC. Check this box if the entity has elected to be treated as a real estate mortgage investment conduit (REMIC). See the Instructions for Form 1066 for more information.

Limited liability company (LLC). An LLC is an entity organized under the laws of a state or foreign country as a limited liability company. For Federal tax purposes, an LLC may be treated as a partnership or corporation or be disregarded as an entity separate from its owner.

By **default,** a domestic LLC with only one member is **disregarded** as an entity separate from its owner and must include all of its income and expenses on the owner's tax return (e.g., **Schedule C (Form 1040)**). Also by default, a domestic LLC with two or more members is treated as a partnership. A domestic LLC may file Form 8832 to avoid either default classification and elect to be classified as an association taxable as a corporation. For more information on entity classifications (including the rules for foreign entities), see the instructions for Form 8832.

 *Do not file Form 8832 if the LLC accepts the default classifications above. **However, if the LLC will be electing S Corporation status, it must timely file both Form 8832 and Form 2553.***

Complete Form SS-4 for LLCs as follows:
• A single-member domestic LLC that accepts the default classification (above) does not need an EIN and generally should not file Form SS-4. Generally, the LLC

should use the name and EIN of its **owner** for all Federal tax purposes. However, the reporting and payment of employment taxes for employees of the LLC may be made using the name and EIN of **either** the owner or the LLC as explained in Notice 99-6. You can find Notice 99-6 on page 12 of Internal Revenue Bulletin 1999-3 at **www.irs.gov/pub/irs-irbs/irb99-03.pdf. (Note:** If the LLC applicant indicates in box 13 that it has employees or expects to have employees, the owner (whether an individual or other entity) of a single-member domestic LLC will also be assigned its own EIN (if it does not already have one) even if the LLC will be filing the employment tax returns.)

• A single-member, domestic LLC that accepts the default classification (above) and wants an EIN for filing employment tax returns (see above) or non-Federal purposes, such as a state requirement, must check the "Other" box and write "Disregarded Entity" or, when applicable, "Disregarded Entity—Sole Proprietorship" in the space provided.

• A multi-member, domestic LLC that accepts the default classification (above) must check the "Partnership" box.

• A domestic LLC that will be filing Form 8832 to elect corporate status must check the "Corporation" box and write in "Single-Member" or "Multi-Member" immediately below the "form number" entry line.

Line 9—Reason for applying. Check only **one** box. Do not enter "N/A."

Started new business. Check this box if you are starting a new business that requires an EIN. If you check this box, enter the type of business being started. **Do not** apply if you already have an EIN and are only adding another place of business.

Hired employees. Check this box if the existing business is requesting an EIN because it has hired or is hiring employees and is therefore required to file employment tax returns. **Do not** apply if you already have an EIN and are only hiring employees. For information on employment taxes (e.g., for family members), see Circular E.

 You may be required to make electronic deposits of all depository taxes (such as employment tax, excise tax, and corporate income tax) using the Electronic Federal Tax Payment System (EFTPS). See section 11, Depositing Taxes, of Circular E and Pub. 966.

Created a pension plan. Check this box if you have created a pension plan and need an EIN for reporting purposes. Also, enter the type of plan in the space provided.

 Check this box if you are applying for a trust EIN when a new pension plan is established. In addition, check the "Other" box in line 8a and write "Created a Pension Plan" in the space provided.

Banking purpose. Check this box if you are requesting an EIN for banking purposes only, and enter the banking purpose (for example, a bowling league for depositing dues or an investment club for dividend and interest reporting).

Changed type of organization. Check this box if the business is changing its type of organization. For example, the business was a sole proprietorship and has been incorporated or has become a partnership. If you check this box, specify in the space provided (including available space immediately below) the type of change made. For example, "From Sole Proprietorship to Partnership."

Purchased going business. Check this box if you purchased an existing business. **Do not** use the former owner's EIN unless you became the "owner" of a corporation by acquiring its stock.

Created a trust. Check this box if you created a trust, and enter the type of trust created. For example, indicate if the trust is a nonexempt charitable trust or a split-interest trust.

Exception. Do **not** file this form for certain grantor-type trusts. The trustee does not need an EIN for the trust if the trustee furnishes the name and TIN of the grantor/owner and the address of the trust to all payors. See the Instructions for Form 1041 for more information.

Do not *check this box if you are applying for a trust EIN when a new pension plan is established. Check "Created a pension plan."*

Other. Check this box if you are requesting an EIN for any other reason; and enter the reason. For example, a newly-formed state government entity should enter "Newly-Formed State Government Entity" in the space provided.

Line 10—Date business started or acquired. If you are starting a new business, enter the starting date of the business. If the business you acquired is already operating, enter the date you acquired the business. If you are changing the form of ownership of your business, enter the date the new ownership entity began. Trusts should enter the date the trust was legally created. Estates should enter the date of death of the decedent whose name appears on line 1 or the date when the estate was legally funded.

Line 11—Closing month of accounting year. Enter the last month of your accounting year or tax year. An accounting or tax year is usually 12 consecutive months, either a calendar year or a fiscal year (including a period of 52 or 53 weeks). A calendar year is 12 consecutive months ending on December 31. A fiscal year is either 12 consecutive months ending on the last day of any month other than December or a 52-53 week year. For more information on accounting periods, see Pub. 538.

Individuals. Your tax year generally will be a calendar year.

Partnerships. Partnerships must adopt one of the following tax years:
• The tax year of the majority of its partners,
• The tax year common to all of its principal partners,
• The tax year that results in the least aggregate deferral of income, or
• In certain cases, some other tax year.

See the Instructions for Form 1065 for more information.

REMICs. REMICs must have a calendar year as their tax year.

Personal service corporations. A personal service corporation generally must adopt a calendar year unless:
• It can establish a business purpose for having a different tax year, or
• It elects under section 444 to have a tax year other than a calendar year.

Trusts. Generally, a trust must adopt a calendar year except for the following:
• Tax-exempt trusts,
• Charitable trusts, and
• Grantor-owned trusts.

Line 12—First date wages or annuities were paid or will be paid. If the business has or will have employees, enter the date on which the business began or will begin to pay wages. If the business does not plan to have employees, enter "N/A."

Withholding agent. Enter the date you began or will begin to pay income (including annuities) to a nonresident alien. This also applies to individuals who are required to file Form 1042 to report alimony paid to a nonresident alien.

Line 13—Highest number of employees expected in the next 12 months. Complete each box by entering the number (including zero ("-0-")) of "Agricultural," "Household," or "Other" employees expected by the applicant in the next 12 months. For a definition of agricultural labor (farmwork), see Circular A.

Lines 14 and 15. Check the **one** box in line 14 that best describes the principal activity of the applicant's business. Check the "Other" box (and specify the applicant's principal activity) if none of the listed boxes applies.

Use line 15 to describe the applicant's principal line of business in more detail. For example, if you checked the "Construction" box in line 14, enter additional detail such as "General contractor for residential buildings" in line 15.

Construction. Check this box if the applicant is engaged in erecting buildings or other structures, (e.g., streets, highways, bridges, tunnels). The term "Construction" also includes special trade contractors, (e.g., plumbing, HVAC, electrical, carpentry, concrete, excavation, etc. contractors).

Real estate. Check this box if the applicant is engaged in renting or leasing real estate to others; managing, selling, buying or renting real estate for others; or providing related real estate services (e.g., appraisal services).

Rental and leasing. Check this box if the applicant is engaged in providing tangible goods such as autos, computers, consumer goods, or industrial machinery and equipment to customers in return for a periodic rental or lease payment.

Manufacturing. Check this box if the applicant is engaged in the mechanical, physical, or chemical transformation of materials, substances, or components into new products. The assembling of component parts of manufactured products is also considered to be manufacturing.

Transportation & warehousing. Check this box if the applicant provides transportation of passengers or cargo; warehousing or storage of goods; scenic or sight-seeing transportation; or support activities related to these modes of transportation.

Finance & insurance. Check this box if the applicant is engaged in transactions involving the creation, liquidation, or change of ownership of financial assets and/or facilitating such financial transactions; underwriting annuities/insurance policies; facilitating such underwriting by selling insurance policies; or by providing other insurance or employee-benefit related services.

Health care and social assistance. Check this box if the applicant is engaged in providing physical, medical, or psychiatric care using licensed health care professionals or providing social assistance activities such as youth centers, adoption agencies, individual/family services, temporary shelters, etc.

Accommodation & food services. Check this box if the applicant is engaged in providing customers with lodging, meal preparation, snacks, or beverages for immediate consumption.

Wholesale–agent/broker. Check this box if the applicant is engaged in arranging for the purchase or sale of goods owned by others or purchasing goods on a commission basis for goods traded in the wholesale market, usually between businesses.

Wholesale–other. Check this box if the applicant is engaged in selling goods in the wholesale market generally to other businesses for resale on their own account.

Retail. Check this box if the applicant is engaged in selling merchandise to the general public from a fixed store; by direct, mail-order, or electronic sales; or by using vending machines.

Other. Check this box if the applicant is engaged in an activity not described above. Describe the applicant's principal business activity in the space provided.

Lines 16a-c. Check the applicable box in line 16a to indicate whether or not the entity (or individual) applying for an EIN was issued one previously. Complete lines 16b and 16c **only** if the "Yes" box in line 16a is checked. If the applicant previously applied for **more than one** EIN, write "See Attached" in the empty space in line 16a and attach a separate sheet providing the line 16b and 16c information for each EIN previously requested.

Third Party Designee. Complete this section **only** if you want to authorize the named individual to receive the entity's EIN and answer questions about the completion of Form SS-4. The designee's authority terminates at the time the EIN is assigned and released to the designee. **You must complete the signature area for the authorization to be valid.**

Signature. When required, the application must be signed by **(a)** the individual, if the applicant is an individual, **(b)** the president, vice president, or other principal officer, if the applicant is a corporation, **(c)** a responsible and duly authorized member or officer having knowledge of its affairs, if the applicant is a partnership, government entity, or other unincorporated organization, or **(d)** the fiduciary, if the applicant is a trust or an estate. Foreign applicants may have any duly-authorized person, (e.g., division manager), sign Form SS-4.

Privacy Act and Paperwork Reduction Act Notice. We ask for the information on this form to carry out the Internal Revenue laws of the United States. We need it to comply with section 6109 and the regulations thereunder which generally require the inclusion of an employer identification number (EIN) on certain returns, statements, or other documents filed with the Internal Revenue Service. If your entity is required to obtain an EIN, you are required to provide all of the information requested on this form. Information on this form may be used to determine which Federal tax returns you are required to file and to provide you with related forms and publications.

We disclose this form to the Social Security Administration for their use in determining compliance with applicable laws. We may give this information to the Department of Justice for use in civil and criminal litigation, and to the cities, states, and the District of Columbia for use in administering their tax laws. We may also disclose this information to Federal and state agencies to enforce Federal nontax criminal laws and to combat terrorism.

We will be unable to issue an EIN to you unless you provide all of the requested information which applies to your entity. Providing false information could subject you to penalties.

You are not required to provide the information requested on a form that is subject to the Paperwork Reduction Act unless the form displays a valid OMB control number. Books or records relating to a form or its instructions must be retained as long as their contents may become material in the administration of any Internal Revenue law. Generally, tax returns and return information are confidential, as required by section 6103.

The time needed to complete and file this form will vary depending on individual circumstances. The estimated average time is:

Recordkeeping	6 min.
Learning about the law or the form	22 min.
Preparing the form	46 min.
Copying, assembling, and sending the form to the IRS	20 min.

If you have comments concerning the accuracy of these time estimates or suggestions for making this form simpler, we would be happy to hear from you. You can write to the Tax Products Coordinating Committee, Western Area Distribution Center, Rancho Cordova, CA 95743-0001. **Do not** send the form to this address. Instead, see **How To Apply** on page 1.

Printed on recycled paper

Form SS-8
(Rev. June 2003)
Department of the Treasury
Internal Revenue Service

Determination of Worker Status
for Purposes of Federal Employment Taxes
and Income Tax Withholding

OMB No. 1545-0004

Name of firm (or person) for whom the worker performed services	Worker's name

Firm's address (include street address, apt. or suite no., city, state, and ZIP code)	Worker's address (include street address, apt. or suite no., city, state, and ZIP code)

Trade name	Telephone number (include area code) ( )	Worker's social security number

Telephone number (include area code) ( )	Firm's employer identification number	Worker's employer identification number (if any)

If the worker is paid by a firm other than the one listed on this form for these services, enter the name, address, and employer identification number of the payer.

Important Information Needed To Process Your Request

We must have your permission to disclose your name and the information on this form and any attachments to other parties involved with this request. **Do we have your permission to disclose this information?** . . . . ☐ **Yes** ☐ **No**
If you answered "No" or did not mark a box, we will not process your request and will not issue a determination.

You must answer ALL items OR mark them "Unknown" or "Does not apply." If you need more space, attach another sheet.

A   This form is being completed by: ☐ Firm ☐ Worker; for services performed _____ to _____ .
                                                             (beginning date)   (ending date)

B   Explain your reason(s) for filing this form (e.g., you received a bill from the IRS, you believe you received a Form 1099 or Form W-2 erroneously, you are unable to get worker's compensation benefits, you were audited or are being audited by the IRS). --------------------------

C   Total number of workers who performed or are performing the same or similar services _____ .

D   How did the worker obtain the job? ☐ Application ☐ Bid ☐ Employment Agency ☐ Other (specify) _____ .

E   Attach copies of all supporting documentation (contracts, invoices, memos, Forms W-2, Forms 1099, IRS closing agreements, IRS rulings, etc.). In addition, please inform us of any current or past litigation concerning the worker's status. If no income reporting forms (Form 1099-MISC or W-2) were furnished to the worker, enter the amount of income earned for the year(s) at issue $ _____ .

F   Describe the firm's business. --------------------------

G   Describe the work done by the worker and provide the worker's job title. --------------------------

H   Explain why you believe the worker is an employee or an independent contractor. --------------------------

I   Did the worker perform services for the firm before getting this position? . . . . ☐ **Yes** ☐ **No** ☐ **N/A**
If "Yes," what were the dates of the prior service? --------------------------
If "Yes," explain the differences, if any, between the current and prior service. --------------------------

J   If the work is done under a written agreement between the firm and the worker, attach a copy (preferably signed by both parties). Describe the terms and conditions of the work arrangement. --------------------------

---

For Privacy Act and Paperwork Reduction Act Notice, see page 5.   Cat. No. 16106T   Form **SS-8** (Rev. 6-2003)

Part I   Behavioral Control

1   What specific training and/or instruction is the worker given by the firm? ....

2   How does the worker receive work assignments? ....

3   Who determines the methods by which the assignments are performed? ....

4   Who is the worker required to contact if problems or complaints arise and who is responsible for their resolution? ....

5   What types of reports are required from the worker? Attach examples. ....

6   Describe the worker's daily routine (i.e., schedule, hours, etc.). ....

7   At what location(s) does the worker perform services (e.g., firm's premises, own shop or office, home, customer's location, etc.)? ....

8   Describe any meetings the worker is required to attend and any penalties for not attending (e.g., sales meetings, monthly meetings, staff meetings, etc.). ....

9   Is the worker required to provide the services personally? . . . . ☐ **Yes** ☐ **No**

10   If substitutes or helpers are needed, who hires them? ....

11   If the worker hires the substitutes or helpers, is approval required? . . . . ☐ **Yes** ☐ **No**
If "Yes," by whom? ....

12   Who pays the substitutes or helpers? ....

13   Is the worker reimbursed if the worker pays the substitutes or helpers? . . . . ☐ **Yes** ☐ **No**
If "Yes," by whom?

Part II   Financial Control

1   List the supplies, equipment, materials, and property provided by each party:
The firm ....
The worker ....
Other party ....

2   Does the worker lease equipment? . . . . ☐ **Yes** ☐ **No**
If "Yes," what are the terms of the lease? (Attach a copy or explanatory statement.) ....

3   What expenses are incurred by the worker in the performance of services for the firm? ....

4   Specify which, if any, expenses are reimbursed by:
The firm ....
Other party ....

5   Type of pay the worker receives: ☐ Salary   ☐ Commission   ☐ Hourly Wage   ☐ Piece Work
☐ Lump Sum   ☐ Other (specify) ....
If type of pay is commission, and the firm guarantees a minimum amount of pay, specify amount $ _____ .

6   Is the worker allowed a drawing account for advances? . . . . ☐ **Yes** ☐ **No**
If "Yes," how often? ....
Specify any restrictions. ....

7   Whom does the customer pay? . . . . ☐ Firm   ☐ Worker
If worker, does the worker pay the total amount to the firm? ☐ **Yes** ☐ **No** If "No," explain. ....

8   Does the firm carry worker's compensation insurance on the worker? . . . . ☐ **Yes** ☐ **No**

9   What economic loss or financial risk, if any, can the worker incur beyond the normal loss of salary (e.g., loss or damage of equipment, material, etc.)? ....

Part III   Relationship of the Worker and Firm

1   List the benefits available to the worker (e.g., paid vacations, sick pay, pensions, bonuses). ----------------------------------

---

2   Can the relationship be terminated by either party without incurring liability or penalty? . . . .   ☐ **Yes**   ☐ **No**
      If "No," explain your answer. --

---

3   Does the worker perform similar services for others?   . . . .   ☐ **Yes**   ☐ **No**
      If "Yes," is the worker required to get approval from the firm? . . . .   ☐ **Yes**   ☐ **No**
4   Describe any agreements prohibiting competition between the worker and the firm while the worker is performing services or during any later
      period. Attach any available documentation. --

---

5   Is the worker a member of a union?   . . . .   ☐ **Yes**   ☐ **No**
6   What type of advertising, if any, does the worker do (e.g., a business listing in a directory, business cards, etc.)? Provide copies, if applicable.

---

7   If the worker assembles or processes a product at home, who provides the materials and instructions or pattern? ----------------

---

8   What does the worker do with the finished product (e.g., return it to the firm, provide it to another party, or sell it)? ----------

---

9   How does the firm represent the worker to its customers (e.g., employee, partner, representative, or contractor)? ----------------

---

10   If the worker no longer performs services for the firm, how did the relationship end? --

---

Part IV   **For Service Providers or Salespersons**—Complete this part if the worker provided a service directly to
                customers or is a salesperson.

1   What are the worker's responsibilities in soliciting new customers? --

---

2   Who provides the worker with leads to prospective customers? --
3   Describe any reporting requirements pertaining to the leads. --

---

4   What terms and conditions of sale, if any, are required by the firm? --
5   Are orders submitted to and subject to approval by the firm? . . . .   ☐ **Yes**   ☐ **No**
6   Who determines the worker's territory? --
7   Did the worker pay for the privilege of serving customers on the route or in the territory? . . . .   ☐ **Yes**   ☐ **No**
      If "Yes," whom did the worker pay? --
      If "Yes," how much did the worker pay? . . . . $ _____ .
8   Where does the worker sell the product (e.g., in a home, retail establishment, etc.)? -----------------------------------

---

9   List the product and/or services distributed by the worker (e.g., meat, vegetables, fruit, bakery products, beverages, or laundry or dry cleaning
      services). If more than one type of product and/or service is distributed, specify the principal one. --------------------------

---

10   Does the worker sell life insurance full time? . . . .   ☐ **Yes**   ☐ **No**
11   Does the worker sell other types of insurance for the firm? . . . .   ☐ **Yes**   ☐ **No**
      If "Yes," enter the percentage of the worker's total working time spent in selling other types of insurance.   . . .   _____%
12   If the worker solicits orders from wholesalers, retailers, contractors, or operators of hotels, restaurants, or other similar
      establishments, enter the percentage of the worker's time spent in the solicitation.   . . . .   _____%
13   Is the merchandise purchased by the customers for resale or use in their business operations? . . . .   ☐ **Yes**   ☐ **No**
      Describe the merchandise and state whether it is equipment installed on the customers' premises. ----------------------

---

Part V   Signature (see page 4)

Under penalties of perjury, I declare that I have examined this request, including accompanying documents, and to the best of my knowledge and belief, the facts
presented are true, correct, and complete.

Signature ▶ _____   Title ▶ _____   Date ▶ _____
                    (Type or print name below)

General Instructions

Section references are to the Internal Revenue Code unless otherwise noted.

Purpose

Firms and workers file Form SS-8 to request a determination of the status of a worker for purposes of Federal employment taxes and income tax withholding.

A Form SS-8 determination may be requested only in order to resolve Federal tax matters. If Form SS-8 is submitted for a tax year for which the statute of limitations on the tax return has expired, a determination letter will not be issued. The statute of limitations expires 3 years from the due date of the tax return or the date filed, whichever is later.

The IRS does not issue a determination letter for proposed transactions or on hypothetical situations. We may, however, issue an information letter when it is considered appropriate.

Definition

Firm. For the purposes of this form, the term "firm" means any individual, business enterprise, organization, state, or other entity for which a worker has performed services. The firm may or may not have paid the worker directly for these services. **If the firm was not responsible for payment for services, be sure to enter the name, address, and employer identification number of the payer on the first page of Form SS-8 below the identifying information for the firm and the worker.**

The SS-8 Determination Process

The IRS will acknowledge the receipt of your Form SS-8. Because there are usually two (or more) parties who could be affected by a determination of employment status, the IRS attempts to get information from all parties involved by sending those parties blank Forms SS-8 for completion. The case will be assigned to a technician who will review the facts, apply the law, and render a decision. The technician may ask for additional information from the requestor, from other involved parties, or from third parties that could help clarify the work relationship before rendering a decision. The IRS will generally issue a formal determination to the firm or payer (if that is a different entity), and will send a copy to the worker. A determination letter applies only to a worker (or a class of workers) requesting it, and the decision is binding on the IRS. In certain cases, a formal determination will not be issued. Instead, an information letter may be issued. Although an information letter is advisory only and is not binding on the IRS, it may be used to assist the worker to fulfill his or her Federal tax obligations.

Neither the SS-8 determination process nor the review of any records in connection with the determination constitutes an examination (audit) of any Federal tax return. If the periods under consideration have previously been examined, the SS-8 determination process will not constitute a reexamination under IRS reopening procedures. Because this is not an examination of any Federal tax return, the appeal rights available in connection with an examination do not apply to an SS-8 determination. However, if you disagree with a determination and you have additional information concerning the work relationship that you believe was not previously considered, you may request that the determining office reconsider the determination.

Completing Form SS-8

Answer all questions as completely as possible. Attach additional sheets if you need more space. Provide information for all years the worker provided services for the firm. Determinations are based on the entire relationship between the firm and the worker.

Additional copies of this form may be obtained by calling 1-800-829-4933 or from the IRS website at **www.irs.gov.**

Fee

There is no fee for requesting an SS-8 determination letter.

Signature

Form SS-8 must be signed and dated by the taxpayer. A stamped signature will not be accepted.

The person who signs for a corporation must be an officer of the corporation who has personal knowledge of the facts. If the corporation is a member of an affiliated group filing a consolidated return, it must be signed by an officer of the common parent of the group.

The person signing for a trust, partnership, or limited liability company must be, respectively, a trustee, general partner, or member-manager who has personal knowledge of the facts.

Where To File

Send the completed Form SS-8 to the address listed below for the firm's location. However, for cases involving Federal agencies, send Form SS-8 to the Internal Revenue Service, Attn: CC:CORP:T:C, Ben Franklin Station, P.O. Box 7604, Washington, DC 20044.

Firm's location:	Send to:
Alaska, Arizona, Arkansas, California, Colorado, Hawaii, Idaho, Illinois, Iowa, Kansas, Minnesota, Missouri, Montana, Nebraska, Nevada, New Mexico, North Dakota, Oklahoma, Oregon, South Dakota, Texas, Utah, Washington, Wisconsin, Wyoming, American Samoa, Guam, Puerto Rico, U.S. Virgin Islands	Internal Revenue Service SS-8 Determinations P.O. Box 630 Stop 631 Holtsville, NY 11742-0630
Alabama, Connecticut, Delaware, District of Columbia, Florida, Georgia, Indiana, Kentucky, Louisiana, Maine, Maryland, Massachusetts, Michigan, Mississippi, New Hampshire, New Jersey, New York, North Carolina, Ohio, Pennsylvania, Rhode Island, South Carolina, Tennessee, Vermont, Virginia, West Virginia, all other locations not listed	Internal Revenue Service SS-8 Determinations 40 Lakemont Road Newport, VT 05855-1555

Instructions for Workers

If you are requesting a determination for more than one firm, complete a separate Form SS-8 for each firm.

 Form SS-8 is not a claim for refund of social security and Medicare taxes or Federal income tax withholding.

If the IRS determines that you are an employee, you are responsible for filing an amended return for any corrections related to this decision. A determination that a worker is an employee does not necessarily reduce any current or prior tax liability. For more information, call 1-800-829-1040.

Time for filing a claim for refund. Generally, you must file your claim for a credit or refund within 3 years from the date your original return was filed or within 2 years from the date the tax was paid, whichever is later.

Filing Form SS-8 does not prevent the expiration of the time in which a claim for a refund must be filed. If you are concerned about a refund, and the statute of limitations for filing a claim for refund for the year(s) at issue has not yet expired, you should file **Form 1040X,** Amended U.S. Individual Income Tax Return, to protect your statute of limitations. File a separate Form 1040X for each year.

On the Form 1040X you file, do not complete lines 1 through 24 on the form. Write "Protective Claim" at the top of the form, sign and date it. In addition, you should enter the following statement in Part II, Explanation of Changes to Income, Deductions, and Credits: "Filed Form SS-8 with the Internal Revenue Service Office in (Holtsville, NY; Newport, VT; or Washington, DC; as appropriate). By filing this protective claim, I reserve the right to file a claim for any refund that may be due after a determination of my employment tax status has been completed."

Filing Form SS-8 does not alter the requirement to timely file an income tax return. Do not delay filing your tax return in anticipation of an answer to your SS-8 request. In addition, if applicable, do not delay in responding to a request for payment while waiting for a determination of your worker status.

Instructions for Firms

If a **worker** has requested a determination of his or her status while working for you, you will receive a request from the IRS to complete a Form SS-8. In cases of this type, the IRS usually gives each party an opportunity to present a statement of the facts because any decision will affect the employment tax status of the parties. Failure to respond to this request will not prevent the IRS from issuing a determination letter based on the information he or she has made available so that the worker may fulfill his or her Federal tax obligations. However, the information that you provide is extremely valuable in determining the status of the worker.

If **you** are requesting a determination for a particular class of worker, complete the form for **one** individual who is representative of the class of workers whose status is in question. If you want a written determination for more than one class of workers, complete a separate Form SS-8 for one worker from each class whose status is typical of that class. A written determination for any worker will apply to other workers of the same class if the facts are not materially different for these workers. Please provide a list of names and addresses of all workers potentially affected by this determination.

If you have a reasonable basis for not treating a worker as an employee, you may be relieved from having to pay employment taxes for that worker under section 530 of the 1978 Revenue Act. However, this relief provision cannot be considered in conjunction with a Form SS-8 determination because the determination does not constitute an examination of any tax return. For more information regarding section 530 of the 1978 Revenue Act and to determine if you qualify for relief under this section, you may visit the IRS website at **www.irs.gov.**

Privacy Act and Paperwork Reduction Act Notice. We ask for the information on this form to carry out the Internal Revenue laws of the United States. This information will be used to determine the employment status of the worker(s) described on the form. Subtitle C, Employment Taxes, of the Internal Revenue Code imposes employment taxes on wages. Sections 3121(d), 3306(a), and 3401(c) and (d) and the related regulations define employee and employer for purposes of employment taxes imposed under Subtitle C. Section 6001 authorizes the IRS to request information needed to determine if a worker(s) or firm is subject to these taxes. Section 6109 requires you to provide your taxpayer identification number. Neither workers nor firms are required to request a status determination, but if you choose to do so, you must provide the information requested on this form. Failure to provide the requested information may prevent us from making a status determination. If any worker or the firm has requested a status determination and you are being asked to provide information for use in that determination, you are not required to provide the requested information. However, failure to provide such information will prevent the IRS from considering it in making the status determination. Providing false or fraudulent information may subject you to penalties. Routine uses of this information include providing it to the Department of Justice for use in civil and criminal litigation, to the Social Security Administration for the administration of social security programs, and to cities, states, and the District of Columbia for the administration of their tax laws. We may also disclose this information to Federal and state agencies to enforce Federal nontax criminal laws and to combat terrorism. We may provide this information to the affected worker(s) or the firm as part of the status determination process.

You are not required to provide the information requested on a form that is subject to the Paperwork Reduction Act unless the form displays a valid OMB control number. Books or records relating to a form or its instructions must be retained as long as their contents may become material in the administration of any Internal Revenue law. Generally, tax returns and return information are confidential, as required by section 6103.

The time needed to complete and file this form will vary depending on individual circumstances. The estimated average time is: **Recordkeeping,** 22 hrs.; **Learning about the law or the form,** 47 min.; and **Preparing and sending the form to the IRS,** 1 hr., 11 min. If you have comments concerning the accuracy of these time estimates or suggestions for making this form simpler, we would be happy to hear from you. You can write to the Tax Products Coordinating Committee, Western Area Distribution Center, Rancho Cordova, CA 95743-0001. **Do not** send the tax form to this address. Instead, see **Where To File** on page 4.

This page intentionally blank.

Form W-4 (2006)

Purpose. Complete Form W-4 so that your employer can withhold the correct federal income tax from your pay. Because your tax situation may change, you may want to refigure your withholding each year.

Exemption from withholding. If you are exempt, complete only lines 1, 2, 3, 4, and 7 and sign the form to validate it. Your exemption for 2006 expires February 16, 2007. See Pub. 505, Tax Withholding and Estimated Tax.

Note. You cannot claim exemption from withholding if (a) your income exceeds $850 and includes more than $300 of unearned income (for example, interest and dividends) and (b) another person can claim you as a dependent on their tax return.

Basic instructions. If you are not exempt, complete the **Personal Allowances Worksheet** below. The worksheets on page 2 adjust your withholding allowances based on itemized deductions, certain credits, adjustments to income, or two-earner/two-job situations. Complete all worksheets that apply. However, you may claim fewer (or zero) allowances.

Head of household. Generally, you may claim head of household filing status on your tax return only if you are unmarried and pay more than 50% of the costs of keeping up a home for yourself and your dependent(s) or other qualifying individuals. See line **E** below.

Tax credits. You can take projected tax credits into account in figuring your allowable number of withholding allowances. Credits for child or dependent care expenses and the child tax credit may be claimed using the **Personal Allowances Worksheet** below. See Pub. 919, How Do I Adjust My Tax Withholding, for information on converting your other credits into withholding allowances.

Nonwage income. If you have a large amount of nonwage income, such as interest or dividends, consider making estimated tax payments using Form 1040-ES, Estimated Tax for Individuals. Otherwise, you may owe additional tax.

Two earners/two jobs. If you have a working spouse or more than one job, figure the total number of allowances you are entitled to claim on all jobs using worksheets from only one Form W-4. Your withholding usually will be most accurate when all allowances are claimed on the Form W-4 for the highest paying job and zero allowances are claimed on the others.

Nonresident alien. If you are a nonresident alien, see the Instructions for Form 8233 before completing this Form W-4.

Check your withholding. After your Form W-4 takes effect, use Pub. 919 to see how the dollar amount you are having withheld compares to your projected total tax for 2006. See Pub. 919, especially if your earnings exceed $130,000 (Single) or $180,000 (Married).

Recent name change? If your name on line 1 differs from that shown on your social security card, call 1-800-772-1213 to initiate a name change and obtain a social security card showing your correct name.

Personal Allowances Worksheet (Keep for your records.)

A Enter "1" for **yourself** if no one else can claim you as a dependent . . . . **A** _____

B Enter "1" if:
- You are single and have only one job; or
- You are married, have only one job, and your spouse does not work; or
- Your wages from a second job or your spouse's wages (or the total of both) are $1,000 or less.

. . **B** _____

C Enter "1" for your **spouse**. But, you may choose to enter "-0-" if you are married and have either a working spouse or more than one job. (Entering "-0-" may help you avoid having too little tax withheld.) . . . . **C** _____

D Enter number of **dependents** (other than your spouse or yourself) you will claim on your tax return . . . . . . **D** _____

E Enter "1" if you will file as **head of household** on your tax return (see conditions under **Head of household** above) . **E** _____

F Enter "1" if you have at least $1,500 of **child or dependent care expenses** for which you plan to claim a credit . . **F** _____
(**Note.** Do **not** include child support payments. See **Pub. 503,** Child and Dependent Care Expenses, for details.)

G **Child Tax Credit** (including additional child tax credit):
- If your total income will be less than $55,000 ($82,000 if married), enter "2" for each eligible child.
- If your total income will be between $55,000 and $84,000 ($82,000 and $119,000 if married), enter "1" for each eligible child plus "1" **additional** if you have four or more eligible children. **G** _____

H Add lines A through G and enter total here. (**Note.** This may be different from the number of exemptions you claim on your tax return.) ▶ **H** _____

For accuracy, complete all worksheets that apply.	• If you plan to **itemize or claim adjustments to income** and want to reduce your withholding, see the **Deductions and Adjustments Worksheet** on page 2.
	• If you have **more than one job** or are **married and you and your spouse both work** and the combined earnings from all jobs exceed $35,000 ($25,000 if married) see the **Two-Earner/Two-Job Worksheet** on page 2 to avoid having too little tax withheld.
	• If **neither** of the above situations applies, **stop here** and enter the number from line H on line 5 of Form W-4 below.

- - - - - - - - - - - - - - - - - - **Cut here and give Form W-4 to your employer. Keep the top part for your records.** - - - - - - - - - - - - - - - - - -

Form **W-4**

Department of the Treasury
Internal Revenue Service

Employee's Withholding Allowance Certificate

▶ **Whether you are entitled to claim a certain number of allowances or exemption from withholding is subject to review by the IRS. Your employer may be required to send a copy of this form to the IRS.**

OMB No. 1545-0074

2006

1 Type or print your first name and middle initial.	Last name		2 Your social security number

Home address (number and street or rural route)	3 ☐ Single ☐ Married ☐ Married, but withhold at higher Single rate.
City or town, state, and ZIP code	**Note.** If married, but legally separated, or spouse is a nonresident alien, check the "Single" box.

4 If your last name differs from that shown on your social security card, check here. You must call 1-800-772-1213 for a new card. ▶ ☐

5 Total number of allowances you are claiming (from line **H** above **or** from the applicable worksheet on page 2) | **5** _____

6 Additional amount, if any, you want withheld from each paycheck . . . . | **6** $ _____

7 I claim exemption from withholding for 2006, and I certify that I meet **both** of the following conditions for exemption.
- Last year I had a right to a refund of **all** federal income tax withheld because I had **no** tax liability **and**
- This year I expect a refund of **all** federal income tax withheld because I expect to have **no** tax liability.

If you meet both conditions, write "Exempt" here . . . . ▶ | **7** _____

Under penalties of perjury, I declare that I have examined this certificate and to the best of my knowledge and belief, it is true, correct, and complete.

Employee's signature
(Form is not valid unless you sign it.) ▶ _____   **Date** ▶ _____

8 Employer's name and address (Employer: Complete lines 8 and 10 only if sending to the IRS.)	9 Office code (optional)	10 Employer identification number (EIN)

For Privacy Act and Paperwork Reduction Act Notice, see page 2.   Cat. No. 10220Q   Form **W-4** (2006)

Form W-4 (2006) Page **2**

Deductions and Adjustments Worksheet

Note. Use this worksheet *only* if you plan to itemize deductions, claim certain credits, or claim adjustments to income on your 2006 tax return.

1	Enter an estimate of your 2006 itemized deductions. These include qualifying home mortgage interest, charitable contributions, state and local taxes, medical expenses in excess of 7.5% of your income, and miscellaneous deductions. (For 2006, you may have to reduce your itemized deductions if your income is over $150,500 ($75,250 if married filing separately). See *Worksheet 3* in Pub. 919 for details.)	**1**	$
2	Enter: { $10,300 if married filing jointly or qualifying widow(er) $ 7,550 if head of household $ 5,150 if single or married filing separately }	**2**	$
3	**Subtract** line 2 from line 1. If line 2 is greater than line 1, enter "-0-"	**3**	$
4	Enter an estimate of your 2006 adjustments to income, including alimony, deductible IRA contributions, and student loan interest	**4**	$
5	**Add** lines 3 and 4 and enter the total. (Include any amount for credits from *Worksheet 7* in Pub. 919)	**5**	$
6	Enter an estimate of your 2006 nonwage income (such as dividends or interest)	**6**	$
7	**Subtract** line 6 from line 5. Enter the result, but not less than "-0-"	**7**	$
8	**Divide** the amount on line 7 by $3,300 and enter the result here. Drop any fraction	**8**	
9	Enter the number from the **Personal Allowances Worksheet,** line H, page 1	**9**	
10	**Add** lines 8 and 9 and enter the total here. If you plan to use the **Two-Earner/Two-Job Worksheet,** also enter this total on line 1 below. Otherwise, **stop here** and enter this total on Form W-4, line 5, page 1	**10**	

Two-Earner/Two-Job Worksheet (See *Two earners/two jobs* on page 1.)

Note. Use this worksheet *only* if the instructions under line H on page 1 direct you here.

1	Enter the number from line H, page 1 (or from line 10 above if you used the **Deductions and Adjustments Worksheet**)	**1**	
2	Find the number in **Table 1** below that applies to the **LOWEST** paying job and enter it here	**2**	
3	If line 1 is **more than or equal to** line 2, subtract line 2 from line 1. Enter the result here (if zero, enter "-0-") and on Form W-4, line 5, page 1. **Do not** use the rest of this worksheet	**3**	

Note. If line 1 is *less than* line 2, enter "-0-" on Form W-4, line 5, page 1. Complete lines 4–9 below to calculate the additional withholding amount necessary to avoid a year-end tax bill.

4	Enter the number from line 2 of this worksheet	**4**	
5	Enter the number from line 1 of this worksheet	**5**	
6	**Subtract** line 5 from line 4	**6**	
7	Find the amount in **Table 2** below that applies to the **HIGHEST** paying job and enter it here	**7**	$
8	**Multiply** line 7 by line 6 and enter the result here. This is the additional annual withholding needed	**8**	$
9	Divide line 8 by the number of pay periods remaining in 2006. For example, divide by 26 if you are paid every two weeks and you complete this form in December 2005. Enter the result here and on Form W-4, line 6, page 1. This is the additional amount to be withheld from each paycheck	**9**	$

Table 1: Two-Earner/Two-Job Worksheet

Married Filing Jointly						All Others	
If wages from **HIGHEST** paying job are—	AND, wages from **LOWEST** paying job are—	Enter on line 2 above	If wages from **HIGHEST** paying job are—	AND, wages from **LOWEST** paying job are—	Enter on line 2 above	If wages from **LOWEST** paying job are—	Enter on line 2 above
$0 - $42,000	$0 - $4,500	0	$42,001 and over	32,001 - 38,000	6	$0 - $6,000	0
	4,501 - 9,000	1		38,001 - 46,000	7	6,001 - 12,000	1
	9,001 - 18,000	2		46,001 - 55,000	8	12,001 - 19,000	2
	18,001 and over	3		55,001 - 60,000	9	19,001 - 26,000	3
				60,001 - 65,000	10	26,001 - 35,000	4
$42,001 and over	$0 - $4,500	0		65,001 - 75,000	11	35,001 - 50,000	5
	4,501 - 9,000	1		75,001 - 95,000	12	50,001 - 65,000	6
	9,001 - 18,000	2		95,001 - 105,000	13	65,001 - 80,000	7
	18,001 - 22,000	3		105,001 - 120,000	14	80,001 - 90,000	8
	22,001 - 26,000	4		120,001 and over	15	90,001 - 120,000	9
	26,001 - 32,000	5				120,001 and over	10

Table 2: Two-Earner/Two-Job Worksheet

Married Filing Jointly		All Others	
If wages from **HIGHEST** paying job are—	Enter on line 7 above	If wages from **HIGHEST** paying job are—	Enter on line 7 above
$0 - $60,000	$500	$0 - $30,000	$500
60,001 - 115,000	830	30,001 - 75,000	830
115,001 - 165,000	920	75,001 - 145,000	920
165,001 - 290,000	1,090	145,001 - 330,000	1,090
290,001 and over	1,160	330,001 and over	1,160

 Printed on recycled paper

APPLICATION TO COLLECT AND/OR REPORT TAX IN FLORIDA

Who must apply?

DR-1
R. 07/05

FLORIDA DEPARTMENT OF REVENUE

You may be required to register to collect, accrue, and remit the taxes or fees listed below if you are engaged in any of the activities listed beneath each tax or fee.

Sales Tax

Complete Sections A, B, and H	Pay $5 fee (in-state only)*

- Sales, leases, or licenses to use certain property or goods (tangible personal property).
- Sales and rentals/admissions, amusement machine receipts, or vending machine receipts for all taxable items.
- Repair or alteration of tangible personal property.
- Leases or licenses to use commercial real property (includes management companies).
- Rental of transient (six months or less) living or sleeping accommodations (includes management companies). A local tourist development tax (bed tax) may also apply. Contact the taxing authority in the county where the property is located.
- Sales or rental of self-propelled, power-drawn, or power-driven farm equipment.
- Sales of electric power or energy.
- Sales of prepaid telephone calling cards.
- Sales of commercial pest control services, nonresidential building cleaning services, commercial/residential burglary and security services, or detective services.
- Sales of secondhand goods. A secondhand dealer registration (Form DR-1S) may also be required.

*Note: If you are registering an in-state business or property location, you must submit a $5 fee with this application. Online registration is free.

Documentary Stamp Tax

Complete Sections A, F, and H	NO fee

- Entering into written financing agreements (five or more transactions per month).
- Making title loans.
- Self-financing dealers (buy here – pay here).
- Banks, mortgage companies, and consumer finance companies.
- Promissory notes.

Use Tax

Complete Sections A, B, and H	NO fee

- Any taxable purchases that were not taxed by the seller at the time of purchase.
- Repeated untaxed purchases through the Internet or from out-of-state vendors.
- Any purchases originally for resale, but later used or consumed by your business or for personal use.
- Use of dyed diesel fuel for off-road purposes.

Unemployment Tax

Complete Sections A, D, and H	NO fee

- Paid wages of $1,500 in any quarter or employed at least one worker for 20 weeks in a calendar year. (Payments made to corporate officers are wages.)
- Applicant is a governmental entity, Indian tribe or tribal unit.
- Hold a section 501(c)(3) exemption from federal income tax and employ four or more workers for 20 weeks in a calendar year.
- Agricultural employer with a $10,000 cash quarterly payroll, or who employs five or more workers for 20 weeks in a calendar year.
- Private home or college club that paid $1,000 cash in a quarter for domestic services.
- Acquired all or part of the organization, trade, business, or assets of a liable employer.
- Liable for federal unemployment taxes.
- Previously liable for unemployment tax in the State of Florida.

Gross Receipts Tax

Complete Sections A, E, and H	NO fee

- Sales of electric power or gas.

Register Online

It's FREE, fast, easy, and secure

You can file this application online, via the Department's Internet site at www.myflorida.com/dor/eservices/apps/register. **There is no fee for Internet registration. See instructions, next page.**

Communications Services Tax

Complete Sections A, G, and H	NO fee

- Sales of communications services (telephone, paging, certain facsimile services, videoconferencing).
- Sales of cable services.
- Sales of direct-to-home satellite services.
- Resellers (for example, pay telephones and prepaid calling arrangements).
- Seeking a direct pay permit.

Solid Waste Fees and Pollutants Tax

Complete Sections A, B, C, and H	Pay $30 fee (drycleaning only)*

- Sales of new tires for motor vehicles.
- Sales of new or remanufactured lead-acid batteries.
- Rental or lease of motor vehicles to others.
- Sales of dry-cleaning services (plants or drop-off facilities). *Note: You must submit a $30 fee with this application. Online registration is free.

How can I register online?

The DR-1 application is on the Department's web site at **www.myflorida.com/dor/eservices/apps/register**. An interactive wizard will guide you through an application from start to finish. Before you begin, gather specific information about your business activities, location, and beginning dates. **There are no fees for online registration.**

Sales and use tax certificate numbers will be issued within three business days of your online submission. After that time, you can return to the site and retrieve your certificate number.

How can I be sure that the information I submit online is secure?

The Department's Internet registration site uses 128-bit secure socket layer technology and has been certified by VeriSign, an industry leader in data security.

If a husband and wife jointly operate and own a business, what type of ownership must we indicate?

Normally, when a husband and wife jointly own and operate a business, the ownership is a "partnership." We suggest you contact the Internal Revenue Service for more information on partnership reporting requirements.

What will I receive from the Department once I register?

1. A *Certificate of Registration* or notification of liability for the tax(es) for which you registered.
2. Personalized returns or reports for filing, with instructions.

3. For active sales tax and communications services tax dealers, an *Annual Resale Certificate* will accompany the *Certificate of Registration.*

What is an *Annual Resale Certificate*?

The Department issues *Annual Resale Certificates* to active, registered sales tax dealers and communications services tax dealers. The *Annual Resale Certificate* allows businesses to make tax-exempt purchases from their suppliers, provided the item or service is purchased for resale. A copy of a current *Annual Resale Certificate* must be extended to the supplier; otherwise, tax must be paid on the transaction at the time of purchase. Tax Information Publication (TIP) 99A01-34 explains the resale provisions for sales and use tax. TIP 01BER-01 explains the resale provisions for communications services tax. Consult the Department's Internet site for further information. **Misuse of the *Annual Resale Certificate* will subject the user to penalties as provided by law.**

What are my responsibilities?

1. You must register for all taxes for which you are liable before beginning business activities, otherwise you may be subject to penalties. For more information, visit our Internet site or contact Taxpayer Services.
2. Complete and return this application to the Florida Department of Revenue with the applicable registration fee. IF MAILING, DO NOT SEND CASH. SEND CHECK OR MONEY ORDER.
3. Collect and/or report tax appropriately, maintain accurate records, post your certificate (if required), and file returns and reports timely. A return/report must be filed even if no tax is due.

4. Notify the Department if your address changes, your business entity or activity changes, you open additional locations, or you close your business.
5. Provide your certificate or account number on all returns, remittances, and correspondence.

What if my business has more than one location?

Sales tax: You must complete a separate application for each location. **Gross receipts tax on electric power or gas:** You have the option of registering all locations under one account number or separately registering each location. **Documentary stamp tax:** You must register each location where books and records are maintained. **Communications services tax and unemployment tax:** You must register each entity that has its own Federal Employer Identification Number (FEIN).

Solid waste fees and pollutants tax (rental car surcharge): You must register for each county where you have a rental location.

What if I am managing commercial or residential rental property for others?

For sales tax, commercial property managers must use this application; residential property managers may use Form DR-1C, *Application for Collective Registration for Rental of Living or Sleeping Accommodations*. Contact Central Registration at 850-488-9750 for assistance.

Are educational seminars offered?

Yes. To get a schedule of upcoming seminars or to register for one, visit us online at **www.myflorida.com/dor** or call the service center nearest you.

Before returning application, remove this page and retain for future reference.

FLORIDA DEPARTMENT OF REVENUE SERVICE CENTERS

CT—Central Time
ET—Eastern Time

Alachua Service Center
14107 US Highway 441 Ste 100
Alachua FL 32615-6390
386-418-4444 (ET)

Clearwater Service Center
Arbor Shoreline Office Park
19337 US Highway 19 N Ste 200
Clearwater FL 33764-3149
727-538-7400 (ET)

Cocoa Service Center
2428 Clearlake Rd Bldg M
Cocoa FL 32922-5731
321-504-0950 (ET)

Coral Springs Service Center
Florida Sunrise Tower
3111 N University Dr Ste 501
Coral Springs FL 33065-5090
954-346-3000 (ET)

Daytona Beach Service Center
1821 Business Park Blvd
Daytona Beach FL 32114-1230
386-274-6600 (ET)

Fort Myers Service Center
2295 Victoria Ave Ste 270
Fort Myers FL 33901-3871
239-338-2400 (ET)

Fort Pierce Service Center
Benton Building
337 N US Highway 1 Ste 207-B
Fort Pierce FL 34950-4255
772-429-2900 (ET)

Hollywood Service Center
Taft Office Complex
6565 Taft St Ste 300
Hollywood FL 33024-4044
954-967-1000 (ET)

Jacksonville Service Center
921 N Davis St A250
Jacksonville FL 32209-6829
904-359-6070 (ET)

Key West Service Center
3118 Flagler Ave
Key West FL 33040-4602
305-292-6725 (ET)

Lake City Service Center
1401 W US Highway 90 Ste 100
Lake City FL 32055-6123
386-758-0420 (ET)

Lakeland Service Center
230 S Florida Ave Ste 101
Lakeland FL 33801-4625
863-499-2260 (ET)

Leesburg Service Center
1415 S 14th St Ste 103
Leesburg FL 34748-6686
352-315-4470 (ET)

Maitland Service Center
Ste 160
2301 Maitland Center Parkway
Maitland FL 32751-4192
407-475-1200 (ET)

Marianna Service Center
4230 Lafayette St Ste D
Marianna FL 32446-8231
850-482-9518 (CT)

Miami Service Center
8175 NW 12th St Ste 119
Miami FL 33126-1828
305-470-5001 (ET)

Naples Service Center
3073 Horseshoe Dr S Ste 110
Naples FL 34104-6145
239-434-4858 (ET)

Orlando Service Center
AmSouth Bank Building
5401 S Kirkman Rd 5th Floor
Orlando FL 32819-7911
407-903-7350 (ET)

Panama City Service Center
703 W 15th St Ste A
Panama City FL 32401-2238
850-872-4165 (CT)

Pensacola Service Center
3670C N L St
Pensacola FL 32505-5217
850-595-5170 (CT)

Port Richey Service Center
6709 Ridge Rd Ste 300
Port Richey FL 34668-6842
727-841-4407 (ET)

Sarasota Service Center
Sarasota Main Plaza
1991 Main St Ste 240
Sarasota FL 34236-5940
941-361-6001 (ET)

Tallahassee Service Center
2410 Allen Rd
Tallahassee FL 32312-2603
850-488-9719 (ET)

Tampa Service Center
Ste 100
6302 E Martin Luther King Blvd
Tampa FL 33619-1166
813-744-6344 (ET)

West Palm Beach Service Center
2468 Metrocentre Blvd
West Palm Beach FL 33407-3105
561-640-2800 (ET)

Central Registration
5050 W Tennessee St
Tallahassee, FL 32399-0100
850-488-9750

Taxpayer Services
800-352-3671 or
850-488-6800
TDD: 800-367-8331

Internet Site
www.myflorida.com/dor

Tax Law Library
www.myflorida.com/dor/law

APPLICATION TO COLLECT AND/OR REPORT TAX IN FLORIDA
SECTION A — BUSINESS INFORMATION

DR-1
R. 07/05
Page 1

Please use BLACK or BLUE ink ONLY and type or print clearly.

Answer ALL questions in the section(s) that apply to your business.

1. This application is for (check all that apply):

✓	Tax Type	Fee Due	Complete Sections
	Sales and Use Tax	$5.00 *	A, B, H
	Use Tax Only	No fee	A, B, H
	Solid Waste Fees and Pollutants Tax	$30.00**	A, B, C, H
	Unemployment Tax	No fee	A, D, H
	Gross Receipts Tax on Electric Power and Gas	No fee	A, E, H
	Documentary Stamp Tax	No fee	A, F, H
	Communications Services Tax	No fee	A, G, H

*The $5 registration fee does not apply if:
- Your business location is outside the State of Florida.
- Your business is moving from one Florida county to another.
- You register online.

**The $30 registration fee applies to drycleaning only. There is no fee for online registration.

2. Indicate whether this is a new registration or a change to an existing registration:

New

A. ☐ New business entity
B. ☐ New business location
C. ☐ New tax obligation at existing location

Provide certificate number if you checked B or C:

☐☐ – ☐☐☐☐☐☐☐ – ☐

Beginning date of business activity:

☐☐ / ☐☐ / ☐☐☐☐
month   day   year

Provide the date this business location or entity became or will become liable for Florida tax(es). Do not use your incorporation date unless that is the date your business became liable for tax. **If you have been in business longer than 30 days prior to registering, contact the DOR service center nearest you.**

Change

D. ☐ Change of county location (Business is moving from one Florida county to another)
E. ☐ Change of legal entity
F. ☐ Change of ownership

If you have checked Box D, E, or F, the Department will cancel your existing certificate(s) and issue a new one. Provide the certificate number(s) to be canceled. (Attach additional sheet if necessary.)

☐☐ – ☐☐☐☐☐☐☐ – ☐

If your business is relocating within the same county, do not use this application. Contact the Department to change your address.

This change is effective (enter date):

☐☐ / ☐☐ / ☐☐☐☐
month   day   year

Receipt Date Stamp

3. If this is a seasonal business (not open year-round), list the months of your open season.

Beginning date: ☐☐ / ☐☐ / ☐☐☐☐   Ending date: ☐☐ / ☐☐ / ☐☐☐☐
              month   day   year   month   day   year

** PLEASE TYPE OR PRINT CLEARLY **

4. Trade, fictitious (d/b/a), or location name:	**Business telephone number:**
5. Legal name of corporation, partnership, or individual (last, first, middle):	**Owner telephone number:**
6. Complete physical address of business or real property. Home-based businesses and non-permanent flea market/craft show vendors must use their home addresses. Listing a post office box, private mailbox, or rural route number is not permitted.	**Fax number:**
City/State/ZIP:	**County:**

7. Mail to the attention of:

Mailing address:

City/State/ZIP:	**Would you like to receive correspondence via e-mail?** ☐ Yes ☐ No	**E-mail address:**

8. If you have a **Consolidated Sales Tax Number** and want to include this business location, please complete the following:

_____
Consolidated registration name on record with the Florida Department of Revenue.
If you want to obtain a new consolidated number, contact the Department and request Form DR-1CON.

8 0 – ☐☐☐☐☐☐☐☐ – ☐
Consolidated registration number

9. Business Entity Identification Number. If an FEIN is not required for your business entity, the social security number of the owner will be accepted. If you are registering for unemployment tax, you **must** have an FEIN. Social security numbers are used by the Department as unique identifiers for the administration of Florida's tax laws. They are confidential under sections 119.0721 and 213.053, Florida Statutes, and are not subject to disclosure as public records.

a. Federal Employer Identification Number (FEIN):
☐☐ – ☐☐☐☐☐☐☐

or

b. Social Security Number (SSN) of owner:
☐☐☐ – ☐☐ – ☐☐☐☐

(If you are required to have an FEIN, but have not yet been assigned one you may call the Internal Revenue Service at 800-829-4933 to request one.)

SECTION A — BUSINESS INFORMATION (CONT'D.)

10. Identify proprietors or owners, partners, officers, members, or trustees. Include the person whose social security number is listed under Question 9. **Without this information, processing of your application may be stopped.**

Name Title	Social security number and Driver license number and state	Home address City/State/ZIP	Telephone number
_ _ _ _ _ _ _ _	_ _ _ _ _ _ _	_ _ _ _ _ _ _	(_ _ _) _ _ _ - _ _ _ _
_ _ _ _ _ _ _ _	_ _ _ _ _ _ _	_ _ _ _ _ _ _	(_ _ _) _ _ _ - _ _ _ _
_ _ _ _ _ _ _ _	_ _ _ _ _ _ _	_ _ _ _ _ _ _	(_ _ _) _ _ _ - _ _ _ _
_ _ _ _ _ _ _ _	_ _ _ _ _ _ _	_ _ _ _ _ _ _	(_ _ _) _ _ _ - _ _ _ _

11. **Type of ownership** - Check the box next to the exact entity structure of your business.

☐ **Sole proprietorship** - An unincorporated business that is owned by one individual.

☐ **Partnership** - The relationship existing between two or more entities or individuals who join to carry on a trade or business. This includes a business jointly owned/operated by a husband and wife.

Check one: ☐ General partnership ☐ Limited partnership
☐ Joint venture ☐ Married couple

☐ **Corporation** - A person or group of people who incorporate by receiving a charter from their state's Secretary of State (includes professional service corporations).

Check one: ☐ C-corporation ☐ S-corporation
☐ Not-for-profit corporation

☐ **Limited liability company** - Two or more entities (or individuals) who file articles of organization with their state's Secretary of State.

Check one: ☐ Single-member LLC ☐ Multi-member LLC
☐ Check here if you elected to be treated as a corporation for federal income tax purposes.

☐ **Business trust** - An entity created under an agreement of trust for the purpose of conducting a business for profit (includes real estate investment trusts).

☐ **Non-business trust/Fiduciary** - An entity created by a grantor for the specific benefit of a designated entity or individual.

☐ **Estate** - An entity that is created upon the death of an individual, consisting of that individual's real or personal property.

Date of death: _____

☐ **Government agency** - A legal government body formed by governing constitutions, statutes, or rules.

☐ **Indian tribe or Tribal unit** - Any Indian tribe, band, nation, or other organized group or community which is recognized as eligible for the special programs and services provided by the United States to Indians because of their status as Indians (includes any subdivision, subsidiary, or business enterprise wholly owned by such an Indian tribe).

12. If a partnership, corporation, or limited liability company, provide your fiscal year ending date: ☐☐ / ☐☐
month   day

13. If incorporated, chartered or otherwise registered to do business in Florida, provide your document/registration number from the Florida Secretary of State:

_____

Provide the date of incorporation, charter, or authorization to do business in Florida:

☐☐ / ☐☐ / ☐☐☐☐
month   day   year

Note: If not incorporated, chartered or registered to do business in Florida, you may be required to do so. Call the Florida Department of State, Division of Corporations at 850-488-9000 for more information.

14. Is your business location rented from another party? Yes ☐ No ☐
If yes, and you **do not operate from your home,** provide the following information.

Owner or landlord's name _____ Telephone number _____

Address _____ City/State/ZIP _____

15.a. What is your primary business activity? _____

   b. What are your taxable business activities? _____

SECTION B — SALES AND USE TAX ACTIVITY — $5 FEE (IN-STATE ONLY)

DR-1
R. 07/05
Page 3

16. Does your business activity include (check all that apply):

a. ☐ Sales of property or goods at retail (to consumers)?

b. ☐ Sales of property or goods at wholesale (to registered dealers)?

c. ☐ Sales of secondhand goods?

d. ☐ Rental of commercial real property to individuals or businesses?

e. ☐ Rental of transient living or sleeping accommodations (for six months or less)?

f. ☐ Management of transient living or sleeping accommodations belonging to others?

g. ☐ Rental of equipment or other property or goods to individuals or businesses?

h. ☐ Renting/leasing motor vehicles to others?

i. ☐ Repair or alteration of tangible personal property?

j. ☐ Charging admission or membership fees?

k. ☐ Placing and operating coin-operated amusement machines at business locations belonging to others?

l. ☐ Placing and operating vending machines at business locations belonging to others?

m. ☐ Purchasing items to be included in a finished product assembled or manufactured for sale?

n. ☐ Providing any of the following services? (Check all that apply.)

n1. ☐ Pest control for nonresidential buildings

n2. ☐ Cleaning services for nonresidential buildings

n3. ☐ Detective services

n4. ☐ Protection services

n5. ☐ Security alarm system monitoring

o. ☐ Purchasing items that were not taxed by the seller at time of purchase (includes, but is not limited to, purchases through the Internet, from catalogs, or from out-of-state sellers)?

p. ☐ Using dyed diesel fuel for off-road purposes?

q. ☐ Operating vending machine(s) owned by you at your business location?

17. What products or services do you purchase for resale? _____

COIN-OPERATED AMUSEMENT MACHINES

18. Are coin-operated amusement machines being operated at your business location? If yes, answer question 19. ☐ Yes ☐ No

19. Do you have a written agreement that requires someone other than yourself to obtain amusement machine certificates for any of the machines at your location? If yes, provide their information below. ☐ Yes ☐ No

Name _____ Address _____ Telephone number _____

Note: You must complete an *Application for Amusement Machine Certificate* (Form DR-18) if you answered YES to question 18 **and** NO to question 19.

CONTRACTORS

20. Do you improve real property as a contractor? If yes, answer questions 21-23. ☐ Yes ☐ No

21. Do you sell tangible personal property at retail? ☐ Yes ☐ No

22. Do you purchase materials or supplies from vendors located outside of Florida? ☐ Yes ☐ No

23. Do you fabricate or manufacture any building component at a location other than contract sites? ☐ Yes ☐ No

MOTOR FUEL

24. Do you sell any type of fuel or use off-road, dyed, diesel fuel? If yes, answer questions 25 and 26. ☐ Yes ☐ No

25. a. Do you make retail sales of gasoline, diesel fuel, or aviation fuel at posted retail prices? ☐ Yes ☐ No

b. If yes to #25a, does this business exist as a marina? ☐ Yes ☐ No

c. If yes to #25a, do you expect to sell more diesel fuel than gasoline? ☐ Yes ☐ No

d. If yes to #25a, provide your Florida Department of Environmental Protection facility identification number for this location. ☐☐☐☐☐☐

26. Do you use dyed diesel fuel for off-road purposes that was not taxed at the time of purchase? ☐ Yes ☐ No

SECTION C — SOLID WASTE FEES AND POLLUTANTS TAX — $30 FEE FOR DRYCLEANING ONLY

27. Do you sell tires or batteries, or rent/lease motor vehicles to others? If yes, answer questions 28-30. ☐ Yes ☐ No

28. Do you make retail sales of new tires for motorized vehicles (either separately or as a part of a vehicle)? ☐ Yes ☐ No

29. Do you make retail sales of new or remanufactured lead-acid batteries sold separately or as a component part of another product such as new automobiles, golf carts, boats, etc.? ☐ Yes ☐ No

30. Are you in the business of renting or leasing vehicles that transport fewer than nine passengers to individuals or businesses? ☐ Yes ☐ No

31. Do you own or operate a dry-cleaning dry drop-off facility or plant in Florida? ☐ Yes ☐ No
If yes, enclose the $30 dry-cleaning registration fee.

32. Do you produce or import perchloroethylene? ☐ Yes ☐ No
If yes, you must complete an *Application for Florida License to Produce or Import Taxable Pollutants* (Form DR-166).

SECTION D — UNEMPLOYMENT TAX — NO FEE

DR-1
R. 07/05
Page 4

If you are registering an additional business location and are already registered with the Florida Department of Revenue for unemployment tax, you do not need to complete this section.

If you need to reactivate a previously assigned unemployment tax (UT) account number, enter your account number and complete items 33-41 below. Make sure that you have entered your FEIN on page 2, item 9.

☐☐☐☐☐☐☐

33. Employer type (check all that apply):

☐ Regular (If a leasing company, attach copy of license.)   ☐ Agricultural (citrus)   ☐ Governmental entity   ☐ Nonprofit organization (501(c)(3) letter must be attached)

☐ Domestic (household)   ☐ Agricultural (non citrus)   ☐ Agricultural crew chief   ☐ Indian tribe / Tribal unit

34. Did your business pay federal unemployment tax in another state in the current or previous calendar year? .... ☐ Yes   ☐ No

If yes, in which state(s) _____   Year(s) _____

35. Do you lease any of your employees? ☐ Yes ☐ No   If yes, check whether all or part of your workforce is leased: .... ☐ All   ☐ Part

Name of leasing company_____ Date leasing began _____   UT account number_____

36. For the current calendar year, how many full or partial weeks have you employed workers? _____

For the previous year, how many full or partial weeks did you employ workers? _____

37. Provide the date that you first employed or will employ workers in Florida. ☐☐/☐☐/☐☐☐☐
                                                                           month   day   year

38. Does another party (accountant, bookkeeper, agent) maintain your payroll? .... ☐ Yes   ☐ No
If yes, provide the following information.

Name of agent _____   Telephone number _____

Address _____   City/State/ZIP _____

39. Provide only your **Florida** gross payroll by calendar quarters. Estimate amounts if exact figures are not available.

	Qtr Ending 3/31	Qtr Ending 6/30	Qtr Ending 9/30	Qtr Ending 12/31
Current year	$	$	$	$
Previous year	$	$	$	$
Next previous year	$	$	$	$
Next previous year	$	$	$	$
Next previous year	$	$	$	$

40. Did you purchase this business from another entity or change your business structure in any way? .... ☐ Yes   ☐ No

If **yes**, complete items **a** through **i** below, providing information about the former entity. Also, complete and submit a *Report to Determine Succession and Application for Transfer of Experience Rating Records* (Form UCS-1S) to the Department of Revenue. This form must be postmarked within 90 days of the acquisition date to be considered timely.

a. Legal name of former entity _____

b. FEIN _____   c. UT account number _____

d. Trade name (d/b/a) _____

e. Address _____

f. Date of purchase/change _____   g. Portion of business acquired: ☐ All ☐ Part ☐ Unknown

h. Was the business in operation at the time the purchase/change occurred? ☐ Yes ☐ No   If no, provide date business closed. _____

i. Was there any common ownership, management, or control at the time the purchase/change occurred? ☐ Yes ☐ No

41. **List the locations and nature of business conducted in Florida. Use additional sheets if necessary.**

Address, city, and county of work site	Principal products / services	Number of employees
_____	_____	_____
_____	_____	_____
_____	_____	_____

Do the above work sites provide support for any other units of the company? .... ☐ Yes   ☐ No

If yes, the services are: ☐ administrative ☐ research ☐ other, specify _____

_____

SECTION E — GROSS RECEIPTS TAX — NO FEE

42. Do you sell electrical power or gas? If yes, answer questions a and b below.. ☐ Yes ☐ No
Do you sell:
a. Electrical power? .... ☐ Yes ☐ No
b. Natural or manufactured gas? .... ☐ Yes ☐ No

SECTION F — DOCUMENTARY STAMP TAX — NO FEE

43. Do you make sales, finalized by written agreements, that do not require recording by the
Clerk of the Court, but do require documentary stamp tax to be paid? If yes, answer questions 44-46......................... ☐ Yes ☐ No

44. Do you anticipate five or more transactions subject to documentary stamp tax per month?...................... ☐ Yes ☐ No

45. Do you anticipate your average monthly documentary stamp tax remittance to be less than $80 per month? .... ☐ Yes ☐ No

46. Is this application being completed to register your **first** location to collect documentary stamp tax?................... ☐ Yes ☐ No
If no, and this application is for additional locations, please list name and address of each additional location.
(Attach additional sheets if needed.)

Location name _____ Telephone number _____

Physical address _____ City/State/ZIP _____

SECTION G — COMMUNICATIONS SERVICES TAX — NO FEE

47. Do you sell communications services? If yes, check the items below that apply... ☐ Yes ☐ No
a. Telephone service (local, long distance, or mobile)... ☐ Yes ☐ No
b. Paging service .... ☐ Yes ☐ No
c. Facsimile (fax) service (not in the course of advertising or professional services)...................................... ☐ Yes ☐ No
d. Cable service... ☐ Yes ☐ No
e. Direct-to-home satellite service .... ☐ Yes ☐ No
f. Pay telephone service.. ☐ Yes ☐ No
g. Reseller (only sales for resale; no sales to any retail customers).. ☐ Yes ☐ No
h. Other services; please describe: _____ ☐ Yes ☐ No

48. Do you purchase communications services to integrate into prepaid calling arrangements?............................. ☐ Yes ☐ No

49. Are you applying for a direct pay permit for communications services? .... ☐ Yes ☐ No

50. Check the appropriate box(es) for the method(s) you **intend** to use for determining the local taxing jurisdictions in which service addresses for your customers are located. If you use multiple databases, check all that apply. If you **only** sell pay telephone or direct-to-home satellite services, provide prepaid calling arrangements, are a reseller, or are applying for a direct pay permit, skip questions 50 and 51.

☐ 1. An electronic database provided by the Department.

☐ 2a. A database developed by this company that will be certified. To apply for certification of your database, complete an *Application for Certification of Communications Services Database* (Form DR-700012).

☐ 2b. A database supplied by a vendor. Provide the vendor's name:

_____

☐ 3. ZIP+4 and a methodology for assignment when ZIP codes overlap jurisdictions.

☐ 4. ZIP+4 that does not overlap jurisdictions. Example: a hotel located in one jurisdiction.

☐ 5. None of the above.

Two collection allowance rates are available.
• Dealers whose databases meet the criteria in items 1, 3, or 4 above are eligible for a .75 percent (.0075) collection allowance.
• Dealers whose databases meet the criteria in item 5 are eligible for a .25 percent (.0025) collection allowance.
• Dealers meeting the criteria in item 2a are eligible for a .25 percent (.0025) collection allowance until the database is certified. Upon certification, the dealer will receive the .75 percent (.0075) collection allowance.
• Dealers meeting the criteria in 2b are eligible for the .75 percent (.0075) collection allowance if the vendor's database has been certified. If not, the .25 percent collection allowance (.0025) will apply.

Dealers with multiple databases may need to file two separate returns in order to maximize their collection allowances.
• If all databases are certified or a ZIP+4 method is used, then the dealer is entitled to the .75 percent (.0075) collection allowance.
• If some databases are certified or a ZIP+4 method is used, and some are not, the dealer has two options for reporting the tax. One is to file a single return for all taxable sales from all databases and receive a .25 percent (.0025) collection allowance. The second option is to file two returns: one reporting taxable sales from certified databases (.75 percent allowance) and a separate return for the taxable sales from non-certified databases (.25 percent allowance).
• If no databases are certified, the dealer will receive a .25 percent (.0025) collection allowance on all tax collected.

51. **If you wish to be eligible for both collection allowances, check the box below to indicate that you will file two separate returns.**

☐ I will file two separate communications services tax returns in order to maximize my collection allowance.

52. Provide the name of the managerial representative who can answer questions regarding filed tax returns.

Name _____ Telephone_____

E-Mail Address_____ Street Address _____

SECTION H — APPLICANT DECLARATION AND SIGNATURE

This application will not be accepted if not signed by the applicant.

If the applicant is a sole proprietorship, the proprietor or owner must sign; if a partnership, a partner must sign; if a corporation, an officer of the corporation authorized to sign on behalf of the corporation must sign; if a limited liability company, an authorized member or manager must sign; if a trust, a trustee must sign; if applicant is represented by an authorized agent for unemployment tax purposes, the agent may sign (attach executed power of attorney). **THE SIGNATURE OF ANY OTHER PERSON WILL NOT BE ACCEPTED.**

Please note that any person (including employees, corporate directors, corporate officers, etc.) who is required to collect, truthfully account for, and pay any taxes and willfully fails to do so shall be liable for penalties under the provisions of section 213.29, Florida Statutes. All information provided by the applicant is confidential as provided in s. 213.053, F.S., and is not subject to Florida Public Records Law (s. 119.07, F.S.).

Under penalties of perjury, I attest that I am authorized to sign on behalf of the business entity identified herein, and also declare that I have read the information provided on this application and that the facts stated in it are true to the best of my knowledge and belief.

SIGN HERE ➤ _____   Title _____

Print name _____   Date _____

Amount enclosed: $ _____

- **$5 fee** – Sales tax registration for business/property located in Florida.
- **$30 fee** – Solid waste registration for dry cleaners.

USE THIS CHECKLIST TO ENSURE FAST PROCESSING OF YOUR APPLICATION.

✓ Complete the application in its entirety.

✓ Make sure that you have provided your FEIN or SSN.

✓ Sign and date the application.

✓ Attach check or money order for appropriate registration fee amount. **DO NOT SEND CASH.**

✓ Mail to: **FLORIDA DEPARTMENT OF REVENUE**
  5050 W TENNESSEE ST
  TALLAHASSEE FL 32399-0100

You may also mail or deliver your application to any service center listed on the inside front cover.

FOR DOR USE ONLY

PM/Delivery	☐☐ / ☐☐ / ☐☐☐	Contract Object (MO)	☐☐☐☐☐☐☐☐
B.P. No.	☐☐☐☐☐☐☐	Contract Object (LO)	☐☐☐☐☐☐☐☐
UT Acct. No..	☐☐☐☐☐☐☐ - ☐	Contract Object (other)	☐☐☐☐☐☐☐☐

NAICS Code(s):
☐
☐
☐

FLORIDA

DEPARTMENT
OF REVENUE

Sales and Use Tax Return

DR-15CS
R. 01/05

Please complete this return.
Attach your check or money order and mail to:

Florida Department of Revenue
5050 W. Tennessee Street
Tallahassee, FL 32399-0120

Certificate Number: _____   **SALES AND USE TAX RETURN**   HD/PM Date: /   /   **DR-15 R. 01/05**

Florida	1. Gross Sales	2. Exempt Sales	3. Taxable Amount	4. Tax Collected
A. Sales/Services	.	.	.	.
B. Taxable Purchases	Include Internet / Out-of-State Purchases →		.	.
C. Commercial Rentals	.	.	.	.
D. Transient Rentals	.	.	.	.
E. Food & Beverage Vending	.	.	.	.

Transient Rental Rate: _____   Surtax Rate: _____   Collection Period _____

5.	Total Amount of Tax Collected	.
6.	**Less Lawful Deductions**	.
7.	Total Tax Due	.
8.	**Less Est Tax Pd / DOR Cr Memo**	.
9.	Plus Est. Tax Due Current Month	.
10.	Amount Due	.
11.	**Less Collection Allowance**	.
12.	Plus Penalty	.
13.	Plus Interest	.
14.	**Amount Due with Return**	.

Due:
Late After:
☐ Check here if payment was made electronically.

Do Not Write in the Space Below

0100 0 20059999 0001003031 0 4999999999 0000 5

Certificate Number: _____   **SALES AND USE TAX RETURN**   HD/PM Date: /   /   **DR-15 R. 01/05**

Florida	1. Gross Sales	2. Exempt Sales	3. Taxable Amount	4. Tax Collected
A. Sales/Services	.	.	.	.
B. Taxable Purchases	Include Internet / Out-of-State Purchases →		.	.
C. Commercial Rentals	.	.	.	.
D. Transient Rentals	.	.	.	.
E. Food & Beverage Vending	.	.	.	.

Transient Rental Rate: _____   Surtax Rate: _____   Collection Period _____

5.	Total Amount of Tax Collected	.
6.	**Less Lawful Deductions**	.
7.	Total Tax Due	.
8.	**Less Est Tax Pd / DOR Cr Memo**	.
9.	Plus Est. Tax Due Current Month	.
10.	Amount Due	.
11.	**Less Collection Allowance**	.
12.	Plus Penalty	.
13.	Plus Interest	.
14.	**Amount Due with Return**	.

Due:
Late After:
☐ Check here if payment was made electronically.

Do Not Write in the Space Below

0100 0 20059999 0001003031 0 4999999999 0000 5

DUE DATE OF RETURN — Your return and payment are **due on the 1st and late after the 20th day of the month** following each collection period. If the 20th falls on a Saturday, Sunday, or state or federal holiday, your return must be postmarked or hand delivered on the first business day following the 20th. **You must file a return even if no tax is due.**

SIGNATURE REQUIREMENT — Sign and date your return. For corporations, the authorized corporate officer must sign. If someone else prepared the return, the preparer also must sign and date the return in the space provided.

Fraud Penalties

FRAUDULENT CLAIM OF EXEMPTION; PENALTIES — Section 212.085, Florida Statutes (F.S.), provides that when any person fraudulently, for the purpose of evading tax, issues to a vendor or to any agent of the state a certificate or statement in writing in which he or she claims exemption from sales tax, such person, in addition to being liable for payment of the tax plus a mandatory penalty of 200% of the tax, shall be liable for fine and punishment as provided by law for a conviction of a felony of the third degree, as provided in s. 775.082, s. 775.083, or s. 775.084, F.S.

SPECIFIC FRAUD PENALTY — Any person who makes a false or fraudulent return with a willful intent to evade payment of any tax or fee imposed under Ch. 212, F.S., in addition to the other penalties provided by law, will be liable for a specific penalty of 100% of the tax bill or fee and, upon conviction, for fine and punishment as provided in s. 775.082, s. 775.083, or s. 775.084, F.S.

FAILURE TO COLLECT AND PAY OVER TAX OR AN ATTEMPT TO EVADE OR DEFEAT TAX — Any person who is required to collect, truthfully account for, and pay over any tax enumerated in Ch. 201, Ch. 206, or Ch. 212, F.S., and who willfully fails to collect such tax or truthfully account for and pay over such tax or willfully attempts in any manner to evade or defeat such tax or the payment thereof; or any officer or director of a corporation who has administrative control over the collection and payment of such tax and who willfully directs any employee of the corporation to fail to collect or pay over, evade, defeat, or truthfully account for such tax will, in addition to other penalties provided by law, be liable to a penalty equal to twice the total amount of the tax evaded or not accounted for or paid over, as provided in s. 213.29, F.S.

I hereby certify that this return has been examined by me and to the best of my knowledge and belief is a true and complete return.

_____   _____   _____   _____
Signature of Taxpayer   Date   Signature of Preparer   Date

Discretionary Sales Surtax (Lines 15(a) through 15(d))

15(a). Exempt Amount of Items Over $5,000 (included in Column 3) .... **15(a).** _____

15(b). Other Taxable Amounts **NOT** Subject to Surtax (included in Column 3) .... **15(b).** _____

15(c). Amounts Subject to Surtax at a Rate Different Than Your County Surtax Rate (included in Column 3) .... **15(c).** _____

15(d). **Total Amount of Discretionary Sales Surtax Collected** (included in Column 4) .... **15(d).** _____

16. Total **Enterprise Zone Jobs Credits** (included in Line 6) .... **16.** _____

17. Taxable Sales/Purchases/Rentals of **Farm Equipment** — 2.5% Rate (included in Line A) .... **17.** _____

18. Taxable Sales/Purchases of **Electric Power or Energy** — 7% Rate (included in Line A) .... **18.** _____

19. Taxable Sales/Purchases of **Dyed Diesel Fuel** — 6% Rate (included in Line A) .... **19.** _____

20. Taxable Sales from **Amusement Machines** (included in Line A) .... **20.** _____

I hereby certify that this return has been examined by me and to the best of my knowledge and belief is a true and complete return.

_____   _____   _____   _____
Signature of Taxpayer   Date   Signature of Preparer   Date

Discretionary Sales Surtax (Lines 15(a) through 15(d))

15(a). Exempt Amount of Items Over $5,000 (included in Column 3) .... **15(a).** _____

15(b). Other Taxable Amounts **NOT** Subject to Surtax (included in Column 3) .... **15(b).** _____

15(c). Amounts Subject to Surtax at a Rate Different Than Your County Surtax Rate (included in Column 3) .... **15(c).** _____

15(d). **Total Amount of Discretionary Sales Surtax Collected** (included in Column 4) .... **15(d).** _____

16. Total **Enterprise Zone Jobs Credits** (included in Line 6) .... **16.** _____

17. Taxable Sales/Purchases/Rentals of **Farm Equipment** — 2.5% Rate (included in Line A) .... **17.** _____

18. Taxable Sales/Purchases of **Electric Power or Energy** — 7% Rate (included in Line A) .... **18.** _____

19. Taxable Sales/Purchases of **Dyed Diesel Fuel** — 6% Rate (included in Line A) .... **19.** _____

20. Taxable Sales from **Amusement Machines** (included in Line A) .... **20.** _____

DEPARTMENT OF REVENUE

┌───┐
│ **DR-15 Sales and Use Tax Return - Instructions for 2005** │
└───┘

DR-15CSN
R. 01/05

Line A, Sales/Services

"Sales" means the total of all wholesale and retail sales transactions. "Sales" includes, but is not limited to:

- Sales, leases, or licenses to use certain property or goods (tangible personal property)
- Sales and rentals/admissions, amusement machine receipts, and vending machine receipts for all items other than food and beverage
- Sales of services including nonresidential pest control, nonresidential maintenance/cleaning services, both residential and nonresidential burglar protection and other protection services, and detective services
- Purchases of machines including vending/amusement machines, machine parts, and repairs thereof
- Sales, purchases, and/or rentals of self-propelled, power-drawn, or power-driven farm equipment (2.5% rate)
- Sales/purchases of electric power or energy (7% rate)
- Sales/purchases of prepaid telephone calling cards (6% rate)
- Sales/purchases of dyed diesel fuel for off-road use, including all vessels (6% rate)

Amusement and Vending Machine Sales - Operators of amusement machines and vending machines containing items other than food and beverage should compute their gross sales by dividing the total receipts from the machine(s) by the appropriate divisor for the county tax rate where the machine(s) is located (see table below). Amusement machine operators must complete Line 20 on the back of the return. Operators of vending machines containing food or beverage items must complete Line E (see Line E instructions).

Sales/Surtax Rate	Amusement Divisor	Other Vended Items Divisor
6.0%	1.040	1.0659
6.25%	1.0425	1.0683
6.5%	1.045	1.0707
6.75%	1.0475	1.0728
7.0%	1.050	1.0749
7.25%	1.0525	1.0770
7.5%	1.055	1.0791

Column 1, Gross Sales

Enter the total amount of gross sales. **Do not include tax collected in this amount.**

Column 2, Exempt Sales

Enter the total amount of tax-exempt sales included in Line A, Column 1. Enter zero, if none. Tax-exempt sales include, but are not limited to, sales for resale, sales of items specifically exempt, and sales to exempt organizations.

Column 3, Taxable Amount

Subtract total exempt sales from gross sales and enter the taxable amount. If you report sales exempt from discretionary sales surtax, complete Line 15(a) or 15(b), see instructions on page 4.

- Report sales, purchases or rentals of self-propelled, power-drawn, or power-driven **farm equipment** (2.5% rate) on **Line 17**.
- Report sales or purchases of electric power or energy (7% rate) on **Line 18**.
- Report sales or purchases of **dyed diesel fuel for off-road use**, including all vessels (6% rate) on **Line 19**.
- Report taxable sales from **amusement machines** on **Line 20**.

Column 4, Tax Collected

Enter the total amount of tax collected, including discretionary sales surtax. Report the discretionary sales surtax collected on Line 15(d) on the back of the return.

Line B, Taxable Purchases

"Use tax" is owed on taxable purchases for goods or services you have used or consumed that were:

- **Internet and Out-of-State purchases not taxed by the seller and NOT purchased for resale.**
- Out-of-State or local purchases not taxed by a supplier and **NOT** purchased for resale whether ordered online, from a catalog, or by telephone.
- Taxable items, originally purchased untaxed for resale, which were later used or consumed by the business, business owner, or employees.

The "use tax" rate is the same as the sales tax rate (6% plus the applicable discretionary sales surtax rate). Use tax and discretionary sales suntax must be remitted on the return for the collection period during which the item is used or consumed.

Note: The following purchases that were not taxed at the time of purchase must be reported on Line A, not Line B.

- Self-propelled, power-drawn, or power-driven farm equipment,
- Dyed diesel fuel for off-road use.
- Electric power or energy used.

Column 1, Gross Sales Not Applicable

Column 2, Exempt Sales Not Applicable

Column 3, Taxable Amount

Enter the total amount of purchases used or consumed that were not taxed by suppliers and not for resale. If you report purchases exempt from discretionary sales surtax, complete Lines 15(a) or 15(b) on the back of the return.

Column 4, Tax Collected

Enter the total amount of use tax owed, including discretionary sales surtax. Report all discretionary sales surtax owed on Line 15(d), see instructions on page 4.

Line C, Commercial Rentals

Taxable commercial rentals include the business of renting, leasing, letting, or the granting of a license to use or occupy any real property, unless specifically exempt under section 212.031, Florida Statutes (F.S.). Contact the Department if you need assistance with commercial rentals.

Column 1, Gross Sales

Enter the total amount of commercial rentals. **Do not include tax collected in this amount.**

Column 2, Exempt Sales

Enter the total amount of tax-exempt commercial rentals included in Line C, Column 1. Enter zero, if none.

Column 3, Taxable Amount

Subtract the total exempt commercial rentals from the total gross commercial rentals and enter the taxable amount.

Column 4, Tax Collected

Enter the total amount of tax collected, including discretionary sales surtax. Report all discretionary sales surtax collected on Line 15(d) on the back of the return. The $5,000 limitation for discretionary sales surtax does not apply to commercial rentals.

Line D, Transient Rentals

Transient rentals are leases or rentals of short term (6 months or less) living accommodations such as hotels, motels, condominiums, apartments, houses, etc. Rental charges for transient accommodations at new trailer camps, new mobile home parks (except mobile home lots regulated under Chapter 723, F.S.), and new recreational vehicle parks are subject to tax until more than 50 percent of the total rental units available are occupied by tenants who have continuously resided there for more than three months. The owner or owner's representative of the camp or park **is required** to declare to the Department that the rental of the transient accommodations at the new camp or park is no longer subject to tax (see section 212.03, F.S.).

Column 1, Gross Sales

Enter the total gross sales of amounts charged for transient rentals only. Do not include tax collected in this amount.

Column 2, Exempt Sales

Enter the total amount of tax-exempt transient rentals included in Line D, Column 1. Enter zero, if none.

Column 3, Taxable Amount

Subtract total exempt transient rentals from total gross transient rentals and enter the taxable amount.

Column 4, Tax Collected

Enter the total amount of tax collected based on the transient rental rate including discretionary sales surtax. Report all discretionary sales surtax collected on Line 15(d) on the back of the return.

Note: Some counties impose a local option tourist development tax in addition to the state's 6% tax. The Department collects the tax for some counties, while in others, dealers remit and report directly to their local county taxing agency.

Line E, Food and Beverage Vending

Operators of food and beverage vending machines should compute their gross sales by dividing the total receipts from the machine(s) by the appropriate food and beverage divisor for the county where the machine(s) is located.

Sales/Surtax Rate	Food and Beverage Divisor
6.0%	1.0645
6.25%	1.06655
6.5%	1.0686
6.75%	1.0706
7.0%	1.0726
7.25%	1.07465
7.5%	1.0767

Column 1, Gross Sales

Enter the total amount of gross sales computed from food and beverage vending machines receipts. Do not include tax collected in this amount.

Column 2, Exempt Sales

Enter the total amount of tax-exempt sales included in Line E, Column 1. Enter zero, if none.

Column 3, Taxable Amount

Subtract total exempt sales from gross sales and enter the taxable amount.

Column 4, Tax Collected

Enter the total amount of tax collected, including discretionary sales surtax. Report all discretionary sales surtax collected on Line 15(d) on the back of the return.

Line 5, Total Amount of Tax Collected

Add all the amounts in Column 4, Lines A through E, and enter the total amount of tax collected. If discretionary sales surtax was collected, it must be included in this amount.

Line 6, Less Lawful Deductions

Enter the total amount of all allowable tax deductions. Do not report sales tax credit memos on this line (see Line 8 instructions).

Lawful deductions include tax refunded by you to your customers because of returned goods or allowances for damaged merchandise, tax paid by you on purchases of goods intended for use or consumption but resold instead, enterprise zone jobs credits, and any other deductions allowed by law.

- Do not include documentation with your return. Documentation to support lawful deductions may be requested later.
- **If you are claiming any enterprise zone jobs credits, you must first complete Line 16 and include this amount on Line 6.**

Line 7, Total Tax Due

Subtract Line 6 from Line 5 and enter the amount. If negative, enter zero (0).

Lines 8-9, Estimated Tax

If you paid $200,000 or more sales and use tax (excluding any discretionary sales surtax) on returns filed for the period July 1, 2003 through June 30, 2004 (Florida's fiscal year), you must make an estimated sales tax payment every month, starting with the December 2004 return due January 1, 2005. Do not pay estimated tax if this is your final return. If you have questions about estimated tax, contact the Department.

Line 8, Less Estimated Tax Paid/DOR Credit Memo

Enter the total amount of estimated tax paid last month and sales tax credit memos issued by the Florida Department of Revenue (DOR). If the DOR credit memo(s) exceeds the total tax due on Line 7, claim the remaining credit memo balance on Line 8 of your next return. If this is your final return, contact the Department to request an Application for Refund (Form DR-26S).

Line 9, Plus Estimated Tax Due Current Month

The percentage factor for calculating estimated tax is 60%. Your estimated tax liability is based only on Florida sales and use tax due (Form DR-15, Line 7, Total Tax Due minus discretionary sales surtax). Note: If you incorrectly calculate or forget to enter your estimated tax, you cannot amend your return.

Compute your estimated tax liability by one of the following methods:

Note: If you correctly calculate your estimated tax using one of the three methods below, you will not be assessed a penalty for underpayment of estimated tax.

Method 1

Calculate 60% of your average sales tax liability for those months during the previous calendar year that you reported taxable transactions.

Example: When completing your December 2004 return, calculate your average sales tax liability for the 2004 calendar year. To calculate your average, complete the following steps:

Step 1. Review all of your 2004 sales tax returns (including December return).

Step 2. Add together the amounts from Line 7 (minus any discretionary sales surtax) for all 2004 returns.

Step 3. Divide the total of all Line 7 amounts by the number of returns filed with tax due on Line 7. This is your 2004 average sales tax liability.

Step 4. Multiply your 2004 average sales tax liability by 60%.

Step 5. Enter the amount determined in Step 4 on Line 9 of each return for 2005.

Method 2

Calculate 60% of your sales tax collected during the same month of the previous calendar year.

Example: When completing your December 2004 return, look at your January 2004 return and multiply the amount from Line 7 (minus discretionary sales surtax) by 60%. Enter that amount on Line 9.

Method 3

Calculate 60% of the tax collected for the collection period following this return.

Example: When completing your December 2004 return, your estimated tax liability is 60% of what you will collect (minus discretionary sales surtax) for the January 2005 return. Enter that amount on Line 9.

Line 10, Amount Due

Subtract the amount on Line 8 from Line 7. Add the amount on Line 9. Enter the result on Line 10. The amount entered on Line 10 cannot be negative. If this calculation results in a negative amount, contact Taxpayer Services.

Line 11, Less Collection Allowance

If your return and payment are filed on time, enter your collection allowance. The collection allowance is 2.5% (.025) of the first $1,200 of the amount due from Line 10, not to exceed $30. If late, enter zero and proceed to Lines 12 and 13.

Line 12, Plus Penalty

The minimum penalty changed to 10% of the Amount Due or $50 whichever is greater. If your return or payment is late, include a penalty of 10% of Line 10 or $50 whichever is greater along with the applicable interest. **The minimum penalty of $50 applies even if you file a late "zero tax due" return.**

Line 13, Plus Interest

If your payment is late, interest is owed on the amount due (Line 10). Florida law provides a floating rate of interest for payments of taxes and fees due, including discretionary sales surtax. The floating rate of interest is established using the formula in section 213.235, F.S., and is updated on January 1 and July 1 each year. To obtain interest rates contact the Department, (see the "Resources" section of these instructions).

To compute interest owed, first calculate the prorated daily interest factor by dividing the interest rate for the filing period by 365 days. Next, estimate the number of days your return is late by counting from the LATE AFTER date listed on the front of the return until the date the return will be postmarked by the U.S. Postal Service or hand delivered to the Department. Finally, multiply the amount of tax due by the number of days late and then by the daily interest rate factor.

Interest Calculation Worksheet			
Tax Due	Days Late	Daily Interest	Interest Due
X	X	*varies =	
*Daily interest = the current interest rate ÷ 365 (366 during leap years)			

Line 14, Amount Due with Return

If your return and payment are filed on time, subtract Line 11 from Line 10 and enter the amount due. If your return or payment is late, add Lines 12 and 13 to Line 10 and enter the amount. Line 14 is the amount you owe, including discretionary sales surtax. Be sure that you have completed **ALL** applicable lines on the back of the return.

Electronic Funds Transfer Check Box

If you made your payment electronically, check the box in the bottom left corner of your DR-15 return.

Instructions for Completing Back of Return Signature

Sign and date your return. For corporations, an authorized corporate officer must sign. If someone else prepared the return, the preparer must also sign and date the return in the space provided.

DR-15CSN
R. 01/05

Lines 15(a) - 15(d), Discretionary Sales Surtax

Discretionary sales surtax must be collected and reported when taxable merchandise or services are sold or delivered to a location within a county imposing surtax. The amount of discretionary sales surtax to be collected and reported depends on where the delivery of the taxable merchandise or service occurs. For real property rentals and transient rentals, it is the county where the property is located.

If your business location is in Florida, the discretionary sales surtax rate printed on your return(s) is the rate in effect for the county where your business is located. If your business is located outside of Florida or you are a registered use tax dealer, your return will not reflect a discretionary sales surtax rate. A dealer (including an out-of-state dealer) who sells, rents, delivers or receives taxable merchandise or services in or at a location within a county imposing a discretionary sales surtax is required to collect or remit the surtax at the rate imposed in the county where the merchandise or service is delivered. Also, the discretionary sales surtax applies to the rental of real property and transient rentals and is collected at the county rate where the property is located.

For motor vehicle and mobile home sales, use the surtax rate of the county where the motor vehicle or mobile home will be registered. For the updated discretionary sales surtax information for 2005, refer to page five. The surtax applies to the first $5,000 of the sales amount on any item of tangible personal property. **The $5,000 limitation does not apply to rentals of real property, transient rentals, or services**.

Discretionary sales surtax must be included with tax reported on Lines A through E in Column 4 of your DR-15 return. Do not remit discretionary sales surtax collected to the County Tax Collector's Office.

Line 15(a), Exempt Amount of Items Over $5,000

Enter the amount in excess of $5,000 or any single taxable item of tangible personal property sold or purchased for more than $5,000. Example: If a single item of tangible personal property is sold for $7,000, enter $2,000 (the amount over $5,000) on Line 15(a). **Remember that the $5,000 limitation does not apply to rentals of real property, transient rentals, or services.**

Line 15(b), Other Taxable Amounts in Column 3 Not Subject to Surtax

Enter the amount of taxable sales or purchases included in Column 3 not subject to discretionary sales surtax. Do not include amounts shown on Line 15(a).

Line 15(c), Amounts Subject to Surtax at a Rate DIFFERENT than Your County Surtax Rate

Enter the amount of taxable sales or purchases on which discretionary sales surtax was collected at a rate other than the rate imposed in the county in which your business is located.

Line 15(d), Total Amount of Discretionary Sales Surtax Collected

Enter the total amount of discretionary sales surtax collected on line 15(d). Do not include state sales tax in this amount.

Enterprise Zone Jobs Credits

If you are claiming any enterprise zone jobs credits on the back of your 2005 DR-15, please note that the method for claiming these credits changed in 2003. ALL enterprise zone jobs credits are now reported on one line, Line 16, and you are no longer required to enter your Enterprise Zone Number.

If you are claiming other sales tax credits (such as tax refunded for returned merchandise, damaged merchandise, etc.) in addition to enterprise zone jobs credits, the total amount for ALL types of credits should be included in the amount on Line 6.

All approved enterprise zone jobs credits must be taken as provided by law. If you have any questions regarding how to request or deduct any enterprise zone jobs credits, call the Return Reconciliation Unit, Department of Revenue, at 850-414-9010.

Line 16, Enterprise Zone Jobs Credits

Enter the total of all enterprise zone jobs credits on Line 16.

Line 17, Taxable Sales/Purchases/Rentals of Farm Equipment

Enter the taxable amount of sales, purchases or rentals of self-propelled, power-drawn, or power-driven farm equipment subject to the 2.5% rate. This amount should also be included in Line A, column 3.

Line 18, Taxable Sales/Purchases of Electric Power or Energy

Enter the taxable amount of sales or purchases, of electric power or energy subject to the 7% rate. If the sale or purchase of electric power or energy occurred in a county that imposes a discretionary sales surtax, the tax rate would be 7% plus the applicable discretionary sales surtax rate.

Line 19, Taxable Sales/Purchases of Dyed Diesel Fuel

Enter the total amount of dyed diesel fuel sales or purchases (subject to sales or use tax) used in self-propelled off-road equipment, including vessels.

Note: For Lines 17, 18, and 19 the tax due from sales or purchases, including discretionary sales surtax if applicable, must be included on the front of the return on Line A, Column 4.

Line 20, Taxable Sales from Amusement Machines

Enter the amount of taxable sales from amusement machines.

Discretionary Sales Surtax Information

These taxes are distributed to local governments throughout the state. **The amount of money distributed is based upon how you complete each tax return.** Dealers should impose the discretionary sales surtax on taxable sales when delivery occurs in a county that imposes surtax. For motor vehicles and mobile home sales, use the surtax rate of the county where the vehicle will be registered. Only the first $5,000 on a single sale of tangible personal property is subject to discretionary sales surtax if the property is sold as a single item, in bulk, as a working unit or as part of a working unit. The $5,000 limitation does not apply to commercial rentals, transient rentals, or services.

Discretionary Sales Surtax Rates for 2005 (as of November 16, 2004)

COUNTY	TOTAL SURTAX RATE		EFFECTIVE DATE	EXPIRATION DATE
Alachua	**.25%**		**Jan 1, 2005**	**Dec 2011 ***
Baker	1%		Jan 1, 1994	None
Bay	.5%		May 1, 1998	Apr 2008
Bradford	1%		Mar 1, 1993	None
Brevard	None			
Broward	None			
Calhoun	1%		Jan 1, 1993	Dec 2008
Charlotte	1%		Apr 1, 1995	Dec 2008
Citrus	None			
Clay	1%		Feb 1, 1990	Dec 2019
Collier	None			
Columbia	1%		Aug 1, 1994	None
Dade			See Miami-Dade for rates.	
De Soto	1%		Jan 1, 1988	None
Dixie	1%		Apr 1, 1990	Dec 2029
Duval	1%	(.5%)	Jan 1, 1989	None
		(.5%)	Jan 1, 2001	Dec 2030
Escambia	1.5%	(1%)	Jun 1, 1992	May 2007
		(.5%)	Jan 1, 1998	Dec 2007
Flagler	1%	(.5%)	Jan 1, 2003	Dec 2012
		(.5%)	Jan 1, 2003	Dec 2012
Franklin	None			
Gadsden	1%		Jan 1, 1996	None
Gilchrist	1%		Oct 1, 1992	None
Glades	1%		Feb 1, 1992	Jan 2007
Gulf	.5%		Jul 1, 1997	Jun 2017
Hamilton	1%		Jul 1, 1990	Dec 2019
Hardee	1%		Jan 1, 1998	None
Hendry	1%		Jan 1, 1988	None
Hernando	**.5%**		**Jan 1, 2005**	**Dec 2014 ***
Highlands	1%		Nov 1, 1989	Oct 2019
Hillsborough	1%	(.5%)	Dec 1, 1996	Nov 2026
		(.5%)	Oct 1, 2001	None
Holmes	1%		Oct 1, 1995	Sep 2006
Indian River	1%		Jun 1, 1989	Dec 2019
Jackson	1.5%	(1%)	Jun 1, 1995	May 2010
		(.5%)	Jul 1, 1996	Jun 2006
Jefferson	1%		Jun 1, 1988	None

COUNTY	TOTAL SURTAX RATE		EFFECTIVE DATE	EXPIRATION DATE
Lafayette	1%		Sep 1, 1991	Aug 2006
Lake	1%		Jan 1, 1988	Dec 2017
Lee	None			
Leon	1.5%	(1%)	Dec 1, 1989	Dec 2019
		(.5%)	Jan 1, 2003	Dec 2012
Levy	1%		Oct 1, 1992	None
Liberty	1%		Nov 1, 1992	None
Madison	1%		Aug 1, 1989	None
Manatee	.5%		Jan 1, 2003	Dec 2017
Marion	**.5%**		**Jan 1, 2005**	**Dec 2009 ***
Martin	None			
Miami-Dade	1%	(.5%)	Jan 1, 1992	None
		(.5%)	Jan 1, 2003	None
Monroe	1.5%	(1%)	Nov 1, 1989	Dec 2018
		(.5%)	Jan 1, 1996	Dec 2015
Nassau	1%		Mar 1, 1996	None
Okaloosa	None			
Okeechobee	1%		Oct 1, 1995	None
Orange	.5%		Jan 1, 2003	Dec 2015
Osceola	1%		Sep 1, 1990	Aug 2025
Palm Bch	**.5%**		**Jan 1, 2005**	**Dec 2010 ***
Pasco	**1%**		**Jan 1, 2005**	**Dec 2014 ***
Pinellas	1%		Feb 1, 1990	Jan 2010
Polk	**1%**	(.5%)	Jan 1, 2004	Dec 2018
		(.5%)	**Jan 1, 2005**	**Dec 2019 ***
Putnam	1%		Jan 1, 2003	Dec 2017
St. Johns	None			
St. Lucie	.5%		Jul 1, 1996	Jun 2006
Santa Rosa	.5%		Oct 1, 1998	Sep 2008
Sarasota	1%		Sep 1, 1989	Aug 2009
Seminole	1%		Jan 1, 2002	Dec 2011
Sumter	1%		Jan 1, 1993	None
Suwannee	1%		Jan 1, 1988	None
Taylor	1%		Aug 1, 1989	Dec 2029
Union	1%		Feb 1, 1993	Dec 2005
Volusia	.5%		Jan 1, 2002	Dec 2016
Wakulla	1%		Jan 1, 1988	Dec 2017
Walton	1%		Feb 1, 1995	None
Washington	1%		Nov 1, 1993	None

* Indicates changed or new information
Please check the rate for **each** county.

DR-15CSN
R. 01/05

Florida Department of Revenue Service Centers
(as of October 2004)

Alachua Service Center
14107 US Highway 441 Ste 100
Alachua FL 32615-6390
386-418-4444 (ET)

Clearwater Service Center
Arbor Shoreline Office Park
19337 US Highway 19 N Ste 200
Clearwater FL 33764-3149
727-538-7400 (ET)

Cocoa Service Center
2428 Clearlake Rd Bldg M
Cocoa FL 32922-5731
321-504-0950 (ET)

Coral Springs Service Center
Florida Sunrise Tower
3111 N University Dr Ste 501
Coral Springs FL 33065-5090
954-346-3000 (ET)

Daytona Beach Service Center
1821 Business Park Blvd
Daytona Beach FL 32114-1230
386-274-6600 (ET)

Fort Myers Service Center
2295 Victoria Ave Ste 270
Fort Myers FL 33901-3871
239-338-2400 (ET)

Fort Pierce Service Center
Benton Building
337 N US Highway 1 Ste 207-B
Fort Pierce FL 34950-4255
772-429-2900 (ET)

Hollywood Service Center
Taft Office Complex
6565 Taft St Ste 300
Hollywood FL 33024-4044
954-967-1000 (ET)

Jacksonville Service Center
921 N Davis St A250
Jacksonville FL 32209-6829
904-359-6070 (ET)

Key West Service Center
3118 Flagler Ave
Key West FL 33040-4602
305-292-6725 (ET)

Lake City Service Center
1401 W US Highway 90 Ste 100
Lake City FL 32055-6123
386-758-0420 (ET)

Lakeland Service Center
230 S Florida Ave Ste 101
Lakeland FL 33801-4625
863-499-2260 (ET)

Leesburg Service Center
1415 S 14th St Ste 103
Leesburg FL 34748-6686
352-315-4470 (ET)

Maitland Service Center
Ste 160
2301 Maitland Center Parkway
Maitland FL 32751-4192
407-475-1200 (ET)

Marianna Service Center
4230 Lafayette St Ste D
Marianna FL 32446-8231
850-482-9518 (CT)

Miami Service Center
8175 NW 12th St Ste 119
Miami FL 33126-1828
305-470-5001 (ET)

Naples Service Center
3073 Horseshoe Dr S Ste 110
Naples FL 34104-6145
239-434-4858 (ET)

Orlando Service Center
AmSouth Bank Building
5401 S Kirkman Rd 5th Floor
Orlando FL 32819-7911
407-903-7350 (ET)

Panama City Service Center
703 W 15th St Ste A
Panama City FL 32401-2238
850-872-4165 (CT)

Pensacola Service Center
3670C N L St
Pensacola FL 32505-5217
850-595-5170 (CT)

Port Richey Service Center
6709 Ridge Rd Ste 300
Port Richey FL 34668-6842
727-841-4407 (ET)

Sarasota Service Center
Sarasota Main Plaza
1991 Main St Ste 240
Sarasota FL 34236-5940
941-361-6001 (ET)

Tallahassee Service Center
2410 Allen Rd
Tallahassee FL 32312-2603
850-488-9719 (ET)

Tampa Service Center
Ste 100
6302 E Martin Luther King Blvd
Tampa FL 33619-1166
813-744-6582 (ET)

West Palm Beach Service Center
2468 Metrocentre Blvd
West Palm Beach FL 33407-3105
561-640-2800 (ET)

CT—Central Time
ET—Eastern Time

For Information and Forms

Information and forms are available on our Internet site at

www.myflorida.com/dor

To receive forms by mail:
- Order multiple copies of forms from our Internet site at **www.myflorida.com/dor/forms** *or*
- Fax your form request to the DOR Distribution Center at 850-922-2208 *or*
- Call the DOR Distribution Center at 850-488-8422 *or*
- Mail your form request to:
  Distribution Center
  Florida Department of Revenue
  168A Blountstown Hwy
  Tallahassee FL 32304-3702

To speak with a Department of Revenue representative, call Taxpayer Services, Monday through Friday, 8 a.m. to 7 p.m., ET, at 800-352-3671 or 850-488-6800.

For a written reply to your tax questions, write:
Taxpayer Services
Florida Department of Revenue
1379 Blountstown Hwy
Tallahassee FL 32304-3716

Hearing or speech impaired persons may call the TDD line at 800-367-8331 or 850-922-1115.

Department of Revenue service centers host educational seminars about Florida's taxes. For a schedule of upcoming seminars,
- Visit us online at **www.myflorida.com/dor** *or*
- Call the service center nearest you.

FLORIDA
DEPARTMENT
OF REVENUE

UCT-83
R. 10/05

To Employees-

- YOUR EMPLOYER

is registered with the Department of Revenue as a liable employer under the Florida Unemployment Compensation Law and you, as employees, are covered by unemployment insurance. **Unemployment taxes, which finance benefits paid to eligible unemployed workers are paid by the employer and, by law, cannot be deducted from employee's wages.**

- You may be eligible to receive unemployment compensation benefits if you meet the following requirements:

  1. You must be totally or partially unemployed through no fault of your own.
  2. You must register for work and file a claim.
  3. You must have sufficient employment and wages.
  4. You must be ABLE to work and AVAILABLE for work.

- You may file a claim for partial unemployment for any week you work less than full time due to lack of work if your wages during that week are less than your weekly benefit amount.

- You must report all earnings while claiming benefits. Failure to do so is a third degree felony with a maximum penalty of 5 years imprisonment and a $5,000 fine.

- Any employee who is discharged for misconduct connected with work may be disqualified from 1 to 52 weeks and until the worker has earned in new work, at least 17 times the weekly benefit amount of his or her claim.

- Any employee who voluntarily quits a job without good cause attributable to the employer may be disqualified until the worker has earned in new work, at least 17 times the weekly benefit amount of his or her claim.

- If you have any questions regarding filing a claim for unemployment compensation benefits, call the Agency for Workforce Innovation at 800-204-2418 or visit the Web site **www.floridajobs.org**.

Agency for Workforce Innovation
Office of Unemployment Compensation
MSC 229
107 East Madison Street
Tallahassee, Florida 32399-4135

This notice must be posted in accordance with Section 443.151(1) of the Florida Unemployment Compensation Law.

Index

D

E

MasterCard, 153
McNamara-O'Hara Service Contract Act, 130
Medicare, 109, 111, 179, 184, 185, 186
merchants, 70, 146, 150, 153, 154, 159, 172
meta tags, 86
metric measurements, 147
migrant labor, 132, 133
misrepresentation of goods, 72, 142, 144, 147, 148
monopolies, 161
mortgages, 50, 61, 66, 151, 192

N

National Labor Relations Act of 1935, 131
new hire reporting, 107, 108
nonprofit corporations, 19, 20, 21
Nutritional Labeling Education Act of 1990, 137

O

Occupational Safety and Health Administration (OSHA), 97, 98, 99
off the books, 130
officers, 18, 19, 21, 76, 157, 162, 182
opt-out procedures, 138, 139
organizational meeting, 21
organizational plan, 38, 40
out-of-state business taxes, 196
overhead, 37
overtime, 2, 122

P

packages, 79, 85, 147, 148, 149, 150, 164, 186
parental consent, 92
partner, 1, 2, 17, 18, 53, 181, 182
partnership, 17, 18, 20, 21, 23, 53, 162, 177, 181, 182, 184, 185, 193
Patent and Trademark Office (PTO), 26, 31, 32, 127, 163, 164
patents, 26, 31, 32, 162, 163, 164, 165
payment, 71, 72, 79, 132, 143, 151, 153, 181, 182, 184, 185, 191
PayPal, 93
pension plan, 111, 112, 122, 123, 124
perpetual existence, 19
polygraph tests, 107
posters, 98, 99, 113, 118, 127, 131, 132
price gouging, 149
pricing, 40, 62, 70, 75, 110, 136, 137, 147, 148, 149, 160, 161
privacy, 91, 92, 95, 96
probationary employment period, 106, 109
products, 2, 3, 37, 38, 39, 40, 42, 50, 58, 77, 83, 84, 87, 88, 89, 91, 94, 100, 101, 106, 109, 126, 127, 130, 136, 137, 147, 153, 160, 161, 162, 164, 169, 170, 171, 173, 174, 180, 190
professional service corporations, 19, 20, 28, 30, 31, 65, 83, 121, 193
profits, 2, 3, 18, 19, 21, 35, 36, 37, 40, 42, 46, 49, 54, 73, 88, 101, 154, 177, 179, 180, 181, 182
promissory note, 151
promotion, 45, 47, 73, 87, 135
proof of purchase, 150
property, 21, 22, 52, 59, 61, 64, 73, 76, 132, 141, 145, 146, 162, 191, 192
    rental, 60, 61, 64, 142, 156, 175
proprietorship, 17, 18, 21, 23, 78, 177, 178, 181, 184
publicity, 3, 25, 62, 81, 83, 85, 87